Church Communications Handbook

A Complete Guide to

Developing a Strategy

Using Technology

Writing Effectively

Reaching the Unchurched

Wanda Vassallo

kregel
PUBLICATIONS

Grand Rapids, MI 49501

Church Communications Handbook

Copyright © 1998 by Wanda Vassallo

Published by Kregel Publications, a division of Kregel, Inc., P.O. Box 2607, Grand Rapids, MI 49501. Kregel Publications provides trusted, biblical publications for Christian growth and service. Your comments and suggestions are valued.

For more information about Kregel Publications, visit our web site at http://www.kregel.com.

Cover design: Alan G. Hartman
Book design: Nicholas G. Richardson

Library of Congress Cataloging-in-Publication Data
Vassallo, Wanda.
   Church communications handbook / Wanda Vasallo.
     p.   cm.
   1. Communication—Religious aspects—Christianity.
2. Communication.
I. Title.
BV4319.V37   1998   254'.3—dc21   97-7363
                                     CIP

ISBN 0-8254-3925-6

Printed in the United States of America

1 2 3 / 04 03 02 01 00 99 98

For Doris and Jerome McIver—
with admiration and gratitude

In appreciation
to the amazing and inspiring men and women
who graciously talked with me about their work
so that I may share their experiences
and expertise with you:

Dr. Richard M. Adams
Mr. George E. Brian, Jr.
Rev. Bruce Buchanan
Sgt. Tony Crawford
Ms. Dana Effler
Dr. Dennis Hochgraber
Rosemary Johnson, LMSW-ACP, LMFT
Rev. Terry Kendrick
Dr. David Kuykendall
Rev. Sam Monzingo
Rev. Dorothy Moore
Rev. Gordon Moore
Rev. Russ Olman
Rev. Ron Raines
Mr. Ron Regan
Dr. Morris Sheats
Dr. Betty Spillman
Ms. Lois Stanley
Ms. Laurie Vassallo
Mr. George Wade
Rev. Jean Warner
Rev. Danny Wegman
Rev. Ed Young

Also to Dean Angel
for continuing to allow me to share
his tremendous expertise
in the field of communication.

And to Dr. Adrienne Stern
for reading the manuscript
and for making valuable suggestions.

Contents

Section V: Communicating with and Through the News Media

Section VI: Communicating Beyond Your Congregation

Index of Forms

Introduction

C hurches and other ministries are located in this world and, therefore, must find ways to relate to this world. Because of this, we should be as "wise as serpents, and harmless as doves" (Matt. 10:16 KJV) as we use current successful communication approaches to get out our message. We should also use every shred of information that is available to help us reach the unsaved and the unchurched and to meet the spiritual needs of those within the body of Christ.

We look backward and foolish when we ignore accepted practices, overlook scientifically conducted research, or fail to meet professional standards of conduct. For example, consider the preacher who yells at a television reporter to "get off this property right now" while the camera is rolling. The minister not only appears idiotic but also contributes nothing to the kingdom of God or to the image of the ministry as a whole.

God has enabled me to obtain training and acquire experiences that can be used to help the church become more effective in communicating its message. I have written this book for that reason.

I am certain that God ordered my career and gave me unusual opportunities that led up to my writing this book. I had been teaching in the Mesquite schools for about six weeks when the district superintendent called and asked me to meet with him. I went into that appointment bursting with curiosity and left in amazement. The superintendent offered me a position for the next year as coordinator of instructional television.

At the time all I knew about television was how to turn one on. But I spent a stimulating and exciting three years learning and doing every facet of television production and programming. I also served as the producer and host for three children's literature series.

Then the Lord led me to apply for a position with the Dallas schools. Upon being accepted, I went back to the classroom to teach speech and music. But after three semesters, I received a telephone call at home one evening. It was the assistant superintendent of communications offering me a job in his department. I had never had a journalism course, not even one in high school. Suddenly I was working as a professional journalist and was once more scrambling to learn everything I could about a totally new field. I served as director of communications and speech writer for the superintendent of the Dallas schools. During those fifteen years, I had rich and wonderful opportunities to learn extensively about many facets of communications with all types of people in all kinds of settings.

I then became the director of communications for a church, where I translated all I had learned in the "real world" and applied it to ministry. The pastor gave me free rein, and we used some "unchurchy" approaches in trying to communicate our message. Since that time, I have had numerous opportunities to attend seminars, observe many ministries, study what experts have to say, and interview numerous ministers about their successful approaches to communicating effectively.

I am convinced that the Lord ordered my steps and gave me rich and unusual opportunities with a purpose. His goal was to enable me to acquire a wealth of information for ministry professionals to help make their communication efforts more effective.

As you read through this book, you will discover that it is a practical guide to church communications. Each section and the chapters they contain cover essential information that will enable your church or parachurch organization to become more effective in communicating its message. Let's take a few moments to overview the contents of the book.

Section 1 deals with communication basics, such as determining what God wants your particular ministry to be doing, developing an overall communications plan, and discovering the unspoken messages you might be sending to others. In section 2, you will learn how to communicate person to person, while section 3 explains how you can communicate more effectively in various settings. Section 4 discusses how to communicate effectively through publications, advertising, and computers, while section 5 deals with communicating with and through the news media. Finally, in section 6, you will learn how to reach outside the four walls of your congregation to the unchurched.

You will discover that parts of this handbook take a how-to approach. For example, the news media operate in a certain manner, and various tasks should be done in specific ways in order to get a message out effectively and to survive in crisis situations. Some chapters deal with publications and give guidelines and tips for preparing professional-looking newsletters, brochures, and other pieces. Other chapters present a wealth of ideas and examples of what several churches have done successfully to reach the unchurched. A number of forms for use in planning and tracking various phases of communication are also included.

This book does not include specific guidelines for selecting a computer, and it does not give precise advice on choosing specific software. Neither does this book tell you how to produce your own television program. With the rapid pace of technological change, such information would be out of date by the time this manuscript was published.

This book is designed as a reference work for you to use as the need arises. Established ministries may find it helpful in fine-tuning and improving some approaches and programs. I'm confident that the stories about the experiences and accomplishments of other ministers will encourage you to launch out in some new and adventurous directions in your service for the Lord.

Wanda Vassallo

SECTION I

Getting Communications Basics in Place

Where there is no vision, the people perish.
—Proverbs 29:18a (KJV)

Catching God's Vision for Your Ministry

Effective communication has to do with sending messages clearly and receiving messages accurately. The key questions to ask are these: what message is being sent, when is it being sent, where is it being sent, and to whom is it being sent? For those in ministry, these are queries that only God can answer. Discovering the mind of Christ for your ministry or catching God's vision for what He wants accomplished by a particular parachurch group in a certain place is foundational and essential.

In writing his book entitled *User Friendly Churches,* George Barna had to interview the leaders of a number of different congregations. He noted that "unless they were driven by God's vision, they were bound to fail. Once in tune with the vision, it became the call to action that motivated clergy and laity alike. That vision became the filter through which all church activities were evaluated. Activities which coincided with the vision were pursued, and those which fell outside the parameters of the vision were rejected."[1]

Proverbs 29:18 tells us: "Where there is no vision, the people perish." But how do you know what God's vision is for your church or parachurch organization? How can you be sure that the direction you are going is ordained by God and not just your own idea? (For more help on answering this question, see the form entitled "Characteristics of a God-Given Vision," which you can find on page 21.) Since discerning God's vision is the initial step in communicating effectively, that's where we'll begin our study.

Vision That Is of God Will Not Go Away

The Rev. Dorothy Moore, founder and director of Reconciliation Outreach in Dallas, says, "If you don't have the Lord's vision for your ministry, it won't bear fruit."

About fifteen or sixteen years ago the Lord began to birth the vision for Moore's ministry—to work with the poor, the downtrodden, and the hopeless in the inner city. Considering her background as a New

15

York debutante and her social standing as the wife of a corporate attorney, that hardly seemed logical. "But," she says, "if it's from God, it just won't go away." She decided to test the waters by serving as a volunteer in Houston's fourth ward at the Martin Luther King Center. To her amazement, she found that she could relate well to the people God had called her to serve, and she felt at home doing it.

Moore describes her experience in fulfilling that vision as being like looking through a telescope. "First you see the overall view, and then gradually the details come into focus."

After moving to Dallas, Moore started Reconciliation Outreach in the inner city on a limited basis. However, it was ten years before the work came to real fruition. Reconciliation Outreach now has a shelter for abused and homeless women; another shelter for drug- and alcohol-addicted men; discipleship, mentoring, and parenting programs; a program serving more than one hundred young people; a thrift shop; an employment agency; and access to many other agencies for services such as health care. She found that during those ten long years, God gave her ministry success a little at a time—just enough to keep her hopeful.

"God doesn't give you anything without your paying a price," Moore reflects. "After all, Jesus had a vision, and it cost Him His life. When the Holy Spirit gets ready to move, it's not work at all. But, in preparation, you have to do all you know to do."[2]

Vision Does Not Change, But Circumstances Do

"When God planted Hopedale Baptist Church (eight miles south of Springfield, Missouri) in 1886 amid eighteen or twenty farms, I believe He planted it for today where it now is in the midst of more than 14,000 lost people." That is the firm belief of Pastor Terry Kendrick, who is convinced that the long-term vision that God has for a church probably will not change. "He has a special purpose for your church in your community," Kendrick states with conviction. He believes that the secret of building an effective ministry lies in finding the vision that God has for your ministry and your church or parachurch organization.

Four non-Christian farmers started Hopedale Baptist Church when they concluded that their area needed some religion. They found a traveling preacher who converted them and made them the first four deacons of the congregation.

In 1983 when Kendrick decided to return to Hopedale, where he had pastored as a student, the membership totaled eighteen people. He says, "The church had just gotten old and tired." They were thirty years behind the culture in which they lived. But the main problem, he believes, was that the church had lost its vision. "We did some research and discovered the church's original vision—to reach everyone in the Hopedale community with the Gospel."

As Kendrick communicated God's vision for the church, people started to get excited. And Hopedale, which he now describes as a "town and country" church in an unincorporated area, began to grow to its present membership of more than three hundred.

How did Kendrick know God's vision and how did he communicate it to the people? He believes that "vision has to be found on your knees before God. It's a supernatural thing. God will say to you, 'This is what I want you to do.'" Then God validates the vision by what happens and by what comes to pass. Kendrick also believes that the answers to the following questions confirm the vision:

- What do you weep about?
- What do you sing about? What enraptures you?
- What do you dream about? What keeps you awake at night?
- What do you think about when you're driving the car?

Kendrick delineates clearly between purpose and vision. He says that purposes are the same for any New Testament church and that they are general in scope. Vision, however, is unique and individual, and it is much narrower in nature.

Kendrick feels that it is just too much to present the entire vision to the congregation or parachurch organization at one time: "I didn't overwhelm them with the total vision." He began by sharing small parts of the vision and by trying to build on small successes. "They don't get excited until they start to see things happen," he comments. "As they begin to see the dream become reality, it becomes *their* vision. They have to see this as authentic—not just a pipe dream. They also have to believe the pastor is capable of leading them there." He believes that a pastor has to earn the trust of the people so that they assume he comes to them with what God wants.

At least once each year Kendrick preaches a state-of-the-church message or a vision sermon. "This includes where we came from, where we are, where we're going—God's purpose here." Also, he's always casting the vision—in other sermons, in classes, and in conversations. For example, Kendrick tells his congregation often that every time he walks through the sanctuary of their new building, he sees it filled with five hundred and fifty people instead of the three hundred who usually come on Sunday morning. He's found that some new members are caught up in the vision after they join, while others are drawn to the church because of the vision.

"The people see that God is in this," Kendrick remarks. And so the vision that God gave to the original founders of Hopedale and confirmed to Kendrick has become the vision of the people.[3]

Vision Is Confirmed and
Directed by God Through People

The Rev. Russ Olmon, copastor of Meadow Creek Community Church in Mesquite, Texas, had a passion for the lost from the moment he was saved. "Within seconds I tried to tell my friends about salvation," he recalls. He believes that at that moment God birthed in him the vision of reaching the lost, even though it would be several years before he became actively involved in a church.

But in retrospect, Olmon sees that God used others—especially the Rev. Ronnie Yarber, his copastor—to guide him in knowing what to do with the vision. This has resulted in a church of more than 650 that is designed in every detail to reach the lost.

While Olmon was a seminary student and member of Yarber's congregation, the latter invited him to lead a mission that the church wanted to start. Olmon was not enthusiastic at all about the idea. He went to one of his seminary professors for counsel, fully expecting him to confirm his decision to tell his pastor and the church board that he would not accept their offer. The professor listened patiently to his story and then, to the amazement of Olmon, responded, "My, you've made a terrible mistake."

"What do you mean?" he meekly asked.

"Well, obviously you're in the wrong church if you're not willing to prayerfully consider what this many committed people believe you should do." The professor continued by saying that God often uses other people to provide His direction in the lives of believers.

That conversation moved Olmon to spend time on his knees in prayer and to decide to become pastor of the mission church.

In the summer of 1996 with the new seekers' church boasting a membership of about three hundred and fifty and poised to build a new, larger building, Yarber approached Olmon again. This time he presented the prospect of merging the two congregations, which harbored the same heart and vision. Again Olmon was less than enthusiastic. But after the two pastors worked through all the reasons why Olmon thought it wouldn't work, the latter decided to submit the possibility to the Meadow Creek board and congregation. To his astonishment, everything fell into place. Yarber and Olmon became copastors of the combined congregations, which grew by more than one hundred new members in the first two-and-a-half months of its existence.

Olmon says, "Ronnie and I are very different, but there's a piece of us that connects. God has used him to direct my life on the curves, at points of critical decisions" (Olmon calls Ronnie both his mentor and a visionary).

Olmon feels that you become almost "a victim of your vision" in the sense that once you know what it is, you can never leave it. "The vision is the basis for all you do. It becomes your values. I ask myself, 'What do I *value* around here?' Then I can communicate the vision to others."

Olmon believes that God calls people. Then he uses other people to call them out to ministry and to recognize their gifts. "He works through leadership and others," he reflects.[4]

Vision Brings Confidence and Endurance

George Barna, in his book *The Power of Vision,* says that in churches where God's vision is the heart of people's efforts, the members feel good about themselves, perform better, have greater endurance, and are less likely to burn out. "Because the people feel empowered by God, they rise to challenges they could not ordinarily dream of confronting. Their performance is generally above average because they recognize that they are pursuing a higher calling and have been granted the stamina and resources to accomplish that end."[5]

Barna also recommends writing out the vision for ministry in a comprehensive manner. He says that even though no one else may ever read it, "by documenting your thoughts in detail you can return to the statement periodically to review whether you are on course, to determine if dimensions or nuances of the vision have been overlooked, to remind yourself of the power and depth of the vision and to become reinvigorated by that reintroduction to His dream for your work." He feels this is especially important when involved in future planning.[6]

Barna believes that helping the church understand the vision is critical. He recommends these strategies for sharing the vision:

- Sermons that constantly reflect the substance of the vision and show how the lives of outstanding biblical characters were molded by their vision.
- Printed materials, such as bulletins, newsletters, brochures, a visitor's packet, and an annual report.
- Letters from the pastor to the congregation that may include the vision statement as part of the church's letterhead.
- Teaching in Sunday school classes, small group studies, new members' classes, meetings, and retreats.
- Multiple vision casters, in addition to the senior pastor, who consistently promote and explain the vision.[7]

Barna concludes, "Vision must be viewed as a direction provided by God and as a strategic framework for ministry. . . . It is a directive that we must obey, praying for His blessing and utilizing all of the energy and resources at our disposal. His vision is His set of marching orders for us to follow."[8]

Vision Brings Motivation and Dedication

Vision, in my own experience, is like a consuming fire within that evokes an intense desire to be fulfilled. I believe that there are eight main steps involved in fulfilling God's vision.

1. A vision begins with an all-out commitment to the Lord, a consecration of talents, a surrender of rights, and a willingness to step up on the potter's wheel. Abraham demonstrated this when he readily left his family and land for an unknown destination at God's command.

2. God gives a vision or a dream. At first you understand its main theme or thrust as through a glass darkly, but you don't see the total picture in detail or understand all its ramifications. It is important to guard your vision carefully at this point, for it will usually sound far-fetched, perhaps even unattainable. Share it only with a few close, mature Christians who will be willing to pray for you, encourage you, and provide godly counsel and direction. We can learn from Joseph's experience in which he shared with his brothers his dream of being in a position of authority over them. They did not like the message, and they did everything possible to keep his dream from becoming a reality.

3. God provides protection. Surely it was God who put the determination into Reuben's heart to keep his brothers from killing Joseph.

4. God provides a time of preparation and opens doors for training. He also sanctifies, purifies, and gets rid of the spiritual dross in the lives of believers. Moses' story is an amazing example of the way in which God provided him with the finest education as well as an intimate knowledge of the ways of the Egyptians.

5. God tests and proves us to find out what is in our hearts and to let us discover the same. Joseph's unjust imprisonment provided a good opportunity for his true character to be revealed.

6. God wants to make certain that the vision does not become more important to us than He is; thus there comes a time for the death of the vision, when it seems that it will not be fulfilled. Abraham had every logical reason to doubt that his vision would ever come

to fruition, when he and Sarah had reached old age without bearing the son whom God had promised and who was necessary for Abraham to become the father of many nations. Perhaps during Moses' long years on the backside of the desert, he also thought his vision would never come to pass.

7. God will grant us favor with others to accomplish His purpose through us. He will open doors that we could never open for ourselves. Joseph was probably more amazed than anyone when he suddenly found himself as a ruler in Egypt, second only to Pharaoh.

8. God fulfills the vision in His own time. Often the wait might seem to us like a painfully long period. Our clocks may be set on central standard time or eastern daylight-savings time, but God operates on everlasting time. In other words, His timing is always perfect. Joseph again provides a good example. The vision that God gave him in two dreams as a boy showed that he would one day occupy a position of great power and authority. But what would have happened if Joseph had become the prime minister of Egypt right after he had climbed out of the well?

Vision becomes the ever-present prescription lenses through which you see everything that happens and evaluate every opportunity presented to you. God gives you a passion to pursue the vision and fulfill it—even when it seems a hopeless dream and an exercise in futility. Your faith and endurance will be tried and tested as by a refiner's fire. While you still have the prerogative to turn away, once you have bought into the vision with all your heart, you probably will not even consider the possibility of ending the pursuit.

Along the way, your desire to fulfill the vision becomes fused with God's desire to bring it to pass in your life. Catching God's vision for your ministry is one of the most motivating, mysterious, and challenging experiences that can happen.

Characteristics of a God-Given Vision

1. The vision won't go away.
2. The vision does not change, even when circumstances do.
3. The vision is confirmed and directed by God through people.
4. The vision brings confidence and endurance.
5. The vision brings motivation and dedication.

2 Developing an Overall Communications Plan

The old saying, "If you don't know where you want to go, any road will lead you there" is a perfect fit when you're talking about church communications. If you're moving, you're going to get somewhere. If you have a church or ministry, you are communicating something. Without a plan, however, the result in both cases may not be all you had hoped for, and certainly not all it could be.

Paramount to the success of any plan is the selection of the person who is going to assume the major responsibility for seeing that it's carried out. Communicating effectively in even a relatively small church is a big job. Ideally it should be given to a full-time staff member or, at least, given as a major responsibility of a staff member who is qualified and enthusiastic about functioning in that role.

The development of an accurate job description, the delineation of the chain of command, and the determination of the authority of the person who is selected should be spelled out clearly. For example, will that person serve as the official spokesperson for the church? Does the work have to be approved before being sent out or printed?

The organization of a communications committee can be helpful in planning, carrying out the plans, and evaluating the projects. The committee might be divided into subgroups to work on specific tasks, such as advertising. The general committee should consider setting overall goals for the program and should look at the events and activities of the year in order to plan a month-by-month calendar for successful communications. (For more help on doing this, see the form entitled "Communications Planning Steps," which you can find on page 30.)

There are five vital principles for developing and implementing an effective plan for communicating the message of your church or other religious group, both to the people within the organization and to those outside of it.

Principle 1: Do Your Homework

Research can tell you much about your community that you may not be aware of, even if you've ministered there for several years. Research, however, doesn't have to be a one-person effort. With a little guidance, a secretary and interested members of your congregation can help you find out what you want to know.

You should begin by defining the boundaries of the community you are trying to reach. If your church is the only one of your denomination in the city, then your community is the corporate limits and beyond. This is also true of the downtown church with little or no residential neighborhood. Otherwise, you will probably want to define an approximate square-mile radius as your target area. If you have programs for persons with special needs, such as for children with disabilities, then the boundaries in that particular area will be much broader. Parents of these children will come a long way to have the needs of their loved ones met.

Once you have defined the parameters, there are many sources you can check for demographic information about your neighborhood. They include:

1. The city, particularly the department of planning.
2. The public library. While the extent of data will vary, every municipal library should have some type of helpful information. Those in major metropolitan centers will have vast information and well-trained, knowledgeable people to assist you. College and university libraries are another possible source.
3. Denominational research departments. Many denominations have research departments that can be of significant help to their member churches.
4. The U.S. Census Bureau, Department of Commerce. The federal census that is conducted every ten years is available in various formats at minimal cost. The bureau also has available other reports based on its continual research efforts.[1] The web site address is http://www.census.gov.
5. States also have government offices that are responsible for providing population and commerce data to other government offices and to state residents. Available information is gleaned from federal, state-funded projects, county and community governments. Information can often be provided for specific geographic areas, such as counties, communities, and zip codes.[2]
6. The public school district.
7. Agencies, such as the United Way.
8. The chamber of commerce.

9. Leg work. It is amazing what you can discover by walking down a street, even if it's one you drive down daily.

10. Another source that may provide useful information is the U.S. Government Printing Office. A catalog of published reports and papers, which must be purchased, may be obtained by calling 202–783–3238. The web site address is www.access.gpc.gov.

11. Also, information may be obtained through the offices of your congressperson and senators. They may be able to identify helpful sources of information you may not be aware of or be of assistance in obtaining facts and statistics. A possible charge might be made for this type of assistance.[3]

Find out which services are available in your area and then decide what's missing. Discover everything possible about your targeted population.

Next, research where there are unmet needs. For example, you may find that your area has an unusually high percentage of senior citizens. Providing programs to meet their special interests and needs could result in an expanded cadre of people with a variety of talents and the time to participate in various ministries.

Consider conducting interviews with selected residents who are not members of your church. Find out about their attitudes toward churches and your church in particular as well as their interests (for instance, what they like to do in their free time, how they feel about their community, and what they value in life; chapter 10 provides more information about how to do this). You may be surprised by what you discover. The information will help you determine how to better communicate with the residents whom you wish to reach.

An analysis of the information you have about your members can also be helpful. Compare data that has been broken down by age group, marital status, special needs, and so forth, with programs that are currently being offered.

If this information is not readily available, consider developing a card to be completed by each member (for more help on doing this, see the form entitled "Member Information Form," which you can find on page 69). In addition to the usual information, such as age and occupation, include such items as past employment, civic and church responsibilities, and special interests and hobbies. You may discover some new talents and needs that you weren't aware of.

Also, consider conducting a survey of members to determine how effective your current efforts are and to generate suggestions for improvement. Chapter 10 discusses how to develop a survey with sample questions and provides suggestions for follow-up.

Principle 2: Identify Your Audiences

Ask yourself this question: "Whom am I trying to reach?" Your identification of the various audiences forms the basis for the strategies that you will develop to reach each of the specific groups.

Note that every church or organization has two main audiences:

- Internal audiences
- External audiences

Internal audiences are church members, staff members, and others who participate in the affairs of the organization on a regular basis. External audiences are all those unaffiliated with the organization.

While these two audiences will vary from church to church, there are some predictable groups; others should be added or deleted to fit your unique situation.

External Audiences

1. general public
2. unsaved
3. unchurched
4. specific ethnic groups
5. various age groups
6. special need groups (for example, unwed mothers, alcoholics, bereaved, and those with disabilities)

Internal Audiences

1. members
2. nonmembers who participate over a period of time
3. visitors
4. various age groups
5. divorced
6. widowed
7. couples with children
8. members at home
9. members with disabilities
10. staff members

Principle 3: Develop a Specific Plan for Reaching Each Audience

Once you've come up with a comprehensive list, then you are ready to develop a specific plan for reaching each segment. An excellent technique for doing this is through the use of brainstorming with staff members, board members, and other representative laypersons (see chapter 8 for further information).

For example, if your goal is to reach unchurched baby boomers, you will probably need to develop some nontraditional, unchurchy sounding approaches. You will want to ask these questions:

- What is the need?
- What messages are we trying to send to this particular group?
- What vehicles will we use?
- How can these approaches be implemented?
- How much will it cost?
- How can we evaluate the effectiveness of our efforts?

Remember that asking those who are participating in a particular area of ministry to help in the development of the plan is critical for its success.

Here is a sample communication project model for the development and implementation of a new program (for more help in doing this, see the form entitled "Communications Project," which you can find on page 30).

Communication Project Model
Project Name: Ministry for the Deaf

1. Briefly state the project: To begin a new ministry for the deaf and hearing impaired.
2. Need for this project: No other church in this area has a ministry of this kind.
3. Purpose of project: To effectively meet the spiritual needs of this group and to provide opportunities for Christian fellowship within the group and with hearing members.
4. Procedures:
   a. Select the director and assistants for the program who know sign language, understand the deaf culture, and, preferably, have some experience working with the deaf.
   b. Identify deaf and hearing-impaired individuals in this general area of the city.
      (1) Contact agencies, such as Deaf Action Center, that provide services for those with this type of disability.
      (2) Contact public and private schools for students who are enrolled in special classes.
      (3) Send news releases to newspapers and radio and television stations giving the details of the program, including what special equipment and services will be available. The news

release could also include a picture and the qualifications of the person who will head the program or a picture of the pastor signing, "I love you."

(4) Contact talk shows on Christian radio stations, and offer to appear as a guest to discuss the proposed program.

  c. Prepare the congregation for a positive reception of the program.

(1) The director will explain the program in a morning service.

(2) Brief deaf awareness presentations will be given to prepare members to relate to future participants in the program. These may include a deaf person giving a brief presentation, a dramatic sketch about deaf culture, and a sign-language interpretation of musical numbers.

  d. Develop the program.

(1) Write personal letters to those who have been identified, inviting them and those who will work with the program to a get-acquainted breakfast or luncheon. Follow up the letter with a personal phone call of invitation.

(2) Purchase assistive listening devices for magnification of sound in the sanctuary and other meeting areas.

(3) Have all services interpreted in sign language.

(4) Install a TTY (equipment that allows the deaf to communicate over the telephone) in the church office or the home of the director of the program.

(5) Offer sign-language classes (at a later date) for other members of the congregation as a means of reaching out to the deaf or hearing-impaired.

5. Needed resources:
  a. Postage for mailing
  b. Pictures for newspapers
  c. Funds for breakfast or luncheon
  d. Cost of special equipment with earphones
  e. Cost of TTY
  f. Identification of those interested in working with the program
  g. Identification of and salary of sign language interpreter, unless a qualified volunteer is available

6. Timing of project:
  a. Identification of workers—date_____
  b. Publicity for project—week of_____
  c. Installation of equipment—date_____
  d. Mailing invitations to breakfast/luncheon—date_____
  e. Breakfast or luncheon—date_____
  f. Beginning of program—date_____

7. Evaluation:
   a. Number of people participating
   b. Completion of anonymous reaction form by participants
   c. Discussion by focus group of participants stating their responses and experiences in the program
   d. Observations of director and workers in program
   e. Use of feedback to fine-tune the program and increase its effectiveness

Principle 4: Make Communications a Specific Item in Your Overall Church Budget

Traditionally, churches have spent little on communicating their message. But if your program is potentially worth a lot, it's certainly worth a commitment of a reasonable amount of time and money to communicate its value. It should not be relegated to "whatever's left over" for its funding.

Appoint a committee of knowledgeable staff members and lay people who have expertise in this area and come up with two lists: components of a plan for effective communications and components of a plan containing essential elements and wish list items. For example, a future goal might be to have a billboard at the freeway or highway exit near your church.

Principle 5: Evaluate the Effectiveness of Your Program and Make Changes and Modifications as Appropriate

Since the process of communications is a cumulative one, it is difficult to evaluate. For example, you may drive by a billboard a dozen times on your way to work before you consciously notice that it's there. There are things you can do, however, to help determine the effectiveness of a certain approach. For instance, add a line on your visitor's card asking the person how he or she heard about the church. This will help you evaluate the impact of advertising, news stories, and the like. In the case of a seminar or similar event, ask on the registration form how the participant heard about the event, whether he or she would be interested in receiving information about future occasions of the same type, and for referrals of others who might like to know about such events.

While everything can't be measured in dollars and cents, another way to evaluate a specific program or approach is to analyze time and money spent on the project in relation to the results. Looking at an effort from that viewpoint may help determine whether the result was worth the effort or whether resources could be used more effectively on other endeavors.

One of the most effective things one church communicator did as far as getting new people to come was to send a flyer about the new church to residents of the neighborhood via marriage mail[4] or cooperative mailing. (This is a relatively inexpensive way to blanket an area.) Several visitors came to the service clutching the flyer and told the ushers that they had received an invitation in the mail. Their enthusiastic response was evidence that the procedure worked and should be used again. Other approaches are evaluation instruments, instant surveys by show of hands, attendance at various events, interviews with small groups from selected audiences, informal conversations, and observable responses. Be imaginative in evaluating, but do evaluate! Otherwise, how will you know whether the time, effort, and money involved are accomplishing your purpose?

Developing a comprehensive, overall plan for communicating effectively requires a commitment of time, energy, and resources on the part of a number of people. The results can provide the necessary information for a giant step forward in the effectiveness and outreach of your ministry.

Communications Planning Steps

1. Specify needs.
2. Identify the audiences.
3. Decide on the messages to be sent.
4. Determine the most appropriate vehicles.
5. Develop a plan of implementation.
6. Implement a schedule.
7. Evaluate the results.

Communications Project

Name of Project_____

1. The need for the project
2. A brief description of the project
3. The purpose of the project
4. The procedures to be followed
5. The resources needed
6. The timing of the project
7. The evaluation of the results

What Unspoken Messages Are You Sending?

3

The Christian Choraliers in concert, 7:00 P.M., November 3, the church sign proudly proclaimed. It sounded like an interesting evening. The problem? It was now November 15.

What message did that church send to passersby? That it didn't keep up with day-to-day business and that it didn't care about the impression that might be left with those who read its sign. Some people may have been irritated. Perhaps they really like the Christian Choraliers and are disappointed that they didn't know about the concert in time to attend. Others may have stored their impression in their subconscious file of "signs not to look at in the future."

Regardless of the individual reaction, the fact is that the church sent a negative message that, doubtless, it didn't intend to transmit. While not keeping a church sign current may seem like a small item amid the countless tasks that must be attended to, that tiny detail can present a negative image for a ministry.

Solomon spoke about the "little foxes that spoil the vine" in Song of Solomon 2:15. He was reminding us that we may do well in the big things but overlook small details like letting the little foxes jump up and ruin the crop. Certainly in the area of ministry there are numerous "little foxes" constantly nipping at our heels, and a fertile ground is in the unspoken messages that every church transmits daily.

The Church Sign

Ask yourself some questions about your sign. Does it stand at right angles to the two-way street so that it may be readily seen by motorists going in either direction? Is the church sign close enough to the street to be easily seen? Does it look contemporary, or is it dated, giving the impression of a church that is out of touch with the times? Does it have the name in large enough letters so that people can easily read them from a distance? Does the church sign contain the ministry's logo? Does it display the times for services along with the phone number of the church? Is it well maintained? Is

31

it lighted at night? Is the post freshly painted? Are the post and the sign in good repair?

Including the words "All Are Welcome" on your sign indicates that you would like to have people with disabilities worship with you and that you can accommodate special needs, such as wheelchair access. The National Organization on Disabilities says that "the phrase now has new meaning."[1]

A message touting an event that is already history not only features worthless information, but it also sends a loud and clear message that the church is careless and not attentive to detail. Certainly it is better not to display any information than to present that kind of negative image.

Information that is kept up over a period of several weeks becomes stale and results in regular passersby becoming programmed to ignore the message. Changing the sign frequently may be a lot of trouble, but it is important if you want any of the messages to be read. And, of course, a misspelled word leaps out for the whole world to see and ridicule.

Coming up with catchy, interest-piquing sermon titles and displaying them on the church sign can create interest. If nothing else, the readers may receive a provocative thought as they hurry by. And who knows? They may eventually find their way inside the sanctuary to hear the rest of the message.

When there is nothing special to feature, many churches have found that a clever, punchy statement will elicit a chuckle, a thought-provoking moment, or a response from those who read it. Drivers who take that route every day will look forward to reading the messages.

Here are some possibilities:

- Coincidence is God's way of remaining anonymous.
- God has a "don't-do-it-yourself" kit.
- Anger is one letter short of danger.
- Never fear tomorrow, for God is already there.
- When God guides, He provides.
- God is your heavenly Father. Call home.
- Fuel up here. God doesn't ration His power.
- Today is the last day of your past.
- The empty vessel makes the greatest sound.
- All sunshine makes the desert.
- Habits are first cobwebs, then cables.
- Is your faith ancient history or current events?
- Let the Son shine in.
- No God, no peace. Know God, know peace.
- The wages of sin have never been reduced.

- For a web begun, God sends thread.
- Call on God, but row away from the rocks.
- One on God's side is a majority.
- What on earth are you doing for heaven's sake?
- Not just a car can be recalled by its maker.

Russ Olmon, copastor of Meadow Creek Community Church in Mesquite, Texas, believes it is important to remember who your audience is for your church sign. He says, "The sign is for the passerby, not for the church member. Most church members drive in the parking lot without even glancing at the sign. The message should be geared toward the unbeliever." He believes that messages such as, "You think it's hot here?" produce a definite negative reaction from the people the church needs to reach.[2]

A professional-looking, additional sign might be appropriate for a special program or project. For example, a colorful banner, complete with balloons, would attract attention for vacation Bible school. For a special event a portable, lighted sign can be effective and worth the rental fee. Or, for fairly frequent use, you might want to consider purchasing your own. If your church is open for prayer at certain times, does a sign let passersby know they are welcome to come inside?

Perhaps you have a sign near the city limits welcoming motorists to your church. What does it look like? Has it stood there for forty years in its original condition? Perhaps it needs a facelift or even a replacement. Is the information current? Also, check out any directional signs pointing the way to your church. Could they use a fresh coat of paint?

In planning any permanent signage, one of the main considerations should be durability and resistance to damage by weather and vandals. Checking with zoning officials in advance about the size of signs that are allowed on the property can save headaches and money in the long run. Needless to say, a marred sign should be repaired or replaced immediately.

The Grounds

What signals do the grounds surrounding your church building send out? "Here is a church that cares about cleanliness, order, and beauty," or "This must be a sloppy, slipshod operation." Of course, people may not actually say those kinds of things, but they will subconsciously form an impression that labels the kind of ministry within the building.

Is the property well landscaped? If not, it would probably be worth the expense to hire a professional landscaper to plan a design that will enhance the beauty and go with the character of the architecture. If the expense of having shrubs and trees planted is too much, perhaps volunteers could do at least some of the work. Have dead trees and shrubs been removed and replaced, or have they been left on the property for some time, thereby marring its overall appearance?

Is there a flower bed? Even one flower bed, perhaps in an area surrounding the sign, adds great eye appeal and grabs the attention of those who pass by. Is the grass kept mowed and neatly edged? Is trash picked up? Are leaves raked up in the fall and disposed of? A well-manicured lawn, neatly trimmed hedges and trees, and seasonal flowers are a natural asset and can be used with landscape lighting to highlight the beauty of your property. If your church has lovely stained-glass windows or an elegant steeple, lighting will provide aesthetic inspiration and admiration from all who see them.

Do drivers need to have their cars' front ends aligned because your church parking lot needs resurfacing? Are parking space lines clearly visible? Are directional arrows painted on the pavement to help traffic flow? Is the lot well lighted at night? If it's gravel, consider including paving in next year's budget. It's expensive, but women with high heels and men with freshly shined shoes will appreciate the tidier and easier-to-walk-on surface. Also, paving eliminates the temptation for children to pick up a few stones and toss them at one another.

Is there accessibility for the dissabled? A sign with the international accessibility logo at the entrance of the parking lot with an arrow pointing the way toward handicapped parking is helpful for those who need this accommodation. And, of course, reserved handicapped-parking places should be clearly marked with the logo. More information about this may be found in chapter 7.

What about the building? Even an old structure can look neat, attractive, and inviting if the trim is kept painted and everything is in good repair. In fact, an older building can be fascinating and interesting to the eye.

Venturing Inside

Intriguing messages on the sign and evidence of pride and caring in the upkeep of the building and grounds may result in observers' deciding to take a closer look. In case they do, will they readily know which door to use? In case there might possibly be any confusion, is there a sign to point the way to the main entrance? Are the buildings clearly marked? Are entrances well lighted? Is provision made for a person in a wheelchair or with limited mobility?

Once inside, what will people see? What will their impressions be? Will their first glimpse inside the doors be inviting and aesthetically pleasing? Will they feel ill at ease or confused, not knowing which direction to go? Perhaps the way to the sanctuary is obvious. If not, a sign with an arrow should give direction. What if they would like to stop by the restroom? Will they perhaps be embarrassed by having to ask a person of the opposite gender, or maybe they'll just have to wander around in hope of running across it. They may need to take babies and toddlers to the nursery or children to a program for their age groups. Will they know which way to go?

A large church that is composed of several buildings would be wise to consider erecting a board with the entire layout of the buildings and floor plans. This should be marked to show the meeting places of various groups and classes. A niche containing flyers with the same printed information could be provided at the bottom of the board.

Will visitors see clean walls that are free of stains and smudges, or will they notice watermarks on the ceiling where the roof leaked two months ago? Will they enjoy walking on a beautiful, clean carpet? Will their eyes feast on quality art work?

It goes without saying that a smiling face should be at the entrance to greet visitors and offer assistance. Name tags with the proper designation of "greeter" or "usher" are important to visitors who are seeking information or assistance.

Bulletin Boards and Displays

An attractive bulletin board can help introduce visitors to your church and its work. If one is used, it should be displayed in a prominent place where it can be easily seen upon entering the building. The bulletin board should be changed frequently; otherwise, people will stop looking at it.

Without some kind of covering, most bulletin boards look deadly dull. Felt, flannel, contact paper, or corrugated board add to the attractiveness of bulletin boards. The use of a couple of contrasting bright colors will draw attention. Also, matting photographs or children's art work on construction paper (which is complementary with your color scheme) will enhance the overall appearance and highlight those elements.

Keep your bulletin-board design simple by using large letters to set the theme and highlight a few large elements. Those walking by should be able to get the message and see the pictures, drawings, or other parts without having to press their noses against the board. Have photographs enlarged, preferably to at least a size of eight-by-ten inches. Too much information or a cluttered look will result in few lookers.

Some possibilities for bulletin-board use include the following:

- pictures of new members with their names in large lettering
- pictures of a special church activity, such as a mission outreach
- announcements and pictures of weddings and new babies
- member of the week with a picture and information
- pictures of a winning sports team sponsored by the church
- spotlight on a certain department or area of ministry
- picture and information about an upcoming seminar or special speaker
- covers from new church library books or book covers on a special theme
- opportunities for service within the church
- church's community projects
- visual representation on how the church dollar is spent
- updates on special offerings
- pictorial report on progress of a new building project
- church members in the news with articles from newspapers and newsletters

You also can take a cue from the supermarkets and have standing exhibits that may be placed as desired—even in the middle of a wide hallway so that attendees will have to notice them. Banners and mobiles on wires are attention-getting devices. You can also buy relatively inexpensive folding table top display units. These come in their own carrying or storage cases and are complete with adjustable shelves. Or, furnish a few hinges and sheets of pegboard or plywood, and get a handyman-type in your church to build your own display unit.

Another alternative to the cork bulletin board is to cover a wall with magnetic paint. This is then covered with a coat of regular wall paint. Small magnets may be used to hold photos and papers. Magnetized plastic alphabets and strips are also available.

The possibilities are limitless as to what you can do with these types of display approaches. Here are a few ideas:

- Take instamatic pictures of new members when they join the church. Have a special new-members spot to display the clearly labeled pictures. This will help the congregation get acquainted with new members and give them special recognition. One large, downtown church displays pictures of new members for more than a year to help others in recognizing them and learning their names.
- Have a display depicting the work of a missionary whom the church supports. This could include pictures as well as real objects to give viewers some idea of their work and the culture.

- Children's drawings and crafts could be displayed. A nice touch would be to include a picture of the young artist beside his or her work.
- An upcoming project of the church could be featured. For example, if the construction of a new gymnasium is beginning, an artist's drawing and a scale model of the finished building could be displayed, along with the floor plan and perhaps photos of the first building phases.
- A successfully completed program could be highlighted. For example, consider a project in which the teens raise money, visit a children's hospital, and give each child a stuffed animal. Pictures might include shots of teens washing cars to make the money, one of the teens sitting in the middle of all the animals, a teen handing an animal to a delighted child, and the happy face of a child who is in a hospital bed and playing with one of the toys.
- The significance of a soon-to-be observed holiday, such as Easter, might be the subject of another display.
- A display highlighting books in the church library would help acquaint worshipers with what's available. Jackets from new books could be used.

A sure-fire attention getter for the foyer is a kiosk, a small free-standing structure housing a screen for projection of video or slides. The frequent changes in images can be used effectively to give visitors as well as members a brief overview of some of the church's interesting programs and projects.

In all of the displays, be sure to have a central focus. This may be one large picture, accompanied by a few smaller ones, rather than a dozen small photos. Also, lettering should be large enough to be easily read without having to come within a foot of it. It also should be at average eye level. Don't make people bend over or stand on tiptoe and crane their necks. More likely than not, they just won't do it.

Velcro® is an amazingly useful material both for bulletin boards and displays of various types. It can be purchased by the yard in many colors. The entire surface of a bulletin board can be covered with brightly colored Velcro® and can display almost anything. The napped surface of the board bonds with the hook tape that can be stuck on most surfaces, which eliminates thumbtacks and pins. Velcro® is remarkably strong and will support somewhat heavy, three-dimensional objects or signs.

In planning all displays, determine your communication purpose. What do you want to say? To whom? What is the most compelling way to display the material? What will you need to do it effectively?

Asking these questions will help you achieve your goal in the most effective way possible.

Finally, finding the right person (namely, someone with imagination and artistic ability) to coordinate this valuable communications approach is critical to its effectiveness.

Within the Sanctuary

Once people are inside the sanctuary, what impression will they get? What is the focal point of the area? Is it aesthetically pleasing? Is it well lighted? Is the environment conducive to worship? What kind of atmosphere has been created by the decor and the music? If hymnals are used, are they in good condition? Are the surroundings bright and cheerful or gloomy? Will what the participants experience with their senses encourage them to make a return visit?

Moving Billboards

Does your church have a bus or a van? This could be a great opportunity to get your name out in the community on a regular basis. Everywhere those vehicles travel, they're providing free advertising. That could be good. Or they could be making a negative statement with every mile they travel. What kind of impression are those vehicles making? Even if they are several years old, they can still look neat and well maintained. If the paint is scratched and faded, perhaps it's time for a new paint job. Are there dents in the fenders and missing hubcaps? Would you really want your child to ride in those vehicles? Would you want them to be your mode of transportation to church? Does a particular vehicle look as though it's ready to fall apart? If the answer to any of these questions is yes, then your vehicles are saying negative things about your ministry.

What about the lettering? Is it professionally done and large enough to be legible at a distance? Does it contain the logo of the church, the street address, city and state, and the telephone number, including area code?

The Answering Machine

Imagine that people write down the telephone number to your church and decide to call for more information. Perhaps no one is in the office, and the answering machine takes the call. Will people hear an enthusiastic voice filled with warmth or a boring monotone? Probably the best voice to use is that of the pastor.

Then what? Few people want to hear a ten-minute recorded message, but many who phone are seeking information about the location of the church and service times. These probably should be included briefly along with an invitation to visit. In giving the location, indicate the number and street along with the nearest intersection. In a metropolitan area where several cities are in close proximity, also give the name of the city in which the facility is located.

If a special event is coming up soon, that can also be mentioned briefly, but don't try to give your schedule of special speakers for the next three months. The caller won't remember the information anyway and may be irritated by such a long message.

If a message is left, make sure someone calls back as soon as possible.

Voice Mail

Many people find voice mail very irritating and extremely impersonal, especially if they are required to enter number after number without ever having the opportunity to speak with a real human being. A church can hardly afford to contribute to the frustration that results and to risk seeming uncaring when just the opposite image is desired. During office hours, having the phone answered by a warm, friendly voice is important. After office hour, voice mail can be effective in routing messages to appropriate mail boxes in the case of a large staff.

Picture the hundreds, perhaps thousands, of eyes and ears that are receiving your unspoken messages everyday, and make sure that the messages you are sending are the ones you really want to convey.

Unspoken Messages Checklist

- Church sign: Is it easily seen and read? Is the message current?
- Grounds: are grounds pleasing to the eye and consistently well maintained? Is the parking lot in good condition and signs positioned for efficient traffic flow?
- Entrance to church: Is the foyer aesthetically pleasing? Will visitors know where to go for various purposes and whom to ask for needed information?
- Bulletin boards and displays: Is information changed frequently to ensure continued interest? Are the elements big, bold, and colorful and the lettering easily read?
- Sanctuary: Is it well lighted and appealing to look at? Are special equipment and seating available so that those with disabilities may fully participate?
- Church van or bus: Is it kept clean and well maintained? Is lettering professionally done and legible at a distance?
- Answering machine: Is the voice friendly and professional sounding? Are location and service times provided in a succinct message?

SECTION II

Communicating
Person to Person

And daily in the temple, and in every house,
they ceased not to teach and preach Jesus Christ.
—Acts 5:42 (KJV)

4 The Stranger in Your Midst

I glanced over the page again. It certainly said all the right things. Nice sentiments. Words such as "love," "welcome," "family of God," and "caring." It was a full-page ad. It wasn't cheap, even at the so-called poverty rate sometimes offered to churches.

"Maybe we ought to go there Sunday," I told my husband, handing him the newspaper. "Sounds okay. Might as well," he agreed.

After several years of attending the same church week in and week out, it was not easy being an outsider looking for a church home. Just deciding where to look next was a real challenge. We were determined to keep an open mind. That decision led us to all kinds of churches—from large ones to tiny ones and everything in between—denominational, nondenominational, racially mixed, congregations of a race other than our own, churches in our neighborhood, and so on.

Sunday morning we eagerly drove into the parking lot of a particular church. The congregation owned a beautiful, well-maintained building. Lovely flowers were on the communion table. The organist played well. The choir, though small, was quite good. The pastor was an excellent speaker, and his message was timely. But when we left, we resolved never to return again.

"Are you sure that's the church in the ad?" my husband queried. We still were dutifully wearing the visitor tags that we had removed from the visitor cards we had filled out. Not a single person had spoken to us. One woman almost returned my smile but then turned quickly away. Several others looked at us coldly as though we were intruders in their sanctuary.

"Did they ever waste their money on that ad," I pointed out. "I wonder whether they could be charged with false advertising. I think that's what's known as the cold shoulder." I lapped up the warm, bright sunshine, feeling as though I had been trapped inside a deep freeze for the past hour and a half. (It should come as no surprise that there was also no response to the visitor's card we had completed and put in the offering plate.)

The pastor of another church we had visited sent us an audiotape, thanking us by name for visiting his church and inviting us back. That was a rather nice, personal touch since I had a tape recorder handy. But I'm not sure I would have gone to the trouble of tracking down a recorder if one had not been readily available. The next thing we heard from that church, though, was an ardent appeal for money. And months later, we were still receiving dramatic pleas for financial help.

One Sunday morning we ventured to a rapidly growing church in our area. We arrived early for the second service. We had to stand outside for several minutes; and when we got into the foyer, the first service had just been dismissed. We were caught in the crush of people rushing into and out of the church simultaneously. At one point, I was nearly knocked down, and I pictured my obituary: "Woman killed in church stampede."

Finally, inside the church, we wandered up and down the aisles, trying to find two seats together. Some of the people sitting near empty seats told us defiantly with scowling faces, "Those seats are saved!" At long last we sank into chairs on different rows, feeling as though we had been in the crush of a dollar clearance sale for one hundred dollar items. It didn't take us long to decide that we didn't want to endure that kind of stress and confusion every Sunday.

A visit to another church provided an intriguing minidrama. We easily found an appropriate place to sit. But one visiting couple a few rows in front of us was not as fortunate. Some regular church members walked in, looked at them quite sternly, and told them in no uncertain terms that they were in the wrong pew and needed to move. The embarrassed pair dutifully changed to another spot.

A moderately sized church invited visitors to a short fellowship after the service. They served coffee and soft drinks, fruit, and pastries. This provided the opportunity for visitors to meet the pastor and his wife, several staff members, and lay leaders. It was a warm, enjoyable fifteen minutes that obviously left those who participated with a favorable impression and a feeling of being welcomed and valued.

We visited another church whose stated primary mission was to reach the unchurched. From the pulpit the pastor welcomed visitors. He mentioned casually that visitors' cards were available if anyone wanted to fill one out, but he did not make an issue of it or ask visitors to stand or raise their hands. The reason? In a conversation after the service, he cited studies which show that the baby-boomer generation—the group which makes up the majority of residents around the church—likes to take a look without having any attention called to themselves. (After the service, the pastor also pointed out an area where participants could meet with laypersons to ask questions and find out more about the church.)

After visiting one large church, we received a phone call from one of the members. He thanked me for visiting and expressed a genuine interest in us as individuals. He asked whether we had any prayer needs and prayed for me over the phone. He also asked whether we would like to receive the church bulletin so that we would know what was going on at their church.

Another large congregation has all of the parking places near the entrance reserved for visitors, while members (except for those with disabilities) are required to park across the street. The moment you get parked, a member dressed in a cheerful red vest opens the door for you and enthusiastically welcomes you to their fellowship. In inclement weather, attendants escort visitors to the door while holding large golf umbrellas over them. Once inside, a greeter also welcomes you and gives directions to the nursery, children's church, or wherever you need to go.

The pastors of two churches we visited used their Sunday morning sermons as an opportunity to soundly upbraid their congregations for their particular shortcomings. We were rather embarrassed to be there and felt as if their correction should have been saved for a special meeting of members. It didn't take long to decide that we would not want to become a part of either church family and be subjected to such tirades.

A Sunday evening solo trek to a medium-sized church proved to be a warm experience. I was greeted at the front door by the pastor, and before I got inside the church, two other people had warmly shaken hands and welcomed me. Two members came over and introduced themselves before the service began, and, afterward, several others spoke. I felt at home. I was blessed, and those members made me feel as though my presence was a blessing to them. Here was a church that really had its act together about how to make an outsider feel welcomed.

We also liked another church we visited several times. The people were warm and friendly. The messages were excellent. It had a lot going for it, but the music was so loud that it actually hurt our eardrums. We mentioned the problem to the pastor, but it was obvious that the volume would not be lowered. We decided that we would either have to wear ear plugs to church or find another place where our hearing would not become impaired.

We also had an interesting experience with a church we had never visited. We had contributed money to help one of its members go on a mission trip with the single's group. Our check was made out to the church. We did not receive an acknowledgment or thank-you, but we did hear from the pastor. He sent us a letter asking for more money. Apparently we were also added to the church's calling list. A recorded voice introduced the pastor. Several of the calls came in during the dinner hour, along with the usual sales calls often made at that time. We were not favorably impressed, made a definite decision not to go there, and wondered what effect such a scenario might have on someone who might not be totally committed to the church.

We were determined to find the "right church." But I cannot help but wonder how many others in a like situation and with similar discouraging experiences have given up and added their names to the roster of church dropouts. And what about those frigid congregations and ministers who might have been instrumental in causing a brother and sister to stumble?

Getting Visitors to Come

How can you get people interested in visiting your church? If they don't know you're there, they certainly can't come. Here are some approaches.

- Use a roadside sign to indicate the location of your fellowship.
- An eye-catching billboard that captures the spirit of your church can be informative and attention getting (see chapter 14 for more information).
- Get your church included in church directories in hotels, motels, and transportation terminals.
- Have your congregation listed on church directory pages in newspapers. While most newspapers charge for the listings, they offer a reduced rate in comparison to commercial advertising. And some smaller weeklies run a church directory page as a community service.
- Purchase a telephone yellow-pages listing. Even better, run an ad in the yellow pages to make your church stand out. Many newcomers to the community will turn to the yellow pages to find out what's available in their type of church preference.
- If your community has a welcome wagon-type program, try to get them to include a packet that has a small gift, your brochure, and a greeting from your church.
- Watch for (and get your members or realtor members of your congregation to assist) new people moving in to the neighborhood around your church. Organize a welcoming committee whose members drop by and give newcomers a gift, such as a homemade loaf of bread or other baked goods, and simply say "We're glad you're here. What can we do to help you get settled?"
- Take out an attention-getting ad in your local newspaper and

33

33

3O6C9D0008FZ

Title	CHURCH COMMUNICATIONS HANDBOOK:
Condition	Good
Location	zone 1 Aisle F Bay 18 Shelf A Item 33
Description	This is a paper back book. The pages have normal wear. We ship Monday-Saturday and respond to inquiries within 24 hours.
Source	STORE 37
SKU	3O6C9D0008FZ
ASIN	0825439256
Code	0825439256
Employee	

have it run outside the religion page or section of the paper. While rates in the big-city dailies can be staggering, costs for advertising in a small weekly will be much more affordable and may be more effective for your purpose (see chapter 14 for more information).

- Get the activities and projects of your church in the newspapers, on radio stations' bulletin-board programs as well as in news stories, and on television (see chapter 17 for more information).
- Be active in community affairs. Join a service club or your local chamber of commerce and participate in public forums. Contacts made in the community can result in the coming of new people to your activities and services.
- Encourage your members to invite friends and family members to special services and other events, such as a drama presentation or a church picnic. George Barna found in his study of several successful, growing churches that visitors came "because of the recommendation, invitation or consistent attendance of a neighbor, friend or work associate."[1]

Barna says that people are most likely to visit churches that have been recommended by someone they trust. He also points out that members in those churches realized that their responsibility extended beyond merely inviting someone to attend. It included accompanying the guest to the church activity and following up on his or her visit. The strategy included hospitality while in the church and a postvisit debriefing. This might be done by inviting the visitor for lunch after the service or having coffee together later in the week.[2]

Asylum Hill Congregational Church in Hartford, Connecticut, has taken an unusual approach to inspiring members to invite their friends to visit the church.

They organized a large number of potluck dinners in members' homes with about 20 members invited to each one. A fellowship time was held before dinner to help participants get better acquainted. After dinner, they were asked, "What brought you to this church for the first time? What brought you back? And have you invited other people to come? What happened when you invited them? What was the message from your discussion?"

After that, the group watched a film on church growth stressing the necessity of church members inviting their friends if new people are going to come to church. Afterwards, a discussion was held. They talked about the scenes they remembered, what was funny, whether there was anything they felt they should do as a result of watching the film.

They were then given a piece of paper and a pencil and were asked to list their unchurched friends, family, and acquaintances. They put them in the order in which they thought they were most likely to respond to an invitation to attend a service. They were then told, "OK, that's your assignment, to call on the first three names on your list and invite them to come to worship with you."

After that, participants broke up into pairs and role played inviting one another to a service. The whole group reassembled, discussed how it went, and what was most helpful. They talked, jotted down notes, and went out and invited their friends.[3]

Cornerstone Church in San Antonio uses an unusual approach to making it easy for members to invite friends and relatives. Once each month, members receive attractive engraved invitations—much like wedding invitations—to give out for the next Sunday's services. Always, dozens of people, carrying their invitations, come to the service saying, "I've been invited to come here today."

Pastor John Hagee says that on those Sundays it is not uncommon for two hundred people to accept Christ. He says that they discovered this successful tactic when their church was dedicated in 1986. In addition to spending a large amount of money on broadcast and print advertising, they handed out similar invitations to the congregation for use in inviting friends and loved ones to the dedication. He asked the sixty-five hundred people who attended how many came in response to the various types of advertising and then, finally, how many came as a result of the invitation. To his amazement, the cards beat the advertising four to one.[4]

Have a "Friend's Day" at your church. Publicize the special service several weeks in advance. Encourage each member of the congregation to bring a friend with her or him that day. You might even want to give a gift to the person or family who brings the most friends.

Once inside your doors, how can you convey to visitors the message of Ephesians 2:19 (KJV): "Now therefore ye are no more strangers and foreigners, but fellow citizens with the saints, and of the household of God."

Here are some practical approaches for making first-time visitors feel glad that they came.

Put Yourself in the Place of the Visitor

Realize that the person may be new to the community or may be briefly in your city. He or she may also be hurting or seeking for God one last time before deciding there's no use. Whatever the situation, going to a new place among strangers makes most people feel rather ill at ease and self-conscious. It's almost like going on a blind date. You are risking the unknown—wondering how you are going to like the other person and what your date will think about you. Regardless of the reasons people have for coming, your fellowship has a responsibility to demonstrate the love of Christ to visitors and to make them feel welcome.

Try out the visitor's role yourself when on vacation by going to a church where no one knows you. Evaluate how you're treated, and compare the positives and the negatives with your own church.

Was parking your car easy or was it such a major chore that your enthusiasm for being there was dampened before you even got inside? Was it clear which door you should enter, or, in the case of a large facility, did you have to wander around trying to find the right building and the sanctuary entrance? Once inside, did you have trouble locating the nursery (if you have a small child), or the restrooms, or even the auditorium? What was the climate into which you stepped? Frigid (but not from too much air conditioning!) or warm and friendly? Of course, the most important question is this: Would you be interested in coming back and considering that fellowship if you were looking for a church home?

John W. Bullock in his article entitled "Evaluating Your Church's Friendliness," says, "The question is not 'Are we friendly?' but 'How friendly do we appear to outsiders?' Every church is friendly to itself. But how do we feel about strangers? How do strangers feel about us?"[5]

Get Your Act Together When It Comes to Traffic Flow and Parking

While this usually does not pose a problem for a small congregation, as the numbers grow, it can become a challenge. This is particularly true for churches with multiple services that result in one group of worshipers coming in while another group is leaving. If the congestion is a real problem, both in the parking lot and inside the foyer, serious consideration should be given to changing the schedule to allow more time between services.

A well-organized parking ministry seeks to direct traffic and assist people in finding a parking space. This can be invaluable in helping people enter the service in a good frame of mind, rather than feeling as though they've just come out of the mall parking lot after the post-Christmas sale.

Consider saving choice spots conveniently located near the front entrance for visitors. That in itself says, "You're special. We're glad you're here." If you have a large number of visitors, you may also want to consider having greeters out in the parking lot to welcome visitors and to show parents, if they're interested, where they can take their kids for children's church.

Place Directional Signs in Prominent Spots

At the entrance to the parking lot, place a directional sign with the international accessibility logo pointing the way to reserved parking for those who are physically disabled.

If yours is a several-building complex, make certain that each building is clearly identified. If there is any possibility for confusion, use a "Sanctuary (or Auditorium) Entrance" sign outside the appropriate door. In a building with several entrances, you may need an additional sign to point the way.

On entrances that are not accessible to a person using a wheelchair, place a sign with the accessibility logo with an arrow pointing to the direction of the nearest accessible doorway.

Once inside, signs indicating the way to the restrooms will be helpful and much appreciated by the newcomer who may be embarrassed to ask for assistance.

Position Enthusiastic Greeters at the Front Door

Greeters should be people who have the special ability to make everyone from the first-time attender to the grouchiest member feel welcomed and appreciated. They also should be thoroughly familiar with the facility so that they can give directions for whatever assistance might be needed. They should know the congregation well enough to spot newcomers and make suggestions so that their visit might be as successful as possible. For example, greeters could say to a couple with a baby, "We have a wonderful nursery. Would you like to leave your little girl there during the service?"

Having the right people as greeters can convince newcomers that "Hey, we're glad you're here," and make them also feel pleased that they came.

Have the Greeter Give Newcomers a Visitor's Card

The greeter could tell visitors that it would be appreciated if they would complete the card and give it to an usher, so that the church can let them know about future programs and activities. Also, a visitor's tag or special ribbon is helpful to members in identifying newcomers before and after the service, if the visitor doesn't mind wearing either of these items. Greeters should be sensitive to negative responses, as demonstrated by body language and other reactions. If the visitor doesn't seem to like an idea, the best thing to do is drop the subject. Some first-timers, especially in the baby boomer age range, prefer to remain anonymous.

In his book entitled *User Friendly Churches,* George Barna points out that the successful churches that he studied did not "humiliate visitors" by showering them with so much attention that it became overwhelming, uncomfortable pressure. He writes that the successful churches "recognized that many people visit a church with trepidation, and with a desire to take things slowly. These cautious visitors often prefer to remain part of the woodwork for awhile, acting as participant-observers, unobtrusive and unfettered."[6]

The visitor's card should ask for such usual information as the newcomer's address, church affiliation, and number and ages of children (a sample card may be found on page 181). It is also helpful to ask what prompted the person's visit. The response can be useful in determining the effectiveness of different types of advertising approaches.

Have the Greeter Give the Visitor Any Literature Available on the Church

This might include a brochure, a current newsletter, and flyers about upcoming events. Many churches have a special visitor's packet with that type of information and, often, a small gift, such as a pen with the church's name on it (see chapter 13 for further information).

These types of informative pieces give the visitor something to do while waiting for the service to begin and provide useful information on the programs and activities of the church. A visitor may see details about the activities of a certain program, such as a drama group or a children's choir, that may spark a special interest for that person or another family member.

The Usher Is Usually the Next Person the Visitor Meets

People with warm personalities and with a gift of hospitality belong in this ministry. The usher is the host to each visitor. Besides greeting the newcomers and handing them the bulletin and/or other information, helping them find a seat to their liking can be helpful, especially if there is a large crowd.

An excellent strategy is for the usher to position the visitor(s) by another couple or single in their age range and introduce them. If possible, the usher should seat a visitor with a disability by someone with a similar disability or by someone whom the usher knows can relate well to that particular person.

Have One Usher Collect the Visitors' Cards and Take Them to the Platform

Before the sermon begins, the pastor can welcome the visitors by name, if there are not too many. The pastor's stating where they are from indicates a personal interest in them and may help church members in striking up a conversation with them after the service. Church-growth researcher Win Arn recommends building a visitor flow by recognizing members who bring newcomers. He suggests saying during the announcements, "If you brought guests today, would you stand and introduce them?" He also says, "Sunday after Sunday it reinforces and rewards those who bring visitors and results in more and more guests/visitors."[7]

Make Sure Visitors Get to Meet the Pastor

Everyone wants to get acquainted with the pastor and see what that person is like once he or she steps out from behind the pulpit. A brief pastor's reception with light refreshments following the service provides an informal time of fellowship for the minister to get acquainted with first-time attenders. This also sends a message that the pastor appreciates the effort the newcomer made to come to the service. If the visitors are there as guests of members, then the members should also be invited to the reception.

Church on the Way in Van Nuys, California, hosts a reception for visitors after the Sunday morning service in a room adjoining the sanctuary. Upon arrival, guests are greeted by a member of the pastoral staff and invited to view a brief video, which includes a welcome, the church's vision and goals, some background on the pastor, and various opportunities for service.[8]

Send the Visitors a Personalized Letter the Week After Their Visit

This may be a carefully worded basic form letter with only the name, address, and salutation personalized. A nice touch, though, is the addition of a handwritten P.S. by the pastor. This is especially effective if the pastor refers to something he and the newcomer talked about or have in common.

Have a Member Call Each Visiting Family Early in the Week

Train a cadre of people to make friendly phone calls to visitors to thank them for coming and to answer any questions they might have about the church. Without seeming to pry, this team can also find out vital information (such as spiritual needs, impressions of the church, and possible interest in becoming members). Whenever possible, callers should be matched with visitors as to general age group and marital status. Without being pushy, the callers should say, "We're interested in you." A summary of the call should be sent to the office, and references should be made to appropriate persons (such as Sunday school teachers) for further follow-up, if it appears to be warranted. (A sample feedback card is included at the end of this chapter.)

Pathway of Life Church in Dallas, Texas, reports good results from delivering a basket of fruit to each visiting family the day after they visit. Volunteers just drop the gift off with a cheery, "We really enjoyed having you with us Sunday. Hope you come back soon." Pastor Danny Wegman says, "We've found at that point in their relationship with our church that they're really not interested in an extended visit."[9]

Place Visitors' Names on Your Mailing List

Be sure that newcomers receive newsletters and special announcements about your church—but not appeals for money. Also, if they never come back, don't indefinitely leave their names on the mailing list.

After a Person or Family Has Visited a Few Times, Call on Them

If a person or family indicates an interest in joining your church, match them with an individual or another family in your congregation who has similar interests. They should help the person or family feel a part of the group and introduce them to other members of the congregation. Also, try to get the person or family involved in a newcomers' class or seekers' group to help acquaint them with the goals, beliefs, and programs of your church (see chapter 5 for further information).

Create a Warm, Friendly Atmosphere for Visitors

Stress to the congregation the importance of each member's being friendly and helpful in welcoming visitors. And remind them frequently that this is a high priority for your church. Members all too easily can fall into the habit of talking only among themselves and ignoring the newcomer. Encourage them not only to speak to visitors but to introduce them to other members, and include them in their conversational group.

Creating a warm atmosphere for newcomers will become a reality, rather than just a nice idea, only when members assume their responsibility in this area. The pastor and other staff members simply cannot do it without the support and participation of other people in the church. Win Arn says that the number-one reason people join churches is that "they felt a sense of belonging. They felt important, 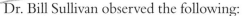 wanted, loved."[10]

Dr. Bill Sullivan observed the following:

A first-time visitor who attends your worship or small group is unfamiliar with the context and unacquainted with your members. Such a situation naturally creates social discomfort. If that discomfort remains at the conclusion of the first contact, the likelihood of your newcomer returning drops markedly. If, however, the social discomfort is gone by the end of the meeting, the chances of this person returning go up dramatically. A church that . . . organizes to overcome the tendency toward social discomfort of newcomers will be much more effective in seeing them eventually involved.[11]

Asking members how they would treat Jesus if He walked into a service might be useful in dramatizing the importance of their actions and attitudes. Realizing that they hold in their hands the reputation of their church and also of Jesus should provide the motivation to reach out in His love to each person or family who ventures into a worship service.

Ken Houts in his book entitled *You Are a Miracle Waiting to Happen,* gives these suggestions for individual church members to use in ministering to visitors.

1. Spend time in fellowship with visitors in church.
2. Ask visitors: "Is there anything I can pray about with you?"
3. Suggest more fellowship. Make an appointment for a specific date, time, and place.
4. Invite the first-time attenders back to church. Let them know their presence and personal happiness are important to you.
5. Go on a "cookie crusade"! Drop by the newcomers' house with a gift of cookies during the week.[12]

Trinity Church in DeSoto, Texas, ran these suggestions for church members in one of its publications.

- If some newcomers are unknown to you, don't be embarrassed to introduce yourself. Even if they are a church member, chances are that if you don't know them, they don't know you and are interested in getting acquainted with you.
- Watch for visitors. Then as soon as possible after the worship service has ended, introduce yourself. Shake the hands of newcomers and invite them to your next Sunday school class.
- Don't assume someone else will greet the visitors. You may be the only one who noticed them. The fact that several persons welcome visitors is not considered bad form, but simply a clear manifestation of a caring congregation.

- Make an overt effort to get to know the people you see Wednesday night or Sunday in worship, even though you have no idea who they are or where they live or work.
- Remember that it is not the fellowship of the pastoral welcome that will positively impress visitors. It's the warmth of your hello and friendly handshake that will convince them that Trinity is filled with friendly people, is a wonderful place to worship, and is an ideal spot to grow in Christ.[13]

Here's one note of caution. If your church is characterized by hugging members, ask them to restrain themselves when it comes to welcoming visitors. Many people feel uncomfortable by that much familiarity from a stranger. Others do not consider that type of contact appropriate between people of opposite genders. And many men would be appalled if another man tried to hug them.

Determine What Happens Before Worship and During the First Minutes of the Service

What kind of atmosphere is created there? Ken Houts says, "Church growth studies have found visitors make up their minds in the first eleven minutes if they are not coming back to a church."[14] That's before the choir sings the beautiful anthem it has rehearsed for weeks and before the pastor delivers that soul-searching sermon prepared after hours of prayer, study, and meditation. That eleven minutes includes the way the visitor is welcomed (or not welcomed), the aura for worship into which that person steps, and the beginning of the service. Incidentally, if dry, dull announcements are being given at the start of the service "to get them out of the way," maybe they should be condensed, rescheduled, or called attention to in printed form for members to read.

Cultivate Repeat Visitors

What about visitors who come the second or third time? Obviously they liked what they saw the first time, or they wouldn't have returned. It's even more important at this stage to help them start making friends and connections to the church, if you want to change their status from visitors to members (see the form entitled "Visitor Contact by Telephone Feedback Card," which appears on page 56). In a medium-sized or large church, tracking repeat visitors is difficult. Nevertheless it is important, for otherwise you would continue to ask newcomers to fill out a visitor's card each time they attended your church.

One way to keep track of visitors is to distribute an attendance sheet during the first part of the service and have every participant sign it.

This form should ask for each person's name, address, phone number, and membership status. This information should be analyzed the next day to see whether there were any visitors who came for the second or third time. The second visit should result in a follow-up letter from the pastor in which he expresses his pleasure that they came back, another phone call with an invitation to a specific group activity, Sunday school class, or church event, and a visit from a staff member. The attendance-sheet approach also gets information from first-time visitors who did not complete a visitor's card.

Ask Someone Who Has Never Attended Your Church to Come as an Anonymous Visitor

Don't tell anyone what you're doing. Give your "mystery shopper" a list of all the aspects you would like to have evaluated. Ask him or her to use an objective eye and make detailed notes about every facet of the experience, including the follow-up of the visit. Then schedule a meeting to discuss frankly that person's reactions and to elicit suggestions for improvement. You may be amazed at what you discover.

Remember the Admonition of Hebrews 13:2

In the King James Version, this verse reads, "Be not forgetful to entertain strangers: for thereby some have entertained angels unawares."

Do you want your church to grow and minister to the needs of those whom God brings your way? If so, then show concern and give careful, loving attention to every newcomer in your midst.

Visitor Contact by Telephone Feedback Card

Date and time of contact _____

Visitor's Name(s) _____

Address _____

Phone number _____

Best time to contact (if known) _____

Impression of and interest in church _____

_____

_____

Needs _____

_____

Suggested follow-up (calls made by appropriate Sunday school teachers, visits made by staff member, and so on) _____

5 Integrating New Members into the Fellowship

Cary and Patricia Arnold had recently moved to Centerville and were searching for a church. They had visited several, but nothing seemed to click. Today, though, they were excited. Their visit to Family First Fellowship had been a great experience. They liked the contemporary, upbeat music, the sermon was relevant to their lives, and, best of all, their five-year-old son and seven-year-old daughter had enjoyed themselves in a spotless, caring atmosphere. "I think our search has ended," Cary said with a sigh of relief. They visited two more times before joining.

Six months later, however, their enthusiasm had waned and disillusionment had set in. "I don't know over three people in the whole church," Patricia complained. "I still feel like a total outsider."

"I know we're not unfriendly people," Cary offered. "But somehow we just don't fit in there."

Family First may be a loving, caring fellowship to its established congregation, but it failed to communicate to Cary and Patricia that they were really wanted and needed within the fold. And so Cary, Patricia, and their two children joined hundreds of others who reenter the revolving church door. As they leave, other newcomers enter. These people visit, and they like what they see and experience. They decide to become members, but somehow they never become a part of the body. Perhaps they would like to get involved, but they can't seem to get inside the "system." Predictably they won't stay. Maybe they'll visit some other churches, or, perhaps, they're just too disappointed to try again.

Reasons Why the Door Revolves

Experts and studies on the subject point out some facts and principles that should provide food for thought for any church that is not keeping the new members it attracts.

Part of the research Flavil Yeakley did for his dissertation at the

University of Illinois included interviewing one hundred lay members. Fifty of them had joined the church and were actively involved. The other fifty joined but then dropped out. He asked each of them how many close friends they had made in the church after they joined. The new members who stayed averaged more than seven new church friends during the first six months. Those who left averaged fewer than two.[1]

Dr. Warren Hartman, in a research project entitled "A Study of the Church School in the United Methodist," asked people who had recently dropped out of church, "Why?" Their most frequent answer was: "Did not feel part of the group."[2]

Elmer L. Towns, based on his study of what he terms ten of today's most innovative churches, says: "New members are best bonded to a new church when they belong to a primary group of the church. The primary group can be any smaller body of the church, such as a Sunday school class, a cell, the ushers, a ladies missionary group or the choir."[3]

Charles E. Fuller of the Institute of Evangelism and Church Growth says in seminars that a new member must be put in a role, task, or activity within six months in order to keep him or her.[4]

William Hendricks points out another area of frequent frustration—the promise or doctrine of spiritual gifts. The Bible teaches that God has given a special ability to every believer so that they can contribute meaningfully to the work of the body (1 Pet. 4:10). Hendricks wrote the following:

> What incredibly good news! It's like telling people that there's a job in the want-ads with their name on it. Naturally they want to find out what that job is. That's when things start to fall apart. . . . How many churches have a "technology" for helping people discover their abilities? . . . This inability to pinpoint people's giftedness only acts to dash people's hopes. Think what a letdown it is to be told that you have a "significant" role to play in the body of Christ, only to discover that you'll be handling a minor chore that, frankly, anyone could do—when what you were hoping for was a task that *only you* could do, one that you were uniquely created and gifted by God to do. It's like answering the aforementioned want-ad, which promised you a position "vital to the future of our company," only to find that your assignment will be the spiritual equivalent of flipping burgers.[5]

Successfully integrating or assimilating new members into the congregation is too critical to be left to chance.

One Church's Approach

When people are received into the congregation as new members at New Life Christian Fellowship in Dallas, they are introduced something like this. "This is Michael Armstrong. You've probably already noticed him playing the saxophone on the platform. He'll be working with the music ministry. And this is his wife, Deborah. She has experience with children's church, and she'll be helping us in this vital area."

At the point of becoming members at New Life, people usually are already active in a cell or small-group ministry that meets one Sunday evening a month. Their gifts and interests have been identified, and they probably have signed up to participate with a particular ministry or are already participating. In other words, they are already plugged in and have begun forming bonds and relationships with members of the congregation.

This kind of involvement doesn't just happen. In fact, it represents several weeks of strategic planning and the work of more than sixty dedicated members who assist in the various facets of the process of connecting people with their church. The success of their efforts is attested to by the fact that since the program started in 1993, membership has more than quadrupled.

George and Sally Wade, who began the program, were elated about New Life when they first made it their church home. But they soon began to wonder why—when it had so much going for it—the church wasn't growing. George, a nurse by profession who chaired a committee at his hospital on customer relations, went to Pastor Richard Buck with the question and a proposal of sorts. "Maybe we need to think about the visitors who come here as our shoppers and find ways to convince them we have the product they need and want."

Buck responded with an invitation for Wade to speak about the importance of a customer-service approach to the congregation. Soon after that Buck called to say that he had noticed an ad from Care Ministries in a minister's magazine and wondered whether that program might be instrumental in meeting their goal. Wade soon found himself in charge of setting up a ministry under the guidance of Care Ministries. "It took about six months before we really got it running smoothly," he recalls.

Basically this is the way it operates. Teams of people work the lobby to ensure that first-time visitors are welcomed and made to feel at home. After the service, they are invited to a hospitality room where refreshments are served and they have an opportunity to meet the pastor, his wife, and other staff members. During the ensuing week, some kind of contact is made each day—a letter from the pastor, home-baked cookies, a card, or a phone call. On Saturday, the person who met them in the lobby calls and invites them back for the next day's service.

About every six or seven weeks, the ministry organizes a Pastor's Fellowship that is held in the pastor's home. All the visitors since the last fellowship are invited for an informal evening of sharing and getting acquainted, complete with delicious goodies. Between ten and thirty people usually show up. Buck will take a few minutes to tell about his background, marriage, and family. Then his wife, Sharon, will introduce other staff members. Each person present is then asked to tell a little about herself or himself. At that time and also in a letter, visitors are invited to attend a six-session Doorway Class to find out more about the church.

The class covers the nondenominational church's doctrine and practices. Participants learn about the four basic temperaments and complete a temperament-personality profile assessment to help them better understand their own strengths and weaknesses and how they might best fit into ministry. They also learn about spiritual gifts and complete a motivational gift test to try to determine which category they match. A Parade of Ministries gives ministry directors a chance to tell about the scope and thrust of their areas of responsibility and various opportunities for service.

Class members are given the opportunity to share about their backgrounds and goals and to form relationships among one another. They are asked to complete a Talent-Skills-Special Abilities inventory on which they indicate previous experience and future desire for service. Small group leaders are invited to the class to try to determine which group members might fit into most appropriately. They then receive a special invitation with the understanding that they are welcome to visit several cell groups before choosing one.

The final step before membership is like a job fair where ministry directors are available to talk with participants, answer questions, share about ministry needs and possibilities for service. The idea is to try to match class participants' talents and aspirations with opportunities for ministry.

Wade believes that there are two key reasons why people will remain at a church. First are relationships. People are connected. They don't feel like outsiders. Second is involvement. Some participation anchors people and fast-forwards assimilation.

Wade muses, "From the moment visitors walk in the door until they join, our goal is to love and care about them. Sometimes I think all that we do is overkill, but it doesn't appear to be. It works. Once visitors become members, the cell group and particular ministry they have signed on with continue the assimilation process."[6]

Making Becoming a Member a Real Happening

Becoming a member of Asylum Hill Congregational Church in Hartford, Connecticut, is an occasion to be remembered. Pastor James L. Kidd meets with new members before the service for prayer and to explain the procedure. Every new member has a sponsor who has special responsibilities for the new member. A ceremony in the worship service gives new members opportunity to make their statements of faith and enter into covenant with the congregants, who, in return, make vows of commitment to the new members. They are given white carnations as a symbol of being washed clean in the love of God in Jesus Christ and forgiven along with a certificate of church membership. Officials of the congregation shake hands with them while a welcoming hymn is sung. Sponsors give them a name tag and a hug.

After the service, a celebration brunch honoring the new members is held. Their friends and family, who have been given a special invitation to the occasion, are also invited to the brunch. A couple of songs are sung to the new members, including "Consider Yourself (one of the family)." Lay leaders stand up and tell about the work of their groups or boards and invite everyone to participate. A couple of long-time members are asked to share what the church has meant to them.

The following week sponsors receive a letter from Kidd reminding them of their obligations—to invite their charges to church, make them welcome, and invite them to meet people for dinner or some other social occasion. Kidd also sends a letter to the new members, again welcoming them and telling them how happy he and the congregation are to have them. Leaders of groups in which the new members probably will be interested are contacted so that they may issue invitations. New members are also asked to serve as greeters at worship in the following weeks which helps them to get acquainted. After three months, they are invited to a reunion brunch with the ministers to see how things are going.

Members of a friendship committee, whose responsibility is helping new members assimilate into the life of the church, call on them to make sure they are participating at the level of their interest.[7]

Providing Ties That Bind

Here are some approaches to new member assimilation that seem to be working well for various churches.

First, membership name tags are worn by all members in the church. One congregation color codes theirs according to the length of membership. New members are easy to pick out because of the color of their tags, but they do not feel "different" since all, except visitors, are wearing a name tag. And in a large church, the name tags help long-time members learn the names of people they may have seen for several months but whose names they do not know.

Second, family pictures are taken of new members the Sunday they join. The following Sunday the names of new members are featured in the bulletin. Their pictures and their names are placed on a special bulletin board, giving members the opportunity to put a name and face together and to learn a bit about those who have just joined. The pictures are kept up until a new batch joins the church or, in some cases, for several months.

Third, a new membership class, which may be called by a variety of names, such as seekers or inquirers, is organized for those who show an interest in finding out more about the church. These are presented in many formats with varying numbers of sessions. However, purposes are usually the same: to present information about the church and its ministry, to answer questions in an informal setting, and to get acquainted with and find out more about those attending. Some churches include assessment tests, such as personality and spiritual-gifts tests, to assist participants in understanding themselves, their motivational gifts, and where they might function most effectively in that particular church.

The purpose and focus of this type of class are entirely different from a new believer's class. If a person is a new believer who is interested in becoming a member, then he or she should be attending both a new believers' class and a new members' class.

Studies conducted by Donald P. Smith show that churches that achieve a high degree of bonding hold new members' classes that total four to seven hours. He notes that "high-loss churches" are more likely to have classes that total only one to three hours.[8]

Fourth, a special friend or new-member sponsor program links frequent visitors with appropriate members of the congregation. The idea is to match a new member with someone in the congregation in similar circumstances (for example, divorced, couples with small children, or seniors who share similar interests). Members have coffee or dinner together with the visitors and get to know one another. The sponsors sit with their newfound friends in services and other church activities, introduce them to other members, and invite them to a small-group fellowship and other events at the church. In short, they help the newcomers get acquainted and feel at home.

One church has sponsors attend a couple of classes of the new members' program with their assignee. Between classes, sponsors check to see whether they have any questions about the class or other functions of the church. Recruitment for new sponsors often is done in the ranks of those who have been successfully assimilated into the life and work of the church only a few months before. After all, they know how it feels to be "a new kid on the block."

Fifth, special social events designed to build relationships among new members and with other members are held throughout the year. These might include such activities as skating, a picnic, a baseball game, pizza, a play, a concert, or a celebration for a special holiday, such as the Fourth of July.

Sixth, a party or celebration is held on the first anniversary of membership for those who have joined. This demonstrates the value that the church places on their being a part of the congregation. If they participated together in some type of indoctrination or new-members' class, they probably formed bonds with one another. This get together provides an additional opportunity for fellowship and strengthening ties.

Seventh, discussion groups or individual interviews with those who have been in the congregation for several months are held. The idea is to discuss their experience in becoming a part of the church. Participants are asked for suggestions on how the process can be improved.

Finally, a specific plan is used for incorporating new members into small groups. This can be accomplished through the use of an interest-and-experience inventory or an information card that new members are asked to complete. (For more help on doing this, see the form entitled "Member Information Form," which you can find on page 69.) Also, information gleaned by sponsors and leaders of new members' classes as well as the results of any tests should be mixed in.

All of this can be studied by a special-assimilation group and by individuals tentatively matched with small groups within the church: an appropriate small fellowship group, a prison ministry, the drama group, hospital visitation, a musical group, an intercessory-prayer group, women's or men's ministry, a nursing-home ministry, the church library, ushers' group, greeters' group, and the list goes on. Referrals may be made to leaders of various ministries and small-fellowship groups so that they may extend a personal invitation to those individuals to visit or become a part of their particular group.

The Wisdom of Small-Group Involvement

Lyle Schaller speaks to the wisdom of this approach. He thinks that newcomers are much more likely to "stick" in a fellowship if they have a place where they are known and would be missed if they didn't show up. He identifies small-groups such as Sunday school classes, choirs, fellowship groups, and sports teams. He says that "the larger the congregation, the more important these small groups are in the assimilation of new members."[9]

Schaller believes that there are three key elements that are essential to membership retention:

1. encouraging new members to join a small group
2. inviting new members to accept some particular task
3. inviting new members to accept a committee assignment or an office in the congregation

Schaller says that if one or another of these does not happen within the first year, members are likely to become inactive.[10]

When new members come into fellowship at New Hope Community Church in Portland, Oregon, they are immediately involved in service. Pastor Dale Galloway finds that members who have not been active for some time are difficult to motivate. "We put new Christians immediately to work," he says. Using immature people doesn't bother him. "We do just like Jesus, who challenged people to take up their cross and follow him."[11]

A study conducted by Donald P. Smith showed that "small groups play a crucial role in membership bonding." The most frequent response given by pastors who were asked to name membership-retention approaches that have been especially helpful was small-group involvement. Smith reports that "members of bonding churches are more likely than members of high-loss churches to belong to three or more organizations, committees, or groups within their churches."[12]

Gordon L. Everette found in his research that "the people least likely to become inactive members were those who became part of a small-group fellowship before entering into formal membership in a church."[13] And Elmer L. Towns says, "If . . . the visitor is helped into a suitable substructure of belonging, then he is likely to stay. He meets not five hundred people, but a dozen. He shares in their conversation. He participates in their activity. He becomes known as a person. . . . What the group is makes little difference, provided it suits his or her talents and interests, and provides a sense of belonging."[14]

How Many Small Groups Are Enough?

Since becoming a part of a small group is apparently a primary key to successfully assimilating new members, a good question to ask is this: "Do we have enough small groups?" Based on his research, Schaller says that the typical congregation of one hundred members needs six to seven face-to-face groups in which members can be involved. He lists the following as the basic criteria:

1. Fewer than thirty-five people participate with five to seven per group as best, eight to seventeen second, and eighteen to thirty-five a distant third.
2. Membership is seen as a positive experience by participants.
3. Close personal friendships have developed within the group.
4. The group meets weekly or at least monthly.
5. Participation makes a significant contribution to the personal and spiritual growth of most of the members.[15]

Schaller also points out several factors that make the need greater for maintaining six to seven small groups per one hundred members ratio:

- a large proportion of new members who come from a background not identical with the background of the members
- a congregation that has been functioning for a long period of time in the same location
- a highly urbanized community[16]

Keeping Tabs on Members

A number of churches find that having all its members renew their commitment each year is an effective way to maintain an active group and discover potential problems. (For more help on doing this, see the form entitled "Member Information Form," which you can find on page 69.) Instead of joining once for life, each person on the roll is asked annually whether he or she wants to continue membership for another year.

First Baptist Church of Fontana, California, calls its approach "covenant membership." Pastor Ross Chenot explains, "It describes the promise each member makes to God and their fellow believers that they will continue to grow spiritually and will use their gifts and abilities for evangelism and nurture."

The church holds a special "Covenant Renewal Sunday" that focuses on recommitment to membership. Those renewing their membership sign and date a "Covenant Membership" card that details their agreement to these responsibilities:

- to attend worship services regularly
- to participate in a small group
- to minister through using their God-given spiritual gifts
- to financially support the church in regular giving, recognizing a tithe as a guideline[17]

Good Shepherd Lutheran Church in Irvine, California, has a similar program. The Board of Congregational Life follows up on those who did not place their cards on the altar on "Covenant Sunday" or mail them to the church. Phone calls are made to ask whether they would like to mail the card in, have someone come by to pick it up, or have one filled out for them, based on their desires. A pastoral visit is made to those who indicate a desire to talk. If they still do not request covenant membership, they are placed on the church's "responsibility list" and at least twice a year receive a visit from a member of the church's Inreach Committee. The following year they are mailed another card and encouraged to reconsider continuing their membership.[18]

Churches with small-group fellowships have a built-in process for keeping up with concerns and crises in the lives of those who participate. Because of the close bonds such groups form, leaders have a real feel for what's going on. Reports of the groups' activities to ministry professionals can include a section on potential problems that seem to be surfacing so that preventive measures can be taken before situations escalate.

New Hope Community Church in Portland, Oregon, uses a phone-calling system. All the members of the church are called every eight weeks along with all the prospects. The information is then fed to the district pastors who are in charge of the cell groups in their area. They, in turn, enlist the lay pastors to help them take care of needs that have been identified. Pastor Dale Galloway explains, "The phone ministry is to care for the people who never get into the call system and who otherwise would fall through the cracks."[19]

Care bearers is the name given to a program at Immanuel United Church of Christ in Shillington, Pennsylvania, whose goal is to increase caring communications between pastors and leaders and the members of the congregation. The congregation is divided into zones and neighborhoods with a care bearer assigned for each neighborhood of approximately ten members. Each care captain oversees ten care bearer units which are entered into the computer for easy retrieval. Care bearers, who receive tips on what to say and how to listen, contact those in their groups at least five times during a year. They remind members of communion services, special events, and certain stewardship or mission emphases. They also provide encouragement and listen to concerns. In turn, the care bearers report to the ministers names of those in need of pastoral services, births and other celebrations, concerns, and persons who move out as well as new residents. Pastor Robert I. Rhoads says, "The care bearers have been the most effective innovation in recent years. The calls have produced a noticeable increase in attendance and contributions, but most important, they have increased the level of trust and feelings of genuine personal care."[20]

Other churches find a lay-shepherd's program to be effective. One approach is to divide the congregation into a manageable number of families. A lay shepherd is given the responsibility of contacting each member of his group at least once a month and monitoring their participation. He reports any problem areas and special needs (such as illness, loss of job, or financial crisis) to the church's staff.

Dr. John Savage, in his videotape entitled "Drop Out Tracks," describes the steps that lead to a person's leaving the church.

1. An "anxiety-provoking event" or cluster of events. This may be a personal tragedy, burnout, a conflict with the pastor or other staff member, another family in the church, or with members of their own family.
2. A verbal cry for help that is ignored.
3. Anger, if there is no response to the cry for help.
4. A feeling of helplessness when no one offers assistance or a feeling of hopelessness in not being able to do anything about the situation.
5. Progressively withdrawing from participation in church activities, ending financial support, and, perhaps, writing a letter of resignation.
6. Sealing off the pain and substituting other activities, especially if no response comes within six to eight weeks after a decision has been made to leave the church.[21]

Donald P. Smith wrote the following:

> The sooner someone recognizes the cry for help and deals with it, the greater the chance of restoring an alienated member and the easier that the restoration will be. However, those who respond to a cry for help must recognize that the presenting issues will not necessarily be the same as the sources of the person's deep underlying pain. And it is that pain they must deal with before resolution of the anxiety is possible. Congregations will be more likely to keep their members if they follow up on absent members quickly and consistently, if they recognize the cries for help and deal with them promptly and skillfully.[22]

Asylum Hill Congregational Church in Hartford, Connecticut, has a group called the calling and caring ministry. Members, who have been trained in listening skills, call on people who have stopped coming to church or whose patterns of involvement and participation have changed. The group also keeps track of new members. Pastor James L. Kidd says, "...that's often where you lose them, about six months after they've been members and they're not fitting in. So we try to have somebody call on them and find out what we can do to help incorporate them into the life and ministry of our church."[23]

The research of Dr. John Savage, who is considered an expert on why people drop out of churches, shows that the inner core group or active members of a church is unlikely to care much about people who are dropping out. In one study, he says, those who were active

> felt that they were "in," and that kind of security produces a major problem. The "in" group was not sensitive to the need of those persons who were aching and leaving the church. That is why 100 percent of the [inactive] group could say, "No one ever came to visit me." The implication of that statement is that the [active] group did not sense the needs of those persons who were drifting away; who were, in fact, crying for help.[24]

Savage also found that after people decide to stop attending church, they will usually wait about six to eight weeks to see whether anyone will contact them to find out why they have left. They go into a kind of holding pattern, not wishing to invest time or energy in exploring other possibilities but waiting to see how their former church will respond. If no one contacts them, they begin to look at other options.[25]

In his book entitled *Exit Interviews,* William D. Hendricks recommends that churches develop a system for listening to people. "Not just the people who are pleased with the program, and not just the potential recruits, but the people on the fringe who are making up their minds whether to stay or leave." He says that system might be simple or complex, depending on the individual situation—everything from the pastor's making a personal visit to sending a neutral representative or a team of laypeople with the right skills to talk with the disaffected. He recommends making listening "a way of life at your church or organization."[26]

What if, in spite of everyone's best efforts, a member who has not moved out of the area decides to call it quits? Conducting an exit interview with that person, if possible, can provide valuable information for use in future planning. Finding out what went wrong and why may be revealing, may point out communication breakdowns, and may help in preventing potential future problems.

And who knows? Realizing that the church is truly interested in "fixing" the problems may result in a decision to stay after all.

Smith sums up well the approaches that successfully integrate and keep members out of the revolving door.

> Churches that meet members' deep needs will attract and keep them. The glue that holds them is there when members experience caring community and discover meaning for living. It is strengthened when they engage in meaningful service and feel that they really belong. There are specific things that congregations believe and are and do that make a difference.[27]

Member Information Form

Name _____

Home Address _____ Home Phone _____

Employer _____ Work Phone _____

Date of birth _____

Is it all right to call you at work? _____

Spouse's name (if married)_____

Names and ages of children _____

_____

Occupation _____

Previous types of positions held _____

_____

Education and special training _____

Membership in organizations _____

Previous service in church _____

_____

Special talents, interests, hobbies _____

_____

Honors, awards, achievements _____

What areas of ministry are you interested in participating in?_____

_____

_____

Would you be interested in serving on a committee? If so, what type? _____

6 Building Bonds Through Small Fellowship Groups

My heart was pounding as I headed for Room 100 at the Dallas School Administration Building. *What if no one shows up?* That thought was quickly followed by an equally disturbing one. *What if someone shows up?*

The year was 1976. I was reluctantly on my way to the first Friday noon Prayer and Share Meeting that God had directed me to start. I had never even been to such a group, much less led one. I felt totally inadequate and was certainly less than enthusiastic about the idea. To make matters worse, a woman who had applied for a position in my department had barged into my office only moments before and had verbally assaulted me for not giving her the job. I felt like I was the one who needed prayer. "Lord, I'll do my best, but I sure need Your help," I muttered as I got on the elevator.

Earlier in the week I had placed invitations in office mail boxes to a number of people I knew to be Christians. My request for a reservation for Room 100 for a "Prayer and Share Group" had been greeted with "a what?" I had to repeat the name three times.

A dozen people came that first day. As we ate our brown-bag lunches, each person gave a little personal information and shared a favorite Scripture and what it meant to her or him. We prayed together, and I asked them to invite others whom they thought might be interested. That was the beginning of an incredible spiritual experience for me and many others at the administration building as, over the next two and a half years, we broke bread together, prayed together, studied the Word, and shared our joys and sorrows each Friday.

Attendance varied from eight to eighty with an average of about twenty to twenty-five. Employees of all races, across the lines of rank—from the grounds keeper to an associate superintendent—participated. We had Catholics, Pentecostals, Charismatics, those from main-line denominations, and those who did not attend a church meet together in love and rich fellowship. Some became Christians as a result.

Each meeting began with a prayer and reading of the "Scripture of the week," which was sent out to the "mailing list" on Tuesday or Wednesday along with the name and background of the speaker, if one had been scheduled, in an invitation. Some weeks a participant would invite his or her pastor or someone with a special testimony. Several of our speakers were school-board members whose faith was of major importance in their lives. I was often amazed as a speaker's subject would be related to the "Scripture of the week." Several times it was the text. Quite a few members of the group talked about their own experiences with the Lord. Other times I conducted a Bible study and led a discussion. Always we prayed together and shared our faith. And God always blessed our meeting in a magnificent way.

I recall feeling disappointment the week we only had eight come. The last one to enter was a lady who had just been released from a psychiatric hospital. She was holding back tears as she blurted out, "I've completely lost my faith in God. Can you help me?" Each person present had something of substance to share with her—a Scripture, a time when his or her faith was low and what helped to restore it, and a word of encouragement. There was no doubt in my mind that God had ordered the number and the ones who came to minister to her. She looked like a different person by the time she left.

My experience with that group convinced me of the value of the bonds that form, the spiritual growth that can occur, and the interaction that can take place only in a small, continuing group setting.

Since then I've had the privilege of leading small, home group fellowships within the church and one that was independent of a church. The latter was composed of people from different fellowships along with those who did not attend a church. We usually sang praise songs, had a short Bible study with group discussion, shared praise reports and prayer needs, prayed together, and had refreshments. We tried to track things we had prayed for with those that had come to pass, which proved to be an edifying and encouraging project. We used impromptu dramatizations, a reader's theater approach to the story of the Crucifixion, and short illustrated lessons using such items as the figures in the manger scene. Before Christmas we usually had a potluck dinner and a party. One evening before Easter we had a Seder dinner with the significance of each part of the meal being explained before it was eaten.

Because of the informality and fellowship aspects of the meetings, some who were not interested in attending church would come. In several cases, they ended up becoming active members of a fellowship.

Benefits and Beginnings

Evangelism, bonding relationships, and luring the once-churched back to church are opportunities that small-group fellowships provide.

The setting is nonthreatening. The atmosphere is warm and caring. Newcomers feel welcome and comfortable.

Win Arn says that in his study of growing churches, "we have found that one common characteristic is the high degree of relational 'glue' among members" and that "the best way to provide for this important quality in a church is through face-to-face, relational groups!" He warns, however, against the mindset that "all we need to do is to begin small groups." He points out that a successful approach must reflect the unique qualities of one's people, one's ministry area, and one's mission priority.[1]

Arn gives these steps to follow in starting new groups:

1. Identify the target group. Who, based on their needs and interests, would benefit from participation in a group?
2. Determine the kind of group. What type of group is most appropriate for this particular audience?
3. Develop a prospect list. Who are the ones who might participate in the group, keeping in mind the interests and characteristics they have in common?
4. Select a group leader with the following qualities: basic leadership skills/gifts, a teachable spirit, a godly reputation, and the ability to identify with other group members.
5. Set up group logistics and purpose, including meeting time and place, frequency of meetings, and activities.
6. Publicize the new group. Issue personal invitations more than once and in different ways, giving the benefits of participation.[2]

Charles E. Fuller, in his Institute of Evangelism and Church Growth, says that there should be seven groups for each one hundred members and that three new groups should be formed for every one hundred new members for merging and replacing old groups that are dying on the vine. He also thinks that one out of every five groups should be less than one year old.[3]

While small groups may be varied, such as sports teams and groups for music or drama, prayer, study, recovery, and service (to name a few), more and more churches are organizing their entire programs around small-cell groups. Most meet in homes and apartments throughout the geographic area covered by the church. Others meet at the church, but in separate locations. Some groups are located at a business or other convenient gathering place. Frequency of meetings will vary—once a month, twice a month, or every week—but on a regular basis. Some churches require members to belong to a cell group, while others encourage affiliation but don't demand it. Some assign members to a certain group, usually geographically, but others allow them to "shop around" and find one that they feel most comfortable in. As a rule, some type of feedback from each meeting is provided to those in charge of the overall program. (For more help on doing this, see the form entitled "Home Fellowship Report," which you can find on page 77.)

Cell Groups— An Integral Part of New Hope Community Church

The Rev. Dale Galloway says that cell groups "are the church" at New Hope Community Church in Portland, Oregon, not just another ministry. When he started the church in the early 1970s, his vision was to have one cell group for every ten members. That ratio still holds true for the TLC (Tender Loving Care) Cells. The groups are more than just "sharing" groups. Galloway believes that groups which exist *only* for the purpose of sharing will eventually run out of steam. TLC groups are task oriented as well as need oriented. He cites the groups' purposes as first, discipling; second, evangelizing; and third, shepherding. Each group is given the goal of bringing at least one new family to Christ every six months. As a reminder, they are asked to leave an empty seat at each meeting to remind the people: "We can grow." Requests for hospital visitation and prayer for the sick, absentees, and other problems are channeled to the lay pastors or cell group leaders. They, in turn, make assignments to those in their group for outreach, nurture, or encouragement.

Lay ministry is emphasized at New Hope. Level one is "lay pastor in training," level two is "lay pastor," and level three is "lay pastor leader," which is someone who supervises five other lay pastors with their groups. Galloway says, "The secret of our TLC groups is leadership. The groups are leadership-centered and multiplication-centered."[4] District pastors are always on the lookout for potential leadership to promote people into greater roles of ministry. He sees his role as preaching on Sunday and making the lay pastors successful.

The church is divided into geographic districts. A district pastor oversees the lay pastors, TLC groups, members, and prospects in that district. Specialty districts function around particular needs or ministries. These include various ministries for different age groups and areas, such as the music ministry.

The groups follow a format beginning with short, conversational prayer. Answers to prayer are shared, so that members can track their progress in the Christian life. Next, members study the Bible with the purpose of applying it to their lives. Lessons are written by Galloway but are not presented for use as a lecture. Instead, lay pastors are provided with two pages of questions to help involve participants in discussion and interaction on the topic. Galloway says, "A good TLC group is where everyone participates. If leaders do all the talking, learning goes down significantly." Lessons are developed in a series and often track the series that congregants are hearing from the pulpit. The third part of the meeting is sharing with one another—what God has done in their lives, a hurt, or a need. They then pray for one another, bring encouragement, and minister to each other. Finally, they have fellowship with something to eat. Galloway describes each of the cell ministries as a "point of entry into the church." Since the cells comprise the church, the whole church is involved in ministry.[5]

Cells—The Primary Focus at Bethany World Prayer Center

Like New Hope, cells provide the structure for ministry at Bethany World Prayer Center in Baker, Louisiana. Pastor Larry Stockstill says that "cells are the primary focus of our congregational life."

In 1993, he began a five-year transition process to a cell-based structure. All competing programs were assigned an attrition life span so they could be phased out as cells became able to take over their functions. Within two years, cells were handling a multitude of ministries, such as follow-up, hospital, benevolence, altar, and ministry to the bereaved.

The program started with six members in each of fifty-four groups with the goal of multiplying in six months. When a group reached twelve members with a trained intern, it was divided into two groups. After only three years, the number of groups had grown to 302.

Five stages of cell life are taught: learning, loving, linking, launching, and leaving. Stockstill explains that each stage lasts a little over a month and corresponds roughly to the biological stages of human cell mitosis: cluster, align, polarize, and multiply. Emphasis is placed on the concept that multiplication is the natural product of a healthy cell group in the church.

New converts at church services and other events are immediately linked up with a cell group and seem to be excited about having an immediate support group. Cell groups assign a sponsor to meet with the new believer for six weeks before he or she is placed in a foundations class.

Stockstill says, "Service functions are also carried out by cell groups. Ushers, greeters, parking lot attendants, nursery workers, and other roles are all handled in rotation by each of the twelve 'zones' of cells, with one zone serving each week." He reports that service ministries are much easier to fill this way since participants are called on to serve only once a quarter rather than once a week.

In switching to a cell-based ministry, Stockstill believes it is unwise to try to force cell groups on the congregation. Rather, he thinks, the transition can be accomplished more smoothly by "starting something successful and letting it gradually replace the existing programs and structure."

Purposes of the Bethany cell groups are twofold: to meet the needs of believers and to reach the lost. Two different meeting formats, which alternate every other week, are used. First, edification meetings feature worship, spiritual gifts, teaching, spiritual warfare for the lost, and planning for the evangelism meeting the following week. Second, the evangelism meetings devote more time to food and fellowship at the first of the meeting so that unbelievers will feel more comfortable. Ice breakers are used to help people relax and get acquainted. Little or no time is devoted to worship, and discussions focus on topics that unchurched people find of interest in daily living. The last item on the agenda is an opportunity for personal ministry.

Stockstill writes the weekly lessons, motivates the pastors and leaders, and keeps the vision of evangelism, prayer, and missions before them. He comments, "We have found that this format change every other week meets the needs of the cell members, while also reminding them of the importance of evangelizing their friends."

Stockstill applauds two features of the cell structure:

- It decentralizes the church in such a way that open hostility cannot affect it as radically, as illustrated by the thriving house-church movement in China.
- It provides "assimilation points" where the church can bring new converts into a relational environment.[6]

Principles for Effective Cell Ministry

How can a church have an effective cell ministry? Dr. Bill Atwood, in seminars he leads on small-group ministry, gives seven key principles for making groups effective.

1. You must have a leader of a group of ten as the primary pastor. Atwood believes that it is important to give people significant responsibility. "They will rise to the occasion," he observes. He recommends using these guidelines for selecting group leaders:
   - a personal commitment to Jesus Christ
   - an articulated commitment to the church and the staff
   - a servant's heart
   - willingness to accept leadership responsibility for a group as a pastor and facilitator and to work with apprentices

2. As numbers grow, you must have support for the leaders. This means providing an apprentice who is preparing to become a group leader. That person provides assistance for the leader and helps her or him stay on track.
3. Every group should always have an empty chair as a reminder to bring others. On the chair is a list of people. Members are reminded to pray for them, form relationships with them, and invite them to the group. The open chair becomes a symbol of outreach.
4. Ministry is a main aspect with the leader's having some contact with each member of the group between meetings.
5. The group has a sense of mission, of looking out beyond the fellowship of the church.
6. The group plans to multiply itself. If a group gets too large, Atwood says, relationships become more superficial except in times of crises. As a result, some will opt to drop out. Atwood gives these suggestions for preparing for multiplying the group. Divide the group into two smaller groups during ministry time, with one group meeting with the leader and the other with the apprentice. Atwood says that after using this approach for six to eight weeks, two circles will emerge. After the group multiplies into two, he recommends a periodic reunion meeting of the two groups or a social.
7. Training for lay pastors must be given on a continuing basis. Atwood breaks it down into two parts:
   • You come to us for vision, problem solving, and skill enhancement.
   • We come to you for coaching, encouragement, and affirmation.[7]

George Barna says that the surveys that are conducted each month by the Barna Research Group repeatedly show a continuing need among people—both Christians and non-Christians—for meaningful personal relationships. He believes that the loneliness that so many are experiencing in today's society can be addressed by intimacy with members of a church congregation. Barna points out that the churches that are growing have learned how to promote interpersonal relationships. He says that this kind of affinity, more often than not, is "accomplished through small-group Bible studies that meet outside the church during the week—for study, prayer, and fellowship." One of their surveys showed that churches with small groups have grown faster, had less turnover in members, and had pastors who were less frustrated with their ministry.[8]

Stockstill sees both cell ministry and public ministry as scriptural and valuable. He cites Acts 2:46 as well as other verses that describe a pattern of meetings that occurred both in the temple and from house to house. He comments as follows:

> Before the Lord's return, the church will be strong again in its public "temple" ministry and its "house to house" ministry. Huge, highly visible, "city churches" will be undergirded by a structure of thousands of relational and evangelistic cells. This can be the church's finest hour as she returns both to her public and her house-to-house functions.[9]

Home Fellowship Report

Date of meeting _____

Location of group _____

Leader of group _____

Number present _____ Number of visitors _____

Special needs of those present _____

_____

Referrals for ministry _____

_____

_____

Comments about meeting _____

_____

_____

7 Communicating with People with Special Needs

"Y es!" Paul shouted with enthusiasm as he noticed the words *ALL ARE WELCOME* on the church sign. "How could I have missed that after driving by here on my way to work for two months?"

Paul and Ellen, who has multiple sclerosis and uses a wheelchair, had been trying to find a church since moving to a new city from their hometown ten weeks before. They had tried to go to several churches but had found the experiences disheartening. One church had reserved parking and an adequate ramp but no restroom that would accommodate a wheelchair. In another, the doorway into the Sunday school class they tried to attend was too narrow for the wheelchair to get through. In the third one, the only place Ellen could sit was behind the last pew. She felt isolated and lonely not being able to worship side-by-side with her husband. The couple went home disappointed.

But Paul knew that the words *ALL ARE WELCOME* probably meant that careful thought had been given to accommodating people with special needs. He glanced at his watch. Yes, he had a few extra minutes. Turning into the parking lot, he saw a sign with the international symbol for disabilities with an arrow pointing toward the reserved handicapped parking spaces. The spaces were wide enough to accommodate their van and the movement of the hydraulic lift necessary for getting the wheelchair in and out of the vehicle. He got out of the van and noticed the ramp. It was sheltered from the weather and covered with nonskid material. Encouraged, he ran up the ramp, which led to a covered porch. The closest door again featured the international symbol with an arrow pointing to the right. A few yards away was the spacious, main entrance.

Unless otherwise noted, information from this chapter is from *That All May Worship: An Interfaith Welcome to People with Disabilities,* a 52-page publication of the National Organization on Disability, edited by Ginny Thornburgh and coauthored by Ann Rose Davie and Ginny Thornburgh, copyright 1992, and used with permission. Copies of this and other publications relating to disabilities are available by calling (202) 293-5960 or writing the National Organization on Disability, 910 16th Street, N.W., Washington, DC 20006.

On Paul's lunch hour he called the church to check on other features inside the building. He didn't want Ellen to be disappointed again. Everything sounded perfect. They went to church the following Sunday, already feeling welcome, knowing that this congregation cared about them and their situation. They were home at last.

An estimated 43 million Americans have disabilities. They need the nurture and fellowship of the local church. And, in return, the church needs them and can benefit significantly from their involvement.

That All May Worship, a publication of the National Organization on Disability (NOD), says the following:

> At some point, lay and religious leaders should publicly declare that people with disabilities are welcome in the congregation. Such a declaration is a celebration of progress toward the goal of becoming a fully inclusive congregation. This welcome should not be delayed until every desirable change has been made, every program is in place or every attitude has been examined.

These are some ways in which NOD recommends your making your commitment known:

In Local Newspaper Advertisements
- Use the accessibility logo.
- Indicate accessible public transportation.
- Advertise services interpreted for worshipers who are deaf.

On Outside Signs and Publicity Posters
- Use the accessibility logo.
- Include the words "ALL ARE WELCOME." The phrase now has new meaning.
- Provide directions to accessible entrances on doorways that are inaccessible.

On Inside Bulletin Boards or Signs
- Remind members about all special accommodations, classes, and opportunities.
- Indicate locations of accessible restrooms.

In Congregational Newsletters and Bulletins
- Print a list of accommodations available to p disabilities.

- Run a story or celebratory announcement about new classes, accommodations, or opportunities.
- Issue periodic open invitations to join the Task Force on Disability Issues (a group which would be sponsored by your church). Publicize meetings.

There are many types of special needs—some temporary, some permanent, but all challenging and all opportunities for the body of Christ to reach out in love. This chapter will provide guidelines and suggestions for making it possible for people with various special needs to attend and to participate successfully in your fellowship. Here are some ways that you can convey that all really are welcome in your church.

First, in the bulletin, regularly print announcements of the following type, describing helpful resources that are available:

- The congregation has a variety of resources available. These include large-print hymnals and Bibles, lap boards, and audio loops. Please speak to an usher if you wish to use any of these resources.
- Everyone is welcome to attend all congregational activities and to participate in our religious education programs. Audio tapes of previous services are also available. If anyone has questions or needs assistance, please speak with an usher or call the office.

Second, provide a comfortable way for people with disabilities within the congregation to offer suggestions for reducing barriers without feeling that they will be labeled as "complainers."

Third, form a Task Force on Disability Issues. NOD recommends inviting as task-force members, people who have:

- various types of disabilities
- a family member with a disability
- responsibility to plan and lead worship
- influence in making policy
- responsibility for managing the building
- skills in carpentry, contracting, or architecture
- responsibility for educational curricula, especially special education skills
- experience in fund raising
- responsibility for community outreach
- skills in writing and communicating

The initial work of the task force could include discussing experiences within the congregation that may be creating barriers for people with disabilities and for their families. The work also includes making lists of access problems encountered by someone with physical or sensory disabilities in trying to enter or use the building.

Other tasks might include considering policies and practices that could be viewed as discouraging to someone with a disability, dividing the list of barriers and problems by type, referring recommendations to the appropriate congregational authority, and planning strategy for fund-raising approaches for the purchase of special equipment or alterations in physical structure.

The formation of such a group will make a strong statement of your church's commitment to meeting the needs of all people. Once formed, encourage those with disabilities to approach task-force members with problems and suggestions.

The task force also could plan and present a workshop for the congregation to promote understanding of various types of disabilities and the challenges they present. Leaders could be people with disabilities within the congregation.

Fourth, use and promote the use of affirming or "people-first language." "People-first" refers to the principle that the person is primary, the disability is secondary. These defined words are frequently misused:

> *Disability*: A permanent physical, sensory, or intellectual impairment that substantially limits one or more of a person's major life activities, including reading, writing, and other aspects of education; holding a job; and managing various essential functions of life such as dressing, bathing, and eating.

> *Handicap*: A barrier society places on the person with a disability. So, one could say, "The stairs in that building will be a handicap for John, who has a disability and uses a wheelchair," but not, "John is handicapped and can't use the stairs." A person uses a wheelchair just as another person uses his or her legs for mobility. Don't say a person is "wheelchair bound" or "confined to a wheelchair."

Certain words and phrases are no longer acceptable. These include: *deaf and dumb, wheelchair bound, victim, invalid,* and categorizations beginning with the word *the,* such as *the disabled, the deaf,* or *the mentally retarded.* Also, it is preferable to describe a person as being "at home" rather than "homebound" or "shut in."

Fifth, learn more about the various conditions and illnesses that are present among members. Consider what special pastoral care may be needed, and train members of the congregation to assist in offering spiritual, moral, and physical support.

Sixth, encourage religious educators to seek out curricula for all ages with thoughtful content and multi-sensory teaching strategies. Seventh, provide a training session for ushers since they are usually the first people to greet and welcome a newcomer. Ask people with disabilities to assist in the training. Eighth, include members with disabilities in worship roles in which other members of the congregation participate. Ninth, make sure that qualified members who happen to have disabilities are offered leadership positions.

Tenth, provide workable transportation arrangements for those without transportation. Transportation is a major barrier for someone with mobility or sight impairment. If possible, give the person with a disability a list of willing drivers in order to provide for personal choice and control. These approaches would be helpful:

- Arrange neighborhood carpools serving the congregation.
- Prearrange assistance for the person with a disability who calls ahead and asks to be met at the car.
- Arrange reserved parking places near the ramped entrances for people with mobility impairments.
- Station someone outside the door to assist persons in and out of cars and to help with doors.
- Recognize and thank publicly those who regularly drive others to church.

Eleventh, understand that many people feel awkward and uncomfortable with those who look or act differently. Too often, many people with disabilities are ignored, isolated, or rejected. Since many people do not know what to do or say around a person with a disability, help them to begin to feel more sure of themselves and encourage interaction. NOD makes these suggestions:

- When someone says, "I don't know what to say when I meet a person with a disability," suggest, "How about 'hello'?"
- Talk directly to the person with a disability, not to the nearby family member, companion, or interpreter.
- Offer assistance but do not impose. Allow a person to retain as much control as possible, doing things for herself or himself, even if it takes longer.
- Ask the person with the disability about the best way to be of assistance. Personal experience makes him or her the expert.

- Do not pretend to understand if the speech or ideas of the person are unclear. Request that the person clarify. Continue speaking to the person rather than asking a companion to answer.
- Work to control reactions of personal discomfort when someone behaves in an unexpected way or looks somewhat different. Try to see the wholeness of spirit underneath and overcome the tendency to turn away or ignore the person with the disability.
- Treat a person with a disability as you would treat any other person.

Finally, follow announcements of general invitation with personal invitations and arrangements for transportation. People with disabilities may not really believe that the invitation includes them, especially if they have had disappointing or isolating experiences in the past.

Different disabilities, of course, present various challenges and needs.

Limited Mobility

An estimated 1.4 million Americans are wheelchair users. And, of course, there are millions of others who use walkers, canes, braces, or crutches. Causes of physical disability range from accidents to genetic conditions or diseases. And, of course, aging increases the chance of broken bones and deteriorating strength.

Ramps, curb cuts, and designated parking spaces make it easier and, often, possible for the mobility impaired to get inside the building. These adaptations can also be helpful for a teacher bringing in supplies on a dolly, parents with strollers or baby carriages, and movers of heavy equipment.

Here are some ways to accommodate those with mobility impairments:

- Provide outside barrier-free access including curb cuts, street level or ramped entrances, and thirty-two-inch doorways with level entry space at least five by five feet. Double doors must be operable by a single stroke or a person with a mobility disability often cannot use them. Doors should be able to be opened by exerting eighty-one pounds of pressure or less.
- Ramps should have protection from the weather, have a nonskid surface, and handrails on at least one side at a height of thirty-two inches above the surface. Ramps should be a minimum of thirty-six inches wide, extending one foot in length for every inch of rise, a 1:12 ratio. Thus, a ramp replacing an eight-inch step must extend eight feet.
- Designate 12' 6" wide parking spaces near accessible entrances and mark them with the international symbol for disabilities.

- Lower elevator control panels with brailled plaques to fifty-four inches or less from the elevator floor with a handrail on at least one side of the elevator.
- Provide an accessible source of water. If a drinking fountain or cooler cannot be lowered, provide a cup dispenser beside it.
- Adapt a bathroom (which may be unisex) by installing grab bars, a raised toilet seat, and a thirty-two-inch door that swings out on the stall. Also necessary are a sink at an appropriate level for a wheelchair with twenty-nine inches of clearance from floor to bottom of the sink, lever-type faucets, a towel dispenser no higher than forty inches from the floor, and an appropriately positioned mirror. A turning space of sixty by sixty inches is necessary to allow for wheelchair turning.
- Equip stairs with rubber treads and handrails on both sides, thirty-two inches above the step. Extend handrails beyond the top or bottom step, a feature helpful to those with braces, crutches, canes, and walkers. Slightly raised abrasive strips on top steps will warn people with limited sight where stairs begin.
- Install firm carpeting, and reduce floor slickness.
- Shorten some pews so that a wheelchair can fit into the main body of the congregation, instead of having to be placed awkwardly in an aisle or behind the last pew. Also, some seating spaces should have extra leg room for people who have casts or use crutches, walkers, or braces.
- Build a ramp to raised areas of the sanctuary, so that those who are mobility impaired can fully participate.
- Move the location of any classroom that is inaccessible.
- Think about room arrangements for all meetings, coffee-hour gatherings, or receptions. Is there clearance in the halls? Are there loose or curling rugs that will impede travel? Are there enough chairs for people who tire easily?
- Have someone available to open heavy doors.
- Offer to provide a note-taker if manual dexterity is impaired.
- Have a supply of straws available for those who have difficulty holding a cup or glass.
- Make available book stands or lapboards for those unable to hold prayer books, hymnals, or Bibles.

Dallas Police Sgt. Tony Crawford, a paraplegic as a result of being shot in the line of duty, has some advice for relating to people who use wheelchairs. He suggests, "Offer to help, but if the person with a disability says 'I can do it,' let him. Don't act like you're pitying him." He says that when a few well-meaning individuals have patted him on the head and said things like "Bless your heart," he's found it rather difficult to maintain a Christian attitude.[1]

Here are some other suggestions for improving personal interactions:

- Sit in order to be at eye level when talking with a person using a wheelchair.
- Be careful not to move a wheelchair, crutches, or walker out of reach. Ask if assistance is needed.
- Do not lean on the wheelchair or otherwise "invade" the person's space.
- When buffet or cafeteria lines cause inconveniences, get suggestions and offer to carry the person's plate or tray.

Blind and Visually Limited

Every congregation will have members with varying degrees of vision. Here are some things you can do to help the blind and those with low vision to be active participants in the worship, education, and social life of the congregation:

- Describe materials being distributed to a group that includes a blind person. Summarize information displayed on a screen.
- Accept a guide dog in the sanctuary as you would any guide.
- Produce bulletins and words to hymns, litanies, and prayers in large print. Provide brailled versions if requested.
- Provide large-print hymnals, Bibles, and prayer books.
- Make available audio tapes of services, sermons, speeches, and lessons.
- Offer a volunteer reader service.
- Improve sanctuary and hallway lighting, especially around staircases and other areas of potential difficulty for people with low vision.
- Place brailled information plaques on elevator panels.

These are some suggestions for improving personal interactions:

- Call a person's name to get his or her attention before speaking. In a group conversation, identify people by name as each one speaks.
- Don't pat a guide dog in harness.
- Feel free to use words such as *see* and *look*.
- When guiding, give verbal clues to what lies ahead, such as steps, curbs, elevators, or doors.
- Let the blind person know when you're leaving.

In Faith Presbyterian Church in Sun City, Arizona, a woman with macular degeneration organized a limited-sight group. They meet regularly and assist people who are losing their vision to get their lives organized. For example, they help people place cooking supplies and utensils in their kitchens so that they can readily find everything. People from other churches frequently come to learn about the program.[2]

Deaf and Hard-of-Hearing

People with varying degrees of hearing acuity will be found in any fairly large group of people, regardless of age. People who are hard of hearing depend on enhanced sound and lip reading to understand what is being said. A person with partial hearing may benefit from assistive listening devices (ALDs), such as a hearing aid, an audio loop worn around the neck, and a small microphone worn on the speaker's lapel.

Those who are deaf prefer interpreted conversation, with American Sign Language (ASL) being the most frequently used language in the United States. ASL is a language with its own syntax and structure. To deaf people, ASL is their native language and is an integral part of what is known as the deaf culture. While many deaf people prefer to worship in a congregation with those who are deaf, others choose a mainstream religious community where interpretation is provided. This is especially true of families with both hearing and deaf members.

These approaches make it possible and comfortable for those who are deaf or have a hearing loss to participate in your programs.

- Provide an interpreter for services and other events.
- Provide reserved seating near speakers and the interpreter.
- Make sure that important announcements are provided in written form as well as interpreted form.
- Use pencil and paper to communicate when necessary.
- Reduce background noise from radios, television sets, and loud fans.
- Purchase a telecommunications device (TDD or TTY) for the church so that a hearing impaired person can call staff members. The devices allow a deaf person to communicate with someone with normal hearing over the telephone lines by using a small terminal with a screen and keyboard similar to a typewriter. The cost is a few hundred dollars.
- Sponsor sign-language classes for interested staff and church members.
- Inform church members about the availability of TDD or TTY relay service through the telephone company. This service converts speech into text on the other end of the line through a

third party and allows those who are deaf to type their response, which is then spoken to the caller.[3]

- Make printed copies of sermons and other material available to the deaf and hearing impaired, since it is nearly impossible to watch an interpreter and take notes at the same time.[4]
- Purchase assistive listening devices (ALDs) for the sanctuary and other meeting areas. Four main types are available: personal and group FM systems (using radio waves), loop systems (using magnetic waves and requiring a hearing aid equipped with a telephone pick-up coil or T-switch), infrared systems (using light waves), and hardwire systems (directly connecting the speaker and listener and requiring that the hard-of-hearing person sit in specific locations where the permanently wired-in earphone jacks are placed).

Barbara A. Buttweiler, advertising manager for Williams Sound Corporation, says, "A hearing assistance system is one of the best ways to increase the signal-to-noise ratio. Assistive listening systems allow you to sit where you like and at the same time be able to hear as if you were right next to the loudspeaker." Using the existing church sound system, "the microphone is placed very close to the sound source, making the desired sound much louder and background noises virtually eliminated. The listener hears the desired sound directly from the sound system through wired headphones or a small wireless receiver and earphone."

Buttweiler points out that the wireless systems have helped overcome the limitations of hardwired systems and have lessened the reluctance of people to use them. Since the listener uses a small portable receiver with an earphone to pick up a transmission anywhere within the church, users may sit wherever they like.

Buttweiler says that infrared systems are a good choice when strong radio interference exists. However, since infrared light is confined by opaque objects, such as walls, the large emitter panels cannot be concealed and may detract from the aesthetic appearance of the church. They also are more expensive than the radio wave systems. She concludes, "Given the ease of installation, relatively low equipment cost and excellent audio performance, FM systems are the logical choice for assistive listening systems."[5] In addition:

- Do a weekly check of batteries in listening devices.
- Encourage those who use equipment to inform an usher if ALDs are not working properly.
- Provide a qualified interpreter for dramatic and musical presentations.

Laurie Vassallo, a sign-language interpreter and teacher of music and drama for deaf students, says that the ideal situation at a performance is to have a reserved section for deaf people in the center section at the front of the auditorium. The interpreter needs to be in the same sight line as the performers so that the viewers will not miss the action of the play or musical while trying to look at the interpreter. Also, there must be enough light on the interpreter's hands so that they may be seen clearly. "The interpreter should be given a script as soon as the actors are," she points out. "Rehearsals should also be open to the interpreter to attend and rehearse with the actors. Interpreters usually make up a sign name for each character, so we don't have to spell the names out each time they're mentioned." She also explains that a bright light behind an interpreter can produce a glare and make it difficult for deaf people to watch the sign language. These suggestions would also apply to interpretation of a video or movie.[6]

Here are some tips for communicating effectively one-on-one:

- To get a person's attention before speaking, tap her or him lightly on the shoulder and speak face-to-face.
- Make eye contact, look at, and speak directly to the person rather than the interpreter. Do not say things to the interpreter, such as, "Tell her for me." Rather, address the deaf person by name. The interpreter may be greeted privately, but, when the interpreter is working, he or she should not be addressed as a participant in the conversation.
- Speak at a moderate pace, clearly but without exaggeration.
- Avoid covering your mouth while speaking.
- Do not stand in front of a window or bright light, since it places the face in a shadow and makes lip reading more difficult.
- Don't pretend to understand if the speech of a person is unclear. Request that the deaf person rephrase the statement until the meaning is certain.

Developmentally Disabled

People with developmental disabilities have lifelong disabling conditions, including mental retardation, spinal-cord injury, epilepsy, sensory impairment, cerebral palsy, autism, and traumatic brain injury, as well as other conditions resulting in limitations.

That All May Worship states the following:

The term "developmental disability" is complicated by the fact that some people with cerebral palsy or autism may have advanced intellectual skills but limited physical development, while people with mental retardation have slower rates of learning and limited capacity for abstract thinking. . . . People with developmental disabilities, especially intellectual disabilities, have often been treated as less than fully human. Today, religious and lay leaders are beginning to understand that those with developmental disabilities . . . have much to offer a welcoming congregation. They may exhibit qualities "that abide," such as faith and hope, and have a meaningful relationship with God.[7]

Here are some of the things your congregation can do to include the developmentally disabled:

- Provide opportunities for participation in all congregational activities.
- Think of concrete ways for the child or adult with retardation to assist before, during, and after the worship service. Some possibilities include: passing out programs and bulletins, filling the water glass for the religious leader, collecting materials left in pews after services.
- Find appropriate ways to increase knowledge and understanding among the members of a congregation, especially among peer groups of children.
- Provide hands-on experiences in social and teaching settings.
- Offer an older child with developmental disability the opportunity to help the teacher of younger children with cutting, pasting, reading, and straightening the classroom.
- Assist persons with developmental disability to participate in denominational activities such as retreats, camping programs, conferences, and assemblies.
- Integrate students with developmental disabilities into regular classes, whenever possible.

Second Baptist of Jacksonville, Arkansas, has a group called the Handi-capables. This is a group for mentally retarded adults who are employed in the community and live in special homes. Church buses provide transportation for all their activities.[8]

Here are some suggestions for improving personal interactions with those with this type of disability:

- Treat adults with developmental disabilities as adults, not as children.
- Talk to the person directly, not through a companion or family member.

- Be patient. Give instructions slowly, in short sentences, and one step at a time.
- Allow those with this type of disability to try tasks on their own, to make mistakes, to take a longer time, and to persevere. Do not impatiently take over doing things for the person that she or he can do alone.

The Rev. Jean Warner, whose Down's syndrome daughter is an adult, suggests that people treat those with this type of handicap like a "real person." She says that it is hurtful when people either ignore her daughter and look quickly away, or, at the other extreme, stare out of curiosity.[9]

Members at Home

How can a congregation nurture, encourage, and care for the spiritual needs of a person who can never come to church and make him or her feel a part of the fellowship?

Central Church, which has more than eight hundred members, has "an intentional pastoral-care ministry" to keep in touch with those at home and those going through a crisis. Each member of the group is responsible for ministering to seven at-homers or others with special needs. This includes visiting them, sometimes helping with grocery shopping, and making monthly reports of needs to the coordinator of pastoral care.

Central also employs a part-time pastoral field-worker who is familiar with community resources, knows how to cut through red tape, assists in filling out forms, and helps in getting appropriate assistance that may be needed.[10]

Calvary Baptist Church in Dallas helps members who are unable to attend services to stay involved and in touch through its Receivers Class, which is conducted through a telephone conference call. Each Sunday morning members of the class eagerly await the call of the telephone operator and wait for the teacher to begin. Members pray together, and hear and discuss the Sunday school lesson. The session is about thirty minutes in length. A permanent list of participants is provided to the telephone company, which charges the church according to the number of participants. The class secretary calls all the members the night before to remind them to be ready for their class on Sunday morning.

Then, on Homebound Day at Calvary, the entire service is broadcast over the conference call arrangement. Homebound workers go out to each home and administer the Lord's Supper at the same time church members are receiving it. Those at home receive a phone call at least once a week and a minimum of one home visit a month.

Another service offered by the church is the Health Assistance Loan Program. A number of wheel chairs, hospital beds, walkers, and other aids are available from the church at no charge.[11]

Here are some other possibilities:

- Think of ways a person at home might assist in the work of the congregation. Examples include: using computer skills, making telephone calls, or writing for the newsletter.
- If the member at home is alert and able to participate in such a group, organize a Bible study that meets in his or her home.
- Make sure that all publications and programs of events are sent to those who cannot attend.
- Tape all services and have a copy delivered to all those at home. Audio tape is good, but video is even better. Since the video tape can be rerecorded, cost is minimal.
- Remember those confined to their homes on special days, such as a birthday, with a floral arrangement or a shower of cards from church members.
- Pair each at-homer with another at-homer as a "buddy" to pray with and talk to on the phone.
- Organize a cadre of caring people to regularly visit and call on members at home and those living in nursing homes.
- Establish a telephone network for older adults who live alone and still are able to get out. Partners can call one another at a predetermined time each morning to make sure that the other person is all right.

Caregivers

For each person with a severe disability and for the majority of those who must remain at home, there is a primary caregiver who, because of his or her role, also has special needs. (For more information about this, see the form entitled "Checklist for Meeting the Needs of Those with Disabilities," which you can find on page 93.) Parents, spouse, siblings, children, and other caregivers often find themselves under enormous emotional and physical strain.

That All May Worship says the following:

It is essential that the caregiver confer dignity, comfort, and hope upon the person with disability, day by day, and not feel like a martyr. To do so, she or he needs multiple sources of personal affirmation. The congregation can be one of the places where the caregiver finds practical and spiritual support that can make all the difference.[12]

Here are some ways that support can be given:

- Provide for someone to take over a few hours so that personal and family business can be accomplished.
- Develop three or four congregational friends or families to provide care on an alternating, regular basis so that the caregiver can have an occasional evening and weekend away.
- Crossroads Christian Church in Corona, California, provides "respite care" for families who take care of children with disabilities. Parents are given time away from their responsibilities by caregivers who come into their homes two Saturday mornings and one Saturday evening every month. No charge is made for the service.[13]
- Be a friend who will listen. Have a nonjudgmental attitude.
- Provide assistance with shopping and running errands.
- Take a casserole or get several people to provide a whole dinner.
- Provide a driver for trips to the hospital or rehabilitation center.
- Encourage creative long-term planning regarding care for the person with disability who is aging. Help mobilize family resources, if such assistance is welcome. Suggest the names of appropriate lawyers, physicians, insurance agents, and religious leaders with problem-solving skills.
- Support the family who must place a member in a residential care facility. Be aware that family members may experience guilt, shame, and loneliness. Provide counseling opportunities during the decision-making period, the initial weeks after placement and, as appropriate, later.

Emergencies

Is your church prepared to handle an emergency medical situation? If not, take a cue from Immanuel United Church of Christ in Shillington, Pennsylvania. The locations of oxygen, first-aid kits, a litter, and blankets and wheelchairs are listed for ushers. Emergency telephone numbers for physicians and nurses are provided. And procedures for the removal and care of persons taken ill during worhip are in place.[14]

At Faith Presbyterian Church in Sun City, Arizona, all ministers have received training in cardiopulmonary resuscitation. In addition, members who are trained in CPR are present in every service in case emergency assistance is needed.[15]

That All May Worship says:

Fortunately, many have learned by effort, luck, and experience that people with disabilities are more like us than unlike us.

We all have similar needs, wants, and fears. We share our humanity. Sometimes we can compensate for problems by ourselves; other times we need family and community support to be ourselves. . . . How much better to regard someone primarily as a person with abilities, and only secondarily as someone who may need assistance to use those abilities.[16]

Checklist for Meeting the Needs of Those with Disabilities

_____ 1. Is the accessibility logo used on signs?

_____ 2. Is a sign directing the way to reserved parking for those with disabilities at the entrance to the parking lot?

_____ 3. Are parking spaces clearly marked and wide enough for vans to use wheelchair lifts?

_____ 4. Have curb cuts been made?

_____ 5. Are ramps protected from the weather, covered with a nonskid surface, and provided with handrails on at least one side?

_____ 6. Do signs point the way to entrances wide enough for wheelchair access?

_____ 7. Are hallways free of obstruction, allowing plenty of room for passage?

_____ 8. Has at least one bathroom been adapted by installing grab bars, a raised toilet seat, a thirty-two-inch door that swings out on the stall, lever-type faucets, a towel dispenser no higher than forty inches from the floor, and an appropriately positioned mirror?

_____ 9. Has an accessible source of water been provided?

_____ 10. Do elevator control panels have brailled plaques no higher than fifty-four inches from the elevator floor with a handrail on at least one side of the elevator?

_____ 11. Do stairs have rubber treads, handrails on both sides, and slightly raised abrasive strips on top steps?

_____ 12. Are there places in the main seating area of the auditorium where those using a wheelchair may be seated with friends or family?

_____ 13. Is a message indicating resources that are available and how to obtain them run in the bulletin?

_____ 14. Have ushers received training on how to welcome and be of assistance to those with disabilities?

_____ 15. Have arrangements been made to arrange transportation to services and other activities for those who are unable to drive?

_____ 16. Is information displayed on a screen summarized orally when a blind person is present?

_____ 17. Are hymnals and other materials available in large print, when needed?

_____ 18. Are services and other events interpreted for the deaf by a qualified sign-language interpreter?

_____ 19. Is a TTY available so that deaf persons can call the church?

_____ 20. Are assistive listening devices available in the sanctuary and other meeting areas?

_____ 21. Are audio and video tapes made of sermons and lessons?

_____ 22. Are members with disabilities included in worship roles in which other members of the congregation participate?

_____ 23. Are qualified members who have disabilities offered leadership positions?

_____ 24. Has a Task Force on Disability Issues been formed?

_____ 25. Are multisensory teaching strategies encouraged?

_____ 26. Is equipment which might be needed in a medical emergency available and its location known by ushers?

_____ 27. Is someone who has had training in CPR present in every service?

Communicating Effectively in Meetings, Through Evaluations, and While Moving

Without counsel purposes are disappointed:
but in the multitude of counsellors they are established.
—Proverbs 15:22 (KJV)

8 Structuring and Conducting Successful Meetings

"N ot another meeting!" That's the reaction of many people today who have too little time to do too many things—especially if they have been subjected to too many long, boring, unproductive meetings. Who can blame them?

Here's probably the most important question to ask before calling another meeting: "Is this meeting really necessary?" Then, unless you can justify it with an unqualified yes, forget it and use a different approach to accomplish your mission. Once a meeting plan passes the litmus test of necessity, stating the purpose and the expected outcome in a single, succinct statement will provide a gyroscope for keeping the meeting on course. After that, there are many decisions to make to ensure that those goals can be met (for more help on doing this, see the form entitled "Checklist for Planning Meetings," which you can find on page 110).

Selecting the Right Spot

A key factor in the success or failure of a meeting is holding it in the most appropriate place for meeting your objectives. Here are some considerations:

1. Select an appropriate room. A too-large facility can seem overwhelming to a small group. On the other hand, one that is too small in proportion to the number of people can make participants feel ill at ease and cramped. Allow about eight hundred square feet for thirty people with tables and chairs and about one thousand square feet for fifty people only. The shape of the room can also be very important. A long, narrow room may be difficult or impossible to arrange effectively if you plan to use group participation or audiovisual approaches.
2. Lighting should be bright enough for reading and writing but not so bright that it causes a glare. Can the lighting be controlled?

Some of the information in this chapter has previously been published in *Speaking with Confidence*, written by the author (Betterway Publications, 1990).

3. Acoustics should enable the speakers to be easily heard in all parts of the room. Carpeting helps. It also makes things easier for a presenter or presider who is going to be standing for some time. It is better not to use microphones unless absolutely necessary. They tend to inhibit some people and can slow down a meeting if a person has to change location in order to speak.
4. Are heating and cooling adequate and reliable?
5. Are there enough electrical outlets and are they appropriately located? This is especially important if audiovisual aids are to be used.
6. Are adequate speaker's stands and appropriate tables readily available?
7. A room without windows provides fewer distractions. A view of the city skyline may be aesthetically pleasing, but it also may be conducive to wandering thoughts, especially if there is a breath-taking sunset or a thunderstorm underway.
8. The room should not have any posts that obstruct vision.

Arranging Seating for Best Effect

The appropriate arrangement of seating for a particular meeting is critical to its success. A good rule of thumb is the closer the participants are to the presenter or presider, the better. It is also easier to generate interaction, enthusiasm, cohesiveness, motivation, and team spirit when members of the group are seated close together and can see one another. If tables are to be used, then they should be narrow.

Here are some good, rather formal arrangements for meetings in which most of the talking will be done from a speaker's stand.

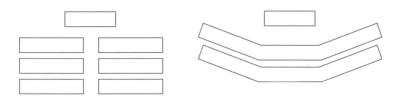

These arrangements encourage good group interaction, since all participants can see one another and are more informal.

This arrangement of furniture facilitates small-group-within-a-group interaction.

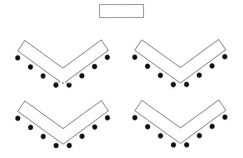

Holding Successful Meetings
Where Business Will Be Conducted

1. Keep the meeting as small as possible by inviting only those who have pertinent information to contribute and/or who will be making decisions.
2. Clearly define the purpose of the meeting and let participants know beforehand exactly what is to be accomplished.
3. Send out an agenda in advance with the most important item at the top.
4. Set a time limit for the entire meeting and for each agenda item. This helps keep the meeting moving in case participants get too long-winded on a particular item.
5. Select an appropriate room for the size and makeup of the group.
6. Be sure that furniture is arranged for optimum interaction.
7. Consider several alternative plans prior to the meeting and develop backup information, costs, and possible outcomes for each option.

During the Meeting

1. Start on time, regardless of who is missing. Waiting for latecomers to arrive reinforces their habit of tardiness. At the next meeting, those who are on time will probably arrive late, too, since they'll think the meeting won't begin at the designated hour anyway.
2. Assign someone to take notes and keep time on each agenda item.
3. Clearly define the purpose of the meeting.
4. Stick with the agenda. Don't allow the meeting to lapse into conversation off the subject.
5. Limit interruptions to emergencies.
6. Restate conclusions for clear understanding and to ensure a commitment of purpose.

7. Make assignments with due dates clearly stated.
8. End on time—even if you have to continue discussion of an agenda item at a later date.

After the Meeting

1. Send notes of the meeting, listing assignments and due dates, to participants and to others affected by decisions.
2. Follow up with progress reports on the implementation of decisions.
3. Have each participant turn in an evaluation of the meeting. An example form may be found at the end of this chapter (page 111).

Using Brainstorming—A Creative Approach

Brainstorming is an effective tool to use for various purposes: to solve a problem, to help your ministry look at new possibilities and break out of ingrained patterns that may no longer be working, to involve people in decision making and carrying out a plan they've helped to create, and to help develop a new program. And most participants enjoy the experience.

As a pastor, perhaps you're faced with a dilemma. Collections have fallen off drastically. It may be understandable in light of the economy and the fact that several members of your congregation have been laid off. However, without a solution soon, it seems inevitable that programs and perhaps staff members will have to be cut.

A brainstorming session at your next board meeting may spark some fresh ideas to help solve the problem. The amazing thing about this technique is that it often generates solutions that neither you nor your members would ever come up with without the structure of this activity.

Brainstorming is a process that is designed to generate as many ideas as possible in a short period of time in a nonjudgmental atmosphere. This approach has been used successfully in the business world for a number of years. In fact, it was first introduced by Walt Disney in the 1920s.

The approach also has tremendous potential for church use in a variety of situations. This is particularly true because of the rapid changes in our society. People will not necessarily respond to programs that were successful in the past. The next time you wonder what to do in a certain area of the church program, consider brainstorming as a vehicle that may help get you where you want to go.

These are some of the advantages of brainstorming:

1. It encourages participation by all members of the group. Even the shyest person will usually contribute within this framework.

Often, he or she will have a worthwhile idea that otherwise might never have been offered.

2. Criticism and negative comments about an idea are ruled out. "Killer phrases," often the death of committee meetings, are forbidden. No one is allowed to make remarks such as:
   - "We've never done it that way before."
   - "We tried it before, and it didn't work."
   - "Too modern."
   - "Too old-fashioned."
   - "You don't understand the problem."
   - "Too much work."
   - "We're too big for that."
   - "We're not big enough for that."

3. Equal value and consideration are given to each idea. No ranking comments, such as, "That's a great idea," or "That's the best suggestion yet," are permitted.

4. Creativity is fostered. In fact, participants are encouraged to think big and say whatever pops into their minds, regardless of how outlandish it may seem. A suggestion can always be tamed down later in the process. One creative idea begets another. Participants often surprise themselves with the fresh approaches they come up with.

5. A great number of ideas can be produced in a short period of time. Quantity is welcomed.

6. An idea of one member may spark a new idea or another direction for someone else.

7. There is no time-wasting discussion of the merits of all ideas. Less effective approaches are automatically eliminated by the process.

8. A plan developed by a group in this manner will usually have the support of all the members. People tend to support what they help create.

9. A sense of unity among members of the group is fostered. Participants usually find the activity to be stimulating and fun. Here's what you'll need:
   - a table or tables to accommodate six to ten people
   - a leader for each table
   - flip charts and felt-tip pens or chalkboards and chalk

If there is more than one group, each one can work on the same problem. Or, you can divide the task into smaller subdivisions in order to design an overall plan. For example, if you want to come up with ways to communicate to your community what your church has to offer, you might divide into groups with each brainstorming a different subtopic. These might include: "How can we communicate effectively with teenagers?" "With people who have physical disabilities?" "With various ethnic groups?"

These are the steps to conducting a successful brainstorming session:

1. State the problem or challenge. Pinpoint the brainstorming subject or subjects in advance. Be sure not to narrow the definition too stringently or you may preclude any number of possibilities. For example, if you've outgrown your space for Sunday school classrooms, don't state the problem as "Where can we build another building?" That rules out looking at present space that may be available but, perhaps, can be used more effectively. Asking, "Where can we find more classroom space?" leaves room for more alternatives. Thus, state the problem in the form of a question. If few people are showing up for your senior citizens' group, don't state the discussion topic as, "No one likes the senior citizens' group." Rather, use something like, "How can we get more senior citizens involved?"

2. Explain what you're going to do. Tell participants that the purpose is to generate as many creative ideas as possible in a short length of time. Comment that the idea doesn't necessarily have to be completely new, that it may be a variation on something that is already being done.

3. Ban any comments—positive or negative—about an idea. The evaluation will come later. One approach is to ring a bell or blow a whistle if someone forgets and criticizes a suggestion.

4. Give the participants a couple of minutes to think about the problem and come up with some ideas.

5. Go around the table in order, having each participant state a suggestion in a brief, complete sentence. Circle the participants as many times as necessary to get everyone's ideas. Some may only want to contribute one or two.

6. Leaders should be cheerleaders. Encourage participants and energize the group with comments such as, "You're doing great," or "John, you look like you have an idea. How about it?"

7. Have recorder(s) list the ideas on newsprint or a chalkboard. Be sure to note every contribution.

8. After all suggestions have been generated, read the list. Then ask whether anyone has another idea he or she would like to add.

9. Once all the ideas have been recorded, consolidate entries that are redundant and eliminate those that simply don't apply. Then have the participants rank the suggestions either by a show of

hands or by written response. Tally the results and identify the most worthwhile suggestions for reaching the stated goal or solving the problem.
10. Now is the time for discussion and putting together a plan.
11. In the case of multiple groups, have each group report on its best suggestions and recommended plan.

One church that was in the process of building a new facility and moving to a new location used brainstorming effectively in coming up with a plan for keeping members involved and informed during the period of transition with good results. Consider this approach for different aspects of your program. You may come up with some creative ways to use the technique of brainstorming in your church.

Be Aware of the Dynamics of Group Communication

Understanding the dynamics of communication in groups and learning to orchestrate and affect those dynamics are tremendous assets for a leader. Being able to recognize the signs that indicate that communication is breaking down and to know how to intervene effectively when the group climate begins to sour, can save a meeting, a program, and perhaps future relationships among participants.

Social scientists have observed that people usually express ideas and information through their words, but their feelings are expressed through subtle body language, tone of voice, facial expression, and so on. The group leader does well to listen with the eyes as well as the ears, to both the person who is talking and to those who are reacting in one way or another. These group dynamics are especially relevant for anyone who is conducting a meeting.

Group Size

Group size is important, for it affects the pattern of communication and determines interaction possibilities. Typically in a small group of five to eight members, each person will participate freely, usually speaking to everyone. Participation is usually open, relaxed, and uninhibited. However, as the size of the group grows, some members will tend to limit their participation. They will interact only with certain other members. The larger the group, the fewer the members who will participate. The atmosphere automatically becomes more formal and more structured.

Enabling and encouraging everyone to participate in a larger group takes effort and skill on the part of the leader. One workable approach is to break the group into smaller units of five to eight people for discussion of a certain point. Then a note-taker from each group can report to the larger group the conclusions of the small-group discussions.

If the larger group is to remain as a single unit, then the leader will have to be creative in finding ways to involve those who are somewhat shy about expressing their opinions and contributing information that may well be valuable to the group. Asking a well-thought-out question that you know such persons can answer without seeming to put them on the spot is a real art. Valuing their reply can go a long way toward giving them the courage to make future contributions without prompting. Of course, sensitive group members can be helpful as well.

Group Participants

Why are the participants there? Motives will vary. Some will participate because they feel they have the background and expertise to help that particular group accomplish its purpose. Others may want to become a part of a group within the church and be involved in some specific effort. Another possibility is that membership on a particular committee may be seen as a prestigious position or a way to network with other members for a variety of reasons. Of course, some may have a combination of motives. Also, participants in a group that meets on a continuing basis may modify or change their expectations.

Doubtless the particular goals of the participants will significantly influence their behavior in the group. Those who want to accomplish a goal will see communicating effectively as a practical, necessary tool for getting the job done. They will want and expect the group to stay on task. However, those who come in order to relate to other members will see communication as an end in itself. They will want to bring personal matters and feelings into the conversation. For those with personal goals to accomplish, communication will be self-expressive and self-serving.

Robert W. Jeambey, former associate synod executive for communication and stewardship in the Presbyterian Church (USA), says that "Every group needs both task-oriented communication and relationship-oriented communication to accomplish its work. Both kinds of behavior contribute to the group's productivity. A group tends to swing back and forth between the two kinds of communication as it adapts to its relationship and task needs."[1]

Group dynamics will change, and the maturity level of the group should grow as it becomes a more cohesive unit. The degree of maturity will affect its communication. Jeambey says that a mature or fully developed group "(1) makes decisions, (2) accepts responsibility for its tasks, (3) is motivated to complete the job, and (4) possesses the knowledge and skills necessary to do so."[2]

Group tensions will exist in any meeting. Initially primary group tension will be present due to the uncertainty and anxiety experienced by not knowing exactly what to expect and how to relate to other members. Usually there will be a great deal of small talk that is tentative, polite, and soft-spoken. The resulting superficial and impersonal communication impedes the productivity of the group. Primary group tension can be overcome by group-building activities, such as get-acquainted and communication games and opportunities.

Secondary tension will develop as the group is structured and begins its work. This stage necessarily evokes differing opinions as to what should be done and how those ends should be accomplished in view of available time, funds, and resources. Personality conflicts may also surface. Ignoring these kinds of tensions can lead to an unpleasant social climate that will doubtlessly undermine the group's productivity.[3]

The climate of the group is the overall feeling or tone that grows out of relationships among the members and the types and degree of tension. The climate necessarily affects the quantity and quality of work that may be accomplished. Unless open, trusting relationships are established, secondary tensions can sabotage the group's efforts. These tensions can result in some members of the group feeling that their views or ideas are threatened or not appreciated and taken seriously. They may begin to perceive the responses of others in the group as hostile, critical, evaluative, or judgmental. The threatened person may, in turn, become aggressive with defensive and offensive statements or dogmatic explanations. Communication can easily become distorted, personalized, self-serving, combative, or devious. These types of reactions can quickly thrust participants into a tailspin of distrust and damaged relationships, leading to major problems and a disruption of group activity.[4]

Creating and maintaining a supportive climate for each participant is critical to the maximum success of the group. If you sense that someone is beginning to feel defensive, you can intervene and often calm troubled waters by elevating that person's status, showing respect, rewarding his or her contributions, pacifying, conveying understanding, expressing agreement (if appropriate), and releasing tension with humor.[5]

Of course, there may be times when, in spite of efforts to be supportive, communications will break down, and discussion will fall apart and even become hostile. When participants bypass one another in the interaction, become defensive, or come into conflict, it may be your cue to intervene. Say something like, "I think it would be wise to get this point straightened out before we go any further." Go back to the original statement that has become a problem and state what you believe it means. Then ask the originator of the idea if that was his or her intent. If not, then ask that person to rephrase the statement, several times if necessary, until the exact meaning is discerned. Then turn to the other party and find out how the message was understood. Urge him or her to express feelings, attitudes, and assumptions about it. Facilitate the exchange between the two parties until it is clear that the speaker and the offended one have come to a clear understanding of the meaning and the intent of the statement. Usually this process will result in a meeting of minds on both sides, and the discussion can go forward once more.

Group Spirit

A team spirit develops as members make the group's purposes and goals their own and as they develop a sense of belonging and oneness with other participants. Overcoming or managing group tension is necessary to this development. This spirit does not equate with conformity or automatic unanimous response to a given situation. It does mean that relationships, commitment to group goals, and an atmosphere of trust have been firmly established so that honest disagreement may take place without deteriorating into pettiness and backbiting. This secure atmosphere is necessary for the group to accomplish its task effectively.

Also, be aware that the dynamics of the group will change somewhat with the addition or subtraction of members. Therefore, it is better to get people who will stay with a particular committee until its work is accomplished. However, in a group that continues year after year, new people may vitalize the group with the addition of new viewpoints and varied experience.

Orchestrating group dynamics, bringing people together, demonstrating supportive behavior, recognizing defensiveness, and intervening when necessary can spell the difference between success and failure for a group.

Handling Different Types of Participants in Meetings

All too often when a discussion is being held, two types of participants will immediately emerge: those who are eager to talk and those who don't want to talk at all. Trying to involve the nontalkers and to keep the talkative ones from dominating a discussion is a real art, requiring great diplomacy and skill. It's definitely to the advantage of the one presiding to remain consistently cool and collected and to give dignity to the participants—even if they are being overbearing.

Here are some suggestions for involving various kinds of participants.

Type of Participants	Solution
Axe Grinders	Discuss the situation if it fits the subject under discussion. Otherwise, indicate an interest in the person's problem and offer to discuss it after the meeting.
Nonstop Talkers	Interrupt when they take a breath and summarize what's been said. Then ask someone else a question. If they persist, say something such as, "Jim might have some insight into this particular question."
Blasé Brendas and Aloof Als	Try to tie the discussion into their areas of expertise or experience. Ask them to share their wisdom on the subject.
Racial or Political Expounders	State that those particular issues cannot be discussed in this meeting.
Whisperers	Stop talking and look at the individuals. Ask a direct question or solicit an opinion.
Illogical Concluders	Say something such as, "That's an interesting perspective."
Stubborn Standers	Recognize that they may not really understand the issue under discussion or the ramifications. Get them to expand on their point of disagreement. Restate your premise. Get others to help you explain. Or, as a last resort, offer to discuss the question with them later.

Participant's Behavior	Solution
Contentious Spirits	Try to ignore their comments by pretending not to hear them. Recognize any legitimate complaints. Offer to discuss it with them after the meeting. Assign someone who has responsibility in the area of their complaint to talk with them privately

	about the problem or concern. Often the group will help you take care of an obvious troublemaker. As a last resort, take them aside and try to enlist their cooperation.
Silent Sams and Samanthas	Ask them a direct, provocative question.
Participants Arguing	Interrupt with a direct question. Bring other audience members into the discussion. Ask that the discussion be limited to the facts.
Strayers from the Subject	Comment, "Someday perhaps we can talk about that, but right now we need to finish our discussion on . . ."
Poor Speakers	Recognize that they may have great ideas but are limited by fear or vocabulary. Restate their contribution by saying something like, "In other words, you think . . ."
Radicals	Say, "Well, of course, you're entitled to your opinion."
Eager Answerers	The person who always wants to answer first can easily sabotage your efforts to involve as many as possible in the discussion, especially if he or she blurts out the answer without being recognized. A good way to handle this type is to say, "After our discussion of this question, I'm going to ask Dale to summarize what's been said."
Shrinking Violets	Ask direct questions that you are sure they can answer. Ask whether they agree with a statement. Comment favorably if they do get the courage to contribute.
Ramblers	When they come up for breath, thank them, rephrase one of their statements, and call on someone else, or go on to the next topic.

Additional Tips for Smooth Meetings

1. Arrive early, at least fifteen minutes before the meeting is scheduled to begin. Attending to last-minute details after most participants arrive gives the impression that you are disorganized and do not care much about the meeting's success.

2. Involve others in planning the meeting. People tend to support what they have a part in planning and carrying out. Ask others for advice and suggestions on ways to improve future meetings, or appoint a committee to assist with planning.

3. Don't conduct every meeting in the same old way. While some people cling to routine, most people find it monotonous over a long period of time. For a group or committee that meets on a continuing basis, add a little festivity occasionally by moving to a more glamorous setting or by serving some really interesting refreshments.

4. Decide in advance on the best seating arrangement in order to accomplish the group's specific tasks.

5. Make certain that everyone clearly understands the purpose of the meeting and what will be discussed before it begins.

6. Be sure that equipment is working and audiovisual material can be easily seen and heard. Probably nothing is more irritating to an audience than mechanical failure and illegible or inaudible media approaches. Also, have a spare bulb available in case one burns out in the middle of a presentation.

7. Ensure that all members have an opportunity to participate. Members who are not aggressive enough to speak up may have some of the best ideas or advice to offer.

8. Set a definite time to end the meeting and stick to it. Most people are simply too busy to attend meetings that drone on and on. They want to know how long the meeting is scheduled to last and that they definitely will be through at that time.

Conducting successful meetings can be challenging, gratifying, and rewarding. Conducting unsuccessful meetings can put a major damper on the effectiveness of your ministry.

Checklist for Planning Meetings

Prior to the meeting

Publicity
____ Notices
____ Letter of invitation
____ Bulletin boards
____ Personal contacts
____ News release
     (if appropriate)

Agenda
____ Plan agenda
____ Plan for involvement
____ Contact those on agenda
____ Previous minutes
____ Committee reports
____ Materials needed
____ Equipment needed

Space and Equipment
____ Reserve space
____ Reserve equipment
____ Sign up equipment, operators, other assistants

Just before the meeting

Space
____ Room arrangement
____ Seating arrangement
____ Extra chairs
____ Climate control

Space and Equipment
____ AV equipment set up, checked
____ Extension cords
____ Microphones
____ Gavel, felt-tip pens, pencils, pads
____ Newsprint or flip charts (if needed to record feedback)
____ Visual aids
____ Agenda, other handouts
____ Name tags (unless participants know each other very well)

At the meeting

____ Meeting, greeting, seating participants, guests
____ Greeting and seating latecomers
____ Handing out materials
____ Operation of equipment
____ Recording meeting (if desired)

End of meeting and after

____ Collect unused materials
____ Return equipment
____ Clean up
____ Thank helpers
____ Read and analyze evaluation, feedback
____ Remind people of follow-up commitments
____ Plan for next meeting: date, place, and so forth
____ Send copy of minutes to participants

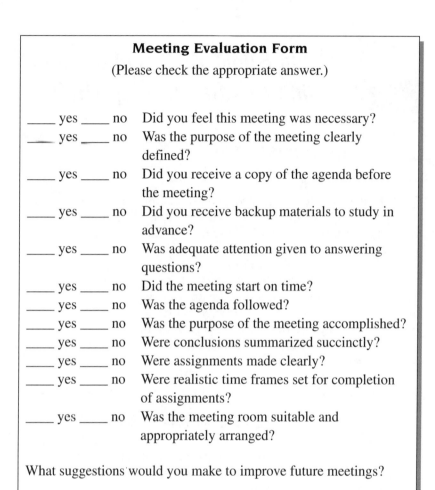

Meeting Evaluation Form
(Please check the appropriate answer.)

____ yes ____ no   Did you feel this meeting was necessary?

____ yes ____ no   Was the purpose of the meeting clearly defined?

____ yes ____ no   Did you receive a copy of the agenda before the meeting?

____ yes ____ no   Did you receive backup materials to study in advance?

____ yes ____ no   Was adequate attention given to answering questions?

____ yes ____ no   Did the meeting start on time?

____ yes ____ no   Was the agenda followed?

____ yes ____ no   Was the purpose of the meeting accomplished?

____ yes ____ no   Were conclusions summarized succinctly?

____ yes ____ no   Were assignments made clearly?

____ yes ____ no   Were realistic time frames set for completion of assignments?

____ yes ____ no   Was the meeting room suitable and appropriately arranged?

What suggestions would you make to improve future meetings?

9 Using Audiovisual Approaches to Communicate More Effectively

The Bell and Howell Corporation offers these statistics as to how people learn: 83 percent learn by sight, 11 percent learn by hearing, 3.5 percent learn by smell, 1.5 percent learn by touch, 1 percent learn by taste. These figures make an excellent case for our giving listeners something to look at.[1]

A "3–M How-To Guide" also speaks to the wisdom of using visual approaches: "When relying on verbalization alone to communicate, an estimated 90 percent of a message is misinterpreted or forgotten entirely. We retain only 10 percent of what we hear. Adding appropriate visual aids to verbalization increases retention to approximately 50 percent."[2]

Fortunately, there is a wide variety of audiovisual aids ready to assist in effectively and precisely communicating your message. However, there are so many different approaches that they can sometimes be confusing. Which one is best to use where, for what effect, and for which purpose can be a good question. Choosing the wrong aid, using it incorrectly, or having poorly prepared visuals can be a distraction instead of an enhancement for the presentation. Nothing is more irritating to an audience than:

- visual material that contains print or detail too small to be seen;
- sound that is distorted, too soft, or excruciatingly loud; and,
- equipment that is not working properly or not being operated correctly.

There are some general rules to keep in mind in the use of audiovisual aids. First remember the three *b*s. Visual material must be: big, bold, and brilliant. A good visual standard to remember is: (1) one idea per visual; (2) six words per line; and, (3) six lines per visual.

Some of the information in this chapter has previously been published in *Speaking with Confidence,* written by the author (Betterway Publications, 1990).

Visual material should be kept simple. One of the most common mistakes is trying to put too much information on each visual. Also, while visual material can provide reinforcement, variety, and interest, monotony can result if the same approach is used repeatedly. For example, arriving at the speaker's stand with a foot-high stack of overhead transparencies can elicit at least internal groans from an audience.

Second, check out your equipment and make sure it's working properly, well in advance of the meeting. Always have extra bulbs at hand in case one burns out. If a projectionist is needed, be sure to have someone who really knows how to operate the equipment—not just the first person who volunteers. When using an aid, such as slides or overhead transparencies, be sure they are numbered, in case they are dropped or have gotten out of order. Be sure to check to ensure that they are in the right order before the meeting begins. Also, run slides to make certain they're not upside down or backward.

Third, make certain that the screen is located where everyone can easily see it. This may require rearranging the room, especially if there are posts involved. Be sure the speaker will not block the screen when it is being used. Make certain projectors are properly loaded and focused before the meeting begins.

Fourth, check the volume level on audio equipment and set it properly in advance. A deafening roar at the beginning or an inaudible first minute of a presentation turns off the listener and negates much of the potential effect.

Fifth, if lights need to be turned off and then back on, assign someone to carry out that important task. Work out in advance all necessary cues with others who are assisting with or participating in the presentation.

Sixth, have someone proof all audiovisual material for errors and for clarity of meaning. Be sure that any material that is used is sharp-looking. A sloppy visual makes a poor impression and should be redone or scratched from the presentation.

Seventh, practice the presentation if there are several pieces to manipulate. A smooth presentation will look easy, but it's not—unless much thought, preparation, and rehearsal have gone into it. If several approaches and more than one person are involved, have a rehearsal beforehand to make sure everything is working properly and everyone understands what to do. Know how much time is required for each aid to be used and include the required number of minutes in the overall presentation time.

Eighth, be cautious about leaving the audience in a darkened room too long—especially after a large meal. Your background music may include several snores.

Ninth, place any aids that the presenter will use near the speaker's stand. This will prevent him or her from having to make long treks back and forth from equipment or a chalkboard.

Tenth, check any tendency to speak toward a visual aid. Always be sure to face the audience. Don't block the audience's view of the visual. To point out a certain area, stand beside a map or chart and use a pointer, holding it in the hand nearest the visual. In the case of an overhead transparency, use a pencil or pen on the stage (the glass surface) of the projector to point out a certain part of the visual rather than going to the screen. Otherwise, you may find yourself blinded by the projector's light and have the Jordan River running down your nose.

Finally, keep the visual up long enough for the viewer to grasp its message. This is especially important if participants are taking notes. Don't forget to interact with the audience while using audiovisual approaches. While this is not possible with some media, such as a movie, other aids lend themselves to audience involvement. Audiovisual material is aptly called an aid. It can be used effectively to help in the communication process, but it can't do the job for you.

Computer-Controlled Presentations

The advent of the computer has brought an amazingly effective resource into the world of audiovisual production.

Jeff Burger, a consultant and prolific author on multimedia, says, "There are several major compelling reasons for making the leap to computer-controlled presentations—malleability, cost-saving, and impact."[3] Some of the flexibility aspects that he points out are: the ability to resort slides with a few mouse clicks rather than having to empty a slide carousel and reposition slides by hand; being able to put together a presentation at the last minute; easily restructuring a presentation for various audiences; and being able to use a master template to change the background font or color scheme of a presentation to appeal to audiences according to gender, age, or ethnic background.[4]

Software packages, such as Microsoft Powerpoint, Astound, Freelance Graphics and SPC's Harvard Graphics, make it possible to execute a presentation directly from the computer. This saves having to go to considerable expense and deal with the time constraints of slide production. Another advantage is that existing elements, such as printed materials and other media, may be used easily.[5]

These are some of the pluses in the area of impact that Burger cites:

- Monitors and most late-model liquid crystal display (LCD) projectors don't require a totally darkened room.

- Many setups can utilize video sources and graphics with a single screen.
- Animation and digital video add interest with effects such as charts growing over a period of time and text and images flying into place.
- Direct support for audio files ensures synchronization with visual material.[6]

In the area of delivery strategies, these are some of the points Burger makes:

- Burger suggests using the same computer that material is developed on to deliver the presentation, since variations from computer to computer can cause unforeseen problems.
- Audience size must be taken into consideration. A standard-sized computer monitor is effective only with a small group of people. Monitors from twenty-five inches to forty inches may be used successfully with a moderate-sized audience. For larger audiences, Burger advises using a projection system or renting one with specific capabilities. Transparent LCD panels that fit on overhead projectors with at least four thousand lumens for proper brightness, contrast, and color fidelity can also be used effectively.[7] A standard overhead projector will not work. It is necessary to rent or buy a super-bright one. LCD projectors are also available. They are less cumbersome to use than the LCD panel with an overhead projector and are growing in popularity.
- Consider transferring the results of computer-generated material onto video tape. Burger says the following:

> Dumping productions created completely within the computer onto tape has the advantage of increased stability. In the case of a power anomaly, for example, a video deck might simply glitch or someone might have to hit the Play button again in the worst case. Computers are typically less tolerant and tend to crash under similar circumstances— forcing a reboot, entailing program reload and [typically] playback from the beginning of the production. Moreover, it's easier for the average person to spec video gear for rental and play tapes than deal with computers.[8]

Characteristics of Various Audiovisual Approaches

Selecting the most appropriate AV aid to do a particular job is critically important. The following information should assist you in deciding on the most appropriate approach for a particular occasion. (For more help on doing this, see the form entitled "Audiovisual Checklist," which you can find on page 128.)

Visual Aid: Overhead Projector

Advantages:

- Transparencies can be used in a lighted room.
- Transparencies can be used with a rather large group of people.
- The speaker can operate the projector and thus maintain complete control over the presentation.
- The speaker can face the audience and does not have to leave the presentation area.
- The speaker can point out features on the transparency with a pen on the stage of the projector itself.
- Transparencies can be used periodically during the presentation by merely flipping on a switch.
- Prepared transparencies can be used with the information being revealed a line at a time when this is desirable.
- The presenter can write on the transparency during the presentation. Feedback from the audience can easily be recorded and projected for the whole group to see and consider.
- Transparencies are relatively inexpensive.
- Professional-looking transparencies can be produced using a computer with large type capabilities and a copying machine—equipment that is usually readily accessible.
- Overhead projectors can be equipped with a two-way acetate roll attachment, which allows the speaker to use a continuous roll of acetate when this would be easier.

Disadvantages:

- Arched effect of image will result unless the projector and screen are carefully positioned.

Tips:

- The screen should be positioned at an angle behind and to the left or right of the speaker. Otherwise, the view of the listener will be blocked.
- Color-highlight film can be used to good effect on portions of the transparency.
- Overlays can be effectively used in showing the parts of a whole.
- Opaque background film gives a dramatic effect, for it looks like the writing or drawing suddenly appears.

- Turn off the projector when it is not in use and while changing transparencies. Projection of only light on the screen distracts from what is being done, for the listener's eye is drawn to the light.
- Beware of using the same repetitious pattern for too long a period. It's a good idea to vary the presentation. For example, two or three transparencies with several items may be used and then followed by a transparency making a single point. Using transparencies throughout an entire presentation can become monotonous.
- Be sure to have a nearby area for storing transparencies before and after use.
- Mounting transparencies in cardboard frames (available at business supply stores) makes them easier to handle. Also limited notes may be written on the frame.
- Humor may be injected by projecting a clever cartoon that helps make a point.

Uses for the Church:
- Sunday school class lessons
- Special seminars
- Business meetings where statistical material may be projected
- Projection of a floor plan proposed for a new building or addition
- Emphasis for a special project or upcoming event by projecting information on a screen before a service
- Before a service as a replacement for announcements
- Projection of lyrics of songs to be sung. Permission to use copyrighted material must be obtained to meet legal requirements (see chapter 16 for more information on copyright laws).
- Projection of prearranged numbers to alert parents they are needed in the church nursery

Audiovisual Aid: Motion Picture Film

Advantages:
- The film can show movement.
- The film can vicariously take the audience to another location and another time in history.
- The film provides a common experience for the audience.
- The film or excerpts from it can serve as a launching pad for a presentation or discussion.
- Many different types of film are available for rental at varying costs.

- Films may be shown to a large group of people, although additional speakers may be necessary in a large auditorium.

Disadvantages:

- The room must be darkened.
- A well-trained projectionist is necessary.
- The speaker loses rapport with the audience, since, as a rule, the film is self-contained and the speaker cannot interact with the participants.

Tips:

- The projector should never be left to run alone.
- The film should be carefully introduced to prepare the viewer for what is important, to note aspects of particular interest to that group, and to emphasize special themes, symbols, or insights.
- Highlights of the film should be summarized afterward.
- The film may be used as an excellent vehicle to launch a group discussion.
- A rear projection screen may be rented in larger cities and should be used with a large audience. However, the rental fee is expensive.
- If only a portion of the film is to be used, make certain it is accuarately cued.

Uses for the Church:

- A number of excellent religious films may be rented and used for various purposes. Copyright laws require that permission be obtained for use of a commercial film in a service or meeting (see chapter 16 for more information).
- A segment from a commercial film might be used to introduce a sermon or a topic that is relevant to contemporary life and around which a whole presentation might be built.

Visual Aid: Slide Projector

Advantages:

- Slides can be used with a large audience.
- With a carousel projector and a remote control, the speaker can operate the equipment.
- The speaker can dwell as long as desired on one particular slide and can go back to that particular slide if there are questions about it.
- Slide presentations can be easily changed and varied to meet the interest and appropriateness of a certain audience or occasion.

Disadvantage:
- The room must be dark or nearly dark.

Tips:
- Cardboard frames on slides are safer than plastic ones, which will sometimes warp when they get hot in the projector.
- The speaker should stand to the right of the screen (audience's left). Since people read from right to left, this is a stronger position for maintaining audience attention.
- A light on the lectern will be needed, especially if the speaker must use notes during the slide presentation.
- A cordless remote slide changer might be purchased, which gives the speaker a great deal more freedom of movement.
- Pace the slide show to maintain audience interest. Keeping one slide on the screen too long invites drifting thoughts. As a rule, six to eight slides per minute will maintain attention.
- Limit the length of the slide show to about ten minutes—fifteen at the most.
- Don't give in to the temptation to use a nearly good slide. Select only those that are top quality and have something to say.
- Check to be sure that the slides are loaded properly. An upside-down shot or one with the letters running backward puts a damper on the whole presentation.

Audio Aid: Audio Tape Recorder

Advantages:
- Audio tapes are inexpensive and easy to use.
- A speaker can back up a point of view with the "expert on the subject's" own voice.
- Music or recorded sounds may be used to illustrate or dramatize a point.
- Music can be used effectively to stimulate, soothe, or set the mood for a particular presentation, or to change the emotional climate during a presentation.
- Prerecorded dialogue may be used to spark discussion or as an example.
- The tape recorder may be used effectively in training when the spoken word is important.

Disadvantages:
- Care must be taken that the tape is played on a recorder with large enough speakers so that all audience members can hear the

recording. When used over a public-address system, precautions should be taken to ensure that the sound will not be distorted.

- The audience may lose interest with nothing to watch, especially if the tape is long.

Tip:

- Don't overlook the audio recorder as a possibility to add color and life to various events and presentations.

Uses for the Church:

- A recording may be used to help children (and adults) learn a new song.
- A brief message from a missionary whom the church supports might be played to encourage further financial giving.
- The pastor or other staff member who is on sabbatical or special assignment could record a brief report and a word of encouragement to be played during a service.
- A sermon may be recorded during the service and, with multiple high-speed tape duplicators, made available for purchase immediately after the service.

Visual Aid: Chalkboard

Advantages:

- Key points and words can be easily and spontaneously emphasized.
- Responses from the audience can be listed and referred to.
- Material can be erased and the board reused immediately.

Disadvantages:

- Chalkboards cannot be used effectively with a large group.
- The audience's attention may be easily lost as the speaker writes with his or her back to the audience.
- Chalkboards are difficult to position so that the entire group can readily see them.
- When the chalkboard is used repeatedly, the chalk residue makes writing progressively more difficult to read.

Tips:

- Be sure that the writing is large enough to be easily read from the back row. With a viewing distance from the chalkboard of thirty-two feet, lettering should be at least two and one-half inches high.

- Limit your writing to key words or phrases.
- While you write, do not remain with your back to the audience more than a few seconds at a time.
- If information is written in advance of the presentation, be sure the chalkboard is turned around or covered. Otherwise, the audience will read instead of listening to the speaker.
- Black chalkboards are easier to read than green ones.
- If a chalkboard is used over and over, ensure that it is washed with a damp cloth during breaks to guarantee increased legibility.
- Once you have written on the chalkboard, move away from it. This is important so that you don't block the listener's view.
- Use a pointer rather than your hand, especially if you wish to emphasize certain written information. This enables you to stand farther away from the board so that the audience will be able to see.
- Erase the chalkboard when you are finished using it. Otherwise, the written information may be distracting.

Visual Aid: Flip Chart

Advantages:
- Flip charts are relatively inexpensive.
- Material can be prepared in advance, using color in drawings, graphs, and charts.
- Key points and words can be easily and spontaneously emphasized.
- Responses from the audience can be listed and referred to.

Disadvantages:
- Flip charts cannot be used effectively with a large group.
- It is easy to lose your audience's attention, especially if you write with your back to the audience for too long a period of time.

Tips:
- Use a blank sheet as you begin your presentation.
- Place blank sheets between pre-prepared sheets so that you may cover the message when you are speaking on a different subject.
- Be sure the writing is large enough (and thick enough) to be easily read from the back row.
- Limit what's written to key words or phrases.
- While writing, do not remain with your back to the audience for more than a few seconds at a time.
- Practice the presentation, including turning the sheets, until it becomes easy and second nature.

- Once you have written on the sheet or turned to the next page, move away from the chart.
- Use a pointer rather than your hand if you wish to emphasize certain written information or a part of a chart or graph.
- Be sure not to block the view of the audience.
- If you prepare charts in advance, be sure to have someone else proof them for errors.
- Know the material on your charts so that you don't have to read from them and end up with a swivel head as a result of looking back and forth at the information and at your audience.

Visual Aid: Flannel, Hook-and-Loop, and Magnet Boards

Advantages:
- Drawings or work of the group may be easily displayed.
- Materials such as cloth, yarn, bits of balsa wood, blotting paper, and sponge will adhere to a flannel board. Hook-and-loop boards allow objects to be firmly attached, yet instantly removed or manipulated. Odd-shaped and heavy objects up to several pounds may also be attached. Small metal objects will adhere to a magnet board, and magnets may be used to hold thin objects of paper or cloth.
- An idea presentation may be built, piece by piece, in an orderly sequence.
- Members of the audience may be involved by asking them to regroup or reposition the objects for a specific reason.
- These boards may be used effectively in teaching a group a particular game, skill, or sport.

Disadvantage:
- Magnet, hook-and-loop, and flannel boards cannot be used effectively with a large group.

Tips:
- Presentations with magnet, hook-and-loop, and flannel boards should be kept simple.
- A flannel board should be tilted slightly back at the top to help materials stick firmly to the flannel surface.
- Be sure to step aside after applying the picture or object to the board's surface so as not to block the audience's line of vision.
- Have a conveniently close working surface available to store visual material before and after use.
- Check the order of visual material and be sure it is separated for easy handling.

Visual Aid: Models and Objects

Advantages:
- Models and objects are good attention-getters and can add realism to a presentation.
- Visual aids that actually do something during the speech are especially interesting.
- The three-dimensional aspect gives models and objects a distinct advantage over pictures.
- Models and objects can usually be handled by the audience, giving a kinesthetic dimension to the presentation.

Disadvantage:
- Models and objects cannot be used effectively with a large group unless they are quite large.

Tips:
- The object or model should be concealed until the time for its discussion in your presentation. Otherwise, it will be distracting and will lose some of its possible impact.
- If it is impossible to let everyone in the group manipulate the object or model during the presentation, provide an opportunity for the other people to do so after you are finished.
- Be sure the object or model is positioned high enough so that those seated on the back row will be able to see it.
- Even something too small to be seen can be used effectively if you want to show just how small it really is.
- Let your imagination run riot in coming up with ideas for the use of real-life objects. For example, a collapsed umbrella could be used to represent the promises of this world, while the Bible could be used to represent God's promises.

Visual Aid: Handouts

Advantages:
- Handouts can be used advantageously to involve listeners in the presentation by giving them a certain graph or chart to look at or a quiz to take.
- Handouts can reinforce the presentation later and can be valuable for future reference.
- Sources and references may be given for those who wish to pursue the subject further.

Disadvantage:

- Handouts can become so absorbing to the audience that it is difficult for the speaker to get members to look at her or him.

Tips:

- Be sure to make arrangements with enough helpers to get the material handed out quickly, quietly, and efficiently.
- Be certain to have more than enough copies available for those present. Audience members become irritated if they don't get a handout—even if they don't particularly want one.
- If the handout is the same as your presentation, do not give it out until after the presentation. Above all, don't stand up and read the handout aloud to your audience.
- If you wish to use the handout to involve the audience during your presentation, leave some blanks so that they can write down key points you want to emphasize.
- If you prepare the material yourself, be sure to have someone else proof the final copy.
- Make sure the reproduction is top quality. A barely legible or ink-smeared copy makes a negative statement about you as a speaker.
- Handout materials should have the name of the item and the speaker's or author's name on each page.
- Place "©" (or "copyright"), the date, and your name on the handout to protect your original work.

Audio Aid: Microphone

Advantages:

- The voice can be amplified to ensure audibility.
- A lavaliere microphone gives the speaker greater flexibility, with a cordless mike providing the maximum ease of movement.
- In a relatively large area, the speaker can speak softly for effect without worrying about not being heard.

Disadvantages:

- Unless excellent equipment is available, the voice can be distorted.
- Use of a stationary mike curtails the movement of the speaker.
- A handheld mike limits the effectiveness of one's gestures.
- Microphones magnify speech defects, such as a hissing sound or smacking of lips.
- Feedback can be disconcerting to an audience. Correct positioning and operation are essential.

Tips:

- The speaker should try out the mike before the meeting begins and get the level set. Realize that a full auditorium will change the sound, and the level will probably need to be adjusted.
- The speaker should know beforehand how to turn the mike on and adjust the height of the stand.
- The speaker must be adept at using a mike effectively. For instance, she or he should back away when speaking louder and move closer when speaking more softly.
- The speaker should remember that she or he cannot really tell how the voice sounds to the audience and must rely on the sound technician to make necessary adjustments.
- The speaker should note that feedback can result if the mike is placed too close to other sound equipment (such as speakers and microphones).

Audio-Visual Aid: Television

Advantages:

- TV can be used in a lighted room.
- Many videocassette tapes on a variety of subjects are now available. However, permission will usually have to be obtained from the copyright owner to use tapes in a meeting or service. (See chapter 16 for further information.)
- The equipment can be easily stopped and started to call attention to a certain point or for discussion.
- Television is particularly helpful in training situations, since feedback can be immediate.
- Material may be edited with appropriate equipment.
- The price of good television equipment is moderate.
- Television shows motion, and is good for demonstrations and for showing close-ups of objects the audience could not otherwise see.

Disadvantage:

- Television cannot be effectively used with a large group of people, unless a large screen is rented. This option can cost several hundred dollars and is only available in larger cities.

Tip:

- If you have a rather large audience, use more than one monitor, and locate them for optimum viewing.

Versatile Video Provides Many Services

Television cameras have been commonplace for a long time in large churches that broadcast their services. Now, however, with video equipment being relatively inexpensive and readily available, even small churches can take advantage of the many services that video can provide. Fortunately, there always seems to be someone in most congregations who has a talent for and a special interest in capturing everything in sight with the camera's eye.

Of course, your projected use determines the quality of the equipment needed. If the plan is to broadcast a church service on television, of course, broadcast quality cameras and editing equipment must be used, and technicians must be able to produce a professionally acceptable product. For internal communications, however, less expensive equipment may be used successfully.

Television's uses are numerous and varied—limited only by vision and imagination. Perhaps you will find some of these approaches helpful for use in your congregation—or maybe they will spark new ideas of your own.

For Those Who Can't Attend

A video of the Sunday morning worship service can be a tremendous way to help those unable to attend to feel that they are a part of their church. Many churches record the sermon on audiotape. While that's good, think how much more involved you would feel if you were a shut-in and actually could see and hear the entire service. The cost would be minimal, for volunteers could pick up the previous week's videotape for reuse when they deliver the video of the most recent service.

This approach would also provide a vital link for missionaries who are overseas to keep them up to date on the progress and activities of their home church. One woman, as part of her mission outreach, faithfully sent several missionaries audiotapes of their church's services. She received many letters of appreciation, saying that they felt less isolated and that the tapes gave them an uplifting means of keeping in touch with their home church. But think how much more effective videocassettes would be. Recipients would be able to see the redecorated sanctuary and feel that they were personally acquainted with the new pastor they've never met.

What about men and women in the armed forces? A videocassette of their home church's service could go a long way toward dispelling loneliness and serve as a reminder of the importance of their faith.

If you were in any of those categories, think how exciting it would be to see and hear the congregation praying for your recovery from illness, your work on the mission field, or your protection in the service. A pastor could even lend a personal touch from time to time by speaking directly to one of the video congregants even as he might address someone in the immediate audience.

For Improvement

There's no doubt that the manner of those on the platform during the service sets the tone for the entire congregation. While all of us mean well and want to do the right thing, often unconscious habits can detract from a worshipful atmosphere or even call attention away from the pastor's message. Using video to give choir members, musicians, and ministers the opportunity to see themselves as others see them can be a revealing experience.

A playback of one such session in a church evoked reactions such as, "I can't believe I did that," and several red faces. Those captured for posterity were surprised to see their sourpuss expressions, the bored looks on their faces, and the distracting mannerisms, such as swinging a foot or whispering to a neighbor. One choir member was appalled to discover that she had pulled on a strand of her long hair throughout most of the sermon. The next time videotaping was done for this purpose, the overall effect had improved dramatically.

Informational Messages

New members and visitors considering membership could be shown a video featuring short segments of various programs offered by the church. This would give them an opportunity to discover which activities various members of their family would find of particular interest. Also a tape could be made of information that is shared frequently, such as an introduction to a premarital counseling session.

Ongoing Informational Program

Skillman Church of Christ in Dallas, Texas, has several hundred members and produces a weekly television program that is shown in each classroom at the beginning of Sunday school. The program is five minutes in length and contains several segments that are introduced by the host and hostess in an informal entertaining style. One program began with information about upcoming events, followed by an interview with a new church member. A layperson chatted with the hostess, giving viewers in the congregation an opportunity to learn the layperson's name and some interesting things about her.

A segment on the church's weekly program of feeding the homeless in downtown Dallas not only informed the congregation about the outreach but also gave credit to those who work weekly in this vital ministry. Another feature was a brief message by a church member who is a psychologist. He suggested ways to be supportive without being intrusive when other church members you don't know well are experiencing a crisis. The program concluded with one of the ministers talking about a new program in the church.

Highlights of the Year Program

Video is a natural for capturing the important events over the span of a year. A tape of those highlights can make an interesting and nostalgic feature for an anniversary banquet or a pastor appreciation event. Including shots of as many members as possible will make it a guaranteed hit. Everyone likes to see what he or she looks like on television.

Documentary on a New Building

A video of the various stages of the construction of a new church building can document an exciting event in the life of a congregation. At the dedication of its new building, one church showed such a program. It began with the uncleared property and captured the various steps in the building process. Appropriate background music enhanced the video. Those who attended felt the video was inspiring when it was played during the dedication service.

Story of Church Outreach and Missionary Efforts

Recording the activities of a church outreach, such as a downtown mission, can be effective in helping to get other members interested in working with and supporting the program. A production on a missionary trip can be tremendously beneficial for informing members and gathering prayer and financial support. Being able to actually see the people who are being helped has a far greater impact than merely hearing about the need.

This is also a great way to report back to those who contribute financially to such a mission. Seeing the ministry in action helps contributors feel a personal involvement above and beyond signing their names on a check.

Special Series

Videotapes of special series, such as a marriage seminar or an outstanding guest speaker (with that person's permission), could be checked out by members on a loan basis. Portions of it could be used later to enhance other presentations dealing with the same or a related subject.

Special Services

During Operation Desert Storm, Hillcrest Church in Dallas, Texas, adopted an army platoon. For July 4, the church held a special service in honor of the men and women in that platoon. The service people and their families were invited to be special guests. Members of the church acted as their weekend hosts. There was patriotic music and recognition for each of those honored. A videocassette captured the spirit and tribute paid to these soldiers. It was also made available to anyone who wanted one.

This, of course, could also be done for a Christmas production, an Easter cantata, a church anniversary, or a children's play.

Model of a Program

Television can be an excellent instrument to use in training people for positions of leadership. For example, a particularly effective home fellowship group could be taped. Other leaders and those interested in leading such a group could learn from the videotape without even being there. Also, outstanding Sunday school teachers could be taped so that their methods and approaches would be available for study and use by other teachers.

A church in Grapevine, Texas, held an especially exciting vacation Bible school. Fortunately, they videotaped the whole series of events—the airplane they built in a classroom to "fly" the children to various cities in Jesus' day; the costumed workers who told the children about their life in Bethlehem, Nazareth, Jerusalem, and Bethany; the temple the children went inside of; the live camel they rented for the children to pet; and so on. Another church interested in having a similar Bible school was glad to have that video to watch instead of just having someone tell them how it was done.

Recruitment of Workers

Do you need more workers for the toddlers' class? Maybe you'd like to extend the hours for your church food bank but just don't have enough hands. An "Opportunities for Service" video, shown at the beginning of the worship service could be just the answer. Some footage of those adorable little tykes clapping their hands and reaching toward the camera or an interview with one of the food-bank "customers" about what the program has meant to her could stir up some interest.

The sky's the limit when it comes to what you can do with that camera and other audiovisual approaches. Using a variety of media creatively and correctly can provide real bonus benefits for services, classes, seminars, business meetings, events, and outreaches. They can be tremendous instruments for improvement, involvement, edification, and coming together for the body of Christ.

Audiovisual Checklist

_____ Have you checked out the meeting room or auditorium for needed adaptive measures and their availability, such as the use of extension cords, the means of darkening the room, and the availability of special stands and adequate screens that will be needed to use certain AV approaches?

_____ Have you allowed plenty of time for making rental arrangements (if necessary) and for setting up and checking out AV equipment?

_____ Have you checked several days in advance of the engagement to be certain that all the equipment is in good working order?

_____ Do you have the equipment in place and in the most advantageous position?

_____ Have you placed electrician's tape over extension cords where people may be walking?

_____ Have you focused any projectors that you might be using?

_____ Have you cued up any tapes or films so that there will be no awkward pause when they are turned on?

_____ Have you made arrangements with someone to turn lights off and on (if necessary), and on cue?

_____ Have you concealed any AV material that you will be using in a manner that will be easy to unmask at the proper time?

_____ Have you tested the level of any sound equipment that you plan to use, including a microphone?

_____ Have you checked out the visibility of your material from all parts of the meeting area?

_____ Have you made arrangements with a competent projectionist to turn on and off the equipment on cue and make certain it is working properly, especially if you cannot operate it yourself?

_____ Do you have spare bulbs on hand in case the one in the projector burns out?

_____ Do you have slides, transparencies, or other material numbered, and have you checked to make sure they are in the proper order?

_____ Do you have an appropriate area to hold transparencies or objects that you will be using during the presentation?

_____ If two or more people are going to be involved in a presentation, have you had a run-through so that everyone understands and can perform her or his function efficiently?

_____ Have you practiced using your AV aids to make certain you can handle them smoothly and professionally?

10 Taking the Pulse of Your Congregation

How long has it been since you had a congregational checkup? While things may seem to be going pretty well, there may be small problems developing that haven't bubbled up to the surface. Some programs may be going smoothly but have lost some of their zip, and may need a good dose of vitamin V for vitality. Certainly, in every organization, there is always room for improvement.

Seeking the counsel of those who are involved with and those who are served by various ministries will give you a good picture of the current wellness of your program and point the way toward planning for future good health and longevity. Of course, there are apparent signs that may be easily read: attendance and enthusiasm evidenced by those who are involved, and some measurable results, such as donations to a food bank that is sponsored by the church.

A great deal of other information may be obtained by asking good questions of members and other regular participants. Everyone has an opinion. And most people like to be asked what they think—if they feel that their views will be taken seriously.

George Barna, in his study of several successful, growing churches, found that the pastors, in addition to getting feedback on the effectiveness of the church programs from staff members, insisted on getting input from the people whom the programs served. Barna says that most of these churches used surveys as a regular part of the evaluation process. In some instances, congregation-wide surveys were used. Others utilized small discussion groups to gain perspectives and to brainstorm ideas for improvement and solving problems[1] (see chapter 8 for more information on conducting a brainstorming session).

Decisions to Make Before Getting Opinions

1. You really want to know how members feel and what they are thinking.
2. You are going to be prepared to receive at least some "bad" news.

After all, a main purpose should be to identify problem areas and opportunities for improvement.

3. You have no qualms about making public the results of the study.
4. You are ready to respond to and follow through on what members say.
5. You realize that the interpretation of the results is as important as the collected data. You will analyze the message from every angle and use the results in future planning. You will not let the report become just something to gather dust on a shelf.

Create Focus Groups

An excellent source of feedback from participants in various aspects of the ministry program is the focus group, which homes in on a particular topic or topics in a concentrated manner. While the discussion itself is informal and unpredictable, the moderator or leader has predetermined and developed specific guidelines for how the discussion should be conducted.

A real key to the success of the focus group is the creation of a comfortable, relaxed, and nonjudgmental atmosphere in which participants feel free and are encouraged to give their opinions and present their suggestions. A successful focus group will include everyone in a frank discussion, instead of posing the same question to each person in the group individually. A great deal of its value rests with the group dynamics that develop among members as the discussion progresses.

The Focus Group Facilitator

The facilitator must be skilled in bringing people together and in creating a climate where they feel at ease and know that their opinions will be valued and respected. Usually the facilitator should not be a member of the staff, especially not the one in charge of the program you wish to evaluate. A layperson with outstanding communication skills who does not participate in that particular program would be a likely candidate. Or you may wish to bring someone in from outside the church. One possibility might be the pastor or a staff member from another church with whom you might trade the responsibility of facilitating such a group in his or her fellowship. Or, if your budget allows, market research companies provide such services.

The responsibilities of the focus-group facilitator include:

- working with the pastor or staff member to develop the selection criteria and screening process and in determining what you wish to find out

- overseeing the selection process
- seeing that participants are sent a note about the meeting and receive a follow-up phone reminder the day before the session (more information about planning and conducting meetings can be found in chapter 8)
- helping to choose an appropriate setting and deciding on the arrangement of the room
- seeing that appropriate refreshments are provided
- developing a discussion guide for use during the session
- welcoming and seating the participants for maximum effectiveness. For example, if two members of the group are best friends, it might be wise to separate them during the session.
- creating a warm, friendly climate where discussion can flow freely. Participants should be informed about any plans to tape the meeting, a good thing to do unless recording the session would seem to hamper the spontaneity of that particular group.
- stating the purpose of the focus group's meeting and the parameters for discussion, such as: one person speaks at a time; each person's viewpoint is valid and desired; everyone has equal opportunity to be heard; disagreement is permitted, for the purpose is not to reach a consensus.
- orchestrating the session by keeping the discussion on target but still allowing for divergent paths when they are of value
- making sure that everyone has the opportunity to participate by drawing out those who may be reticent and by using tactful approaches to keep one or two from dominating the discussion
- following people's thought processes during the session and probing for further information when it will be productive to the discussion
- analyzing the discussion and translating insights into a report for use in the evaluation and decision-making process

The Participants

If the focus group is being used to help evaluate a program within the church, the selection process is relatively simple. The program director knows the participants, information about them that might be pertinent, and whether they fit the profile that is needed. The leader also knows which people would provide a good cross-section of viewpoints within the group. In that case, it is usually just a matter of finding out whether those who have been identified are interested in being a part of the group and determining a convenient time. If, however, you are trying to find out the community's perception of your church among a certain age group, the search can be long, tedious, and expensive, especially if you hire someone to do it for you. Also, you probably will have to pay the participants for their time.

One Church's Approach

Wooddale Church, located in the Minneapolis suburb of Eden Prairie, Minnesota, used an interesting approach to determine the perception of others by recruiting outsiders to visit the church. Task force members each asked a neighbor, co-worker, or friend to visit one service during a six-week period. Most of the participants did not attend church or were from a vastly different tradition. They were asked in advance if they would be willing to participate in a post-visit interview to learn their impressions. No one in the church knew who the visitors might be nor when they would show up.

After their visits, a facilitator conducted a focus group meeting in a rented room at a marketing research company. Members of the task force listened and watched through a one-way mirror. They talked about what they had experienced, what had impressed them, and their likes and dislikes about their visit. Some of their comments were serious, some silly. Parts of what they had to say were affirming, and others pointed out what they perceived as problem areas. One unabashedly irreligious man commented, "That's my kind of church, and I'm going back." Pastor Leith Anderson said the point was to see the story from an outsider's perspective. "It is one more piece to putting together the puzzle that gives a picture of the story."

Anderson also suggests a simple way to do a quick survey of the congregation. "Pass out 3x5 cards and request each person to write four or five words that best describe the church. Collate the answers to see the frequency of words listed." He says if frequent responses are words like "loving," "caring," "supportive," and "family," it would probably indicate that the church has a compassionate and strong internal connection. Terms such as "outreaching," "evangelistic," and "open" would indicate an awareness of the importance of reaching out to others outside the church. He says the answers may reflect "reality, perception, or the topic of last Sunday's sermon." The results won't tell you everything, but it will give you part of the picture.[2]

Size and Location of Group

Having the right people and the right number are critical to the success of the group's work. The ideal number is from eight to ten. More than ten limits participation, and fewer than eight loses some of the group dynamics of interaction.

The location is also important. While the meeting can be held at the church, a neutral location is probably better. The room should be large enough to avoid feeling cramped, but not so large that the group is dwarfed by the size of the space. It is extremely important that there are no distracting noises or interruptions. Members should be seated in a circle or oval, preferably around a table.

Hold One-on-One Interviews with Members

A great deal of information can be gleaned by taking the time and making the effort to meet with an individual who is convinced that you want an honest opinion. This can be especially helpful in a situation where you just can't quite put your finger on what's wrong in a certain area or how things could be improved.

If one can be arranged, an exit interview with a member leaving the church for whatever reason can be especially helpful and revealing. There's always the possibility that your concern in the case of a misunderstanding might turn things around and that person might stay after all.

Conduct a Formal Survey of Church Members

Surveying your church members can be revealing of:

- overlooked areas of need
- approaches that can work better with slight modification
- worthwhile ideas for improvement from participants
- considerations of value in long-range planning

Then, too, it's always nice to learn that certain aspects of your church program are going great.

A well-conducted opinion survey can mean the difference between guessing and knowing how the members feel about the programs and approaches of your church.

Preparing the Questionnaire

Asking the right questions is critical to the success of any survey. Making certain that questions are objective and do not call for biased answers is extremely important. One person should be charged with the responsibility of phrasing and finalizing the instrument. A small committee, composed of staff members, board members, and, perhaps, a couple of interested laypersons, should act in an advisory capacity. Brainstorming can be used effectively in this project.

Committee members must decide, first of all, what specifically they want to find out. Probably the best approach is to identify broad areas, such as:

1. atmosphere of the church
2. opportunities for fellowship

3. opportunities for participation in ministry and service
4. extent to which needs are being met
5. effectiveness of communication approaches
6. evaluation of specific programs
7. allocation of funds

Once broad areas are identified, then specific types of questions can be formulated. Questions in these kinds of categories should be multiple choice for ease in tabulation. Choices should usually number from three to five. These are some examples of workable multiple-choice questions.

I feel that the atmosphere at our church is:
   a. Very warm and friendly
   b. Warm
   c. Lukewarm
   d. Cool
If I had a serious problem, I believe help would be:
   a. Immediately available
   b. Available
   c. Difficult to get
   d. Unavailable
I think that the number of guest speakers and other types of guest ministry are:
   a. Too many
   b. About right
   c. Too few
I believe that the nursery facilities and care offered for infants and toddlers is:
   a. Excellent
   b. Very good
   c. Good
   d. Fair
   e. Poor

To foster creative thinking, other questions should be open-ended. While the analysis of this type of query is more difficult, it will provide valuable ideas for future planning and food for thought. Here are some ideas for open-ended responses.

1. What would you like to see offered or done at our church that is not presently a part of the program?
2. Do you think anything should be eliminated from the present program? If so, what?

3. The thing(s) I like most about our church is (are):
4. The thing(s) I like least about our church is (are):
5. From my observation, I would say that the main reason(s) people have left our church in the past has (have) been:
6. I think new members would be attracted to our church if:
7. What do you think the major goals for our church should be this year?
8. What do you think the major goals for our church should be for the next five years?
9. What other suggestions do you have for the improvement of our church program?

Armed with input from the committee, the survey developer will then study the suggestions and come up with the first draft of the survey. Six special suggestions are in order:

1. To ensure candid responses, do not ask for the respondee's name.
2. Begin the survey with an interesting question.
3. Keep the survey as brief as possible while covering the information you want to elicit. Page after page of questions will be overwhelming to some members, and they will not want to complete your questionnaire.
4. Use concise, simple language.
5. Limit each question to one topic.
6. Place questions about personal characteristics at the end of the survey. They will be less threatening and more frequently answered.

This is the type of demographic information you will want to know about each person who completes the survey:

I am a:
   a. Male
   b. Female
My age is:
   a. Under 20
   b. 20–30
   c. 30–40
   d. 40–50
   e. Over 50
I have been a member of this church:
   a. Less than a year
   b. 1 to 2 years

    c. 3 to 4 years
    d. 5 or more years
I am:
    a. Married
    b. Single
    c. Divorced
    d. Widowed
I have children in the following age brackets:
    a. 0–2 years
    b. 3–5 years
    c. 6–8 years
    d. 9–12 years
    e. 13–15 years
    f. 16–18 years
I attend church on the average of:
    a. Nearly every service
    b. Morning service only
    c. Once a month
    d. Several times a year

Once the first draft is completed, the committee should meet once more to go over the instrument, question by question. These are good questions for committee members to consider in evaluating the instrument.

- Is the meaning of each question absolutely clear?
- Is the vocabulary simple enough to be readily understood?
- Will the responses to a particular question result in information that will be valuable? If not, delete that one.
- Is all desired information covered by the questions?

Based on committee recommendations, the developer would then finalize the survey and administer it to a few volunteers to make absolutely certain that it is easily understood and elicits the desired information.

Administering the Survey

You'll probably get close to 100 percent response of those present if the survey is completed at the church. Here are some suggestions.

1. Select a service or meeting with the largest attendance. Tell the members in advance when the survey will be conducted and what to expect. An article in the church newsletter a couple of weeks in advance would be helpful.
2. Be sure to have an ample supply of pencils handy.

3. Explain the purpose of the survey, how it was developed, and its potential value in making improvements and in future planning. Assure the respondents that the analysis will be shared with members.
4. State that only members and nonmembers who usually attend the church should complete the survey.
5. Emphasize that respondents should not write their names on the instrument and that a frank opinion is desired.
6. Ask respondents to circle the letter of the response of their choice.
7. Go over a few questions with respondents. Include open-ended questions as well as multiple choice. An excellent approach would be to use an overhead projector with parts of the survey projected on a screen.
8. Request that respondents answer all questions, if possible.
9. Explain how the results will be analyzed—overall, by age groups, marital status, responses of parents with children of certain ages, and so forth—and give examples of how the program might be improved as a result. For instance, if divorcees indicate there are not enough opportunities for fellowship, new approaches might be developed for that particular group to meet that need.
10. Stress that staff members and those in leadership really want to know respondents' opinions and insights in order that improvements can be made.
11. In order to give members not in attendance an opportunity to respond to the survey, participants should be asked to sign a separate list. The instrument can then be mailed to members not listed, with a cover letter explaining the purpose and asking them to return the completed survey by mail for anonymity.
12. Set a realistic time limit for completion, warn the respondents when the time is nearly up, and collect all questionnaires before moving on to the next activity.

Compiling the Results

Tabulating the results of the survey, even one administered to a relatively small number of respondents, can be a time-consuming task. Totals should be run on all questionnaires and then according to various special groups, such as age, sex, length of membership, and so forth. Tallies of open-ended questions require judgment calls about which responses can be grouped together. This probably should be done by one person.

Once the results have been tabulated, a report should be prepared. The heading should give the name of the church and "Summation of Questionnaire Results." This could be followed by the date that the survey was conducted, the number of people who participated, and the purpose. After that, a description (based on the information at the end of the instrument) of the respondees should be given (for example, the number of males and females and the number in various age groups).

Responses to multiple-choice questions can be reported by copying the question and responses with the number of people who circled each letter placed beside it. Answers to open-ended questions may be stated in sentence form. For example: The things most frequently mentioned that people like best about the church are: the friendly atmosphere, 52; sermons, 103; training opportunities, 47; and so forth.

After the results of the entire group are reported, then the results from smaller groups may be compared with the overall response. For example, these could include: responses from singles compared with overall responses and comparison of responses by men with those of women. These are probably more easily understood when expressed in percentages.

The report should end with some statements summarizing the general tone of response to the survey. For example: An overwhelming number of respondents expressed an optimistic opinion about the future of the church. The report should be made available to all participants as well as to other members. Results and their implications should be discussed.

Analyzing the Results

Now comes the critical part of the church survey—analyzing what it really means and deciding what to do as a result. The same committee with perhaps some additions, such as leaders in various areas of ministry, should come together and carefully go over the responses from every angle. Deductions can be categorized. These might include areas such as: weaknesses in the program, unmet needs, considerations for future planning, and facility improvements.

Appropriate subcommittees might then be named to meet with staff members who have been charged with the responsibility in each area to discuss short-term and long-range improvements and solutions. Here again, brainstorming can be used effectively in coming up with specific, workable plans (see chapter 8 for more information about this).

A summary of some of the highlights of the survey could make an interesting article for the church newsletter. It could include quotes from the pastor about what changes might be made as a result and its value in future planning.

Arranging focus groups, holding individual interviews, and conducting a church survey require a commitment of time, effort, and resources on the part of a number of people. However, the reward in a better and smoother-running church program can far outweigh the investment. That is, if you really want to know and are willing to act on the results.

11 On the Move to a New Location

A curious sight to the eyes of American tourists in the Holy Land is the Bedouin tent-dwellers. The dirty, worn tents with holes near the top for ventilation stand determinedly in the stark, arid desert. Usually a woman tending a small herd of sheep and goats will be nearby.

It seems that a number of years earlier the government decided to improve the lot of these wanderers. They built and furnished nice apartment houses for the Bedouins, and officials assisted them in moving into their new homes—the height of luxury in comparison with their battered tents. Everyone was pleased with the way the nomads had been helped to improve their way of living.

Several days later the officials went back to check on the Bedouins and see how they were doing. To their surprise, the apartments were full of animals. Where were the Bedouins? Back in their tents, living exactly as they had for centuries. They refused to give up their old ways for a better life. But they did decide that the apartments would make good pens for their sheep and goats.

This story illustrates the resistance to change that seems to be built into human nature—in every culture. Consider how many people sit in the same pew every Sunday at church and become visibly upset if a visitor happens to make the terrible mistake of sitting in their place. And how many of us drive exactly the same route to and from work every day, not varying our path by even one turn?

Because we are people of habit, successfully moving a church to a new location presents some of the greatest challenges in communicating effectively. Certainly there are many opportunities for excitement and elation, but there are also numerous chances for misunderstanding and conflict.

How do you make the journey from one building to another successfully with as little disruption and turmoil as possible? Here are some suggestions:

1. Keep people informed every step of the way so that it becomes their project.
2. Use brainstorming (see chapter 8 for more details) as you consider possibilities in initial stages of planning. People tend to support what they feel involved in and have a part in creating.
3. Involve as many people as possible on various committees.
4. As soon as the property is purchased, have an attractive sign made and placed on it with a message such as, "Future Home of _____."
5. Display architectural drawings and, if possible, a scale model of the building or complex in a prominent place in the church as soon as they are available.
6. Make absolutely certain that all plans meet city codes and specifications and that the necessary permits have been obtained.
7. Have committees report frequently to keep everyone informed on the progress of all phases of the project.
8. Run articles in the newsletter. Consider publishing a special edition about the building program periodically.
9. Hold events, such as a picnic and worship service, on the property before anything is built, to help people start feeling at home there.
10. Conduct tours of the new property.
11. Be sure to bring new members up-to-date on the building program.
12. Hold a ground-breaking ceremony when it's time for construction to begin.
13. Announce a realistic, projected date for completion.
14. Send out periodic news releases on the purchase of the property, ground breaking, and, of course, dedication of the new facility.
15. Speak about the move frequently in sermons and in other meetings. Preach faith-building sermons.
16. Keep city and civic leaders informed about your plans and what they will mean to the community.
17. Keep a video record of the building progress from the unimproved land, activities on the property, ground-breaking, and various stages of construction to the completed, landscaped building. Have the video edited and consider showing it as a part of the dedication ceremony.
18. Schedule the dedication service on a Sunday afternoon so that people outside your congregation can come. Send out formal invitations to city officials, other ministers, the architect and other key people in the actual construction, and friends of the church. Have a special program with a picture of the new facility on the front. Include a brief history of the church in the program with

a longer version presented as a part of the service. Serve refreshments after the service. Have trained guides take people on a tour of the facility.

19. Plan special events, such as a concert, as a part of the opening events. People who won't come to a regular service may be interested in attending a musical program and seeing the new church they've watched being constructed. Also, it provides an opportunity for members to invite friends and family members to an informal evening of entertainment.

Learning about how other pastors made the transition should make your move easier and smoother.

Moving and Merging Two Congregations

Much happened during the week after the ground-breaking ceremony for a larger building on the same property of Meadow Creek Church in Mesquite, Texas. Members were excited about having more room and about moving upward and onward in their mission of reaching the unsaved in their community.

So it was with some trepidation that Pastor Russ Olmon told his congregation the following Sunday about the desire of Gross Road Baptist to "marry" with their church. "They were shocked and stunned," he recalls. He explained the benefits: a seven-acre tract of land located on a major thoroughfare two blocks from a freeway and in the middle of an area which would soon be dotted with restaurants and the largest theater in the entire area, and a facility of sixty-one thousand square feet, complete with a twenty thousand square-foot community center with a gymnasium—something Meadow Creek could not hope to build for several years. Most important was the fact that the two congregations shared the same vision—that of reaching the lost.

Olmon says that within two weeks people were already seeing the potential. They began having meetings about the possible move and offered tours of the new facility. There were many questions. Will things be the same? Will the contemporary services change? What's it going to be like? What will be the name? Who will be the pastor? What about the staff?

These issues were brought before numerous focus groups in both churches. Out of those meetings emerged these decisions. The name would become Meadow Creek Community Church. Both senior pastors would become copastors. Current staff members of both churches would become the staff of the new church. Major responsibilities in areas such as missions, administration, staff management, shepherding, and budget management were defined. The four hundred thousand dollars in Meadow Creek's building fund and the revenue from the sale of their current building and property would be used to make major renovations and updates of the Gross Road facility.

A few weeks later both congregations voted on whether to merge. The Meadow Creek congregation voted 100 percent in favor, and Gross Road only had four dissenters. The same Sunday another church balloted to buy the Meadow Creek property. Tension was high as each of the three churches waited expectantly to find out the decisions of the other two.

Members of Meadow Creek had a month to get used to the idea, and another month to prepare for the move. During that time both congregations worked hard to get to know each other. Each group helped with the other's vacation Bible school and attended each other's events. They also held three joint events, such as a big picnic, to assist in the getting-acquainted process. At that point Olmon says his congregation was so eager that it was like "holding back wild horses."

Just a little over two months after the "marriage," Meadow Creek Community Church had already added about one hundred new participants in their Sunday morning services.

Olmon is amazed at the smooth transition of not only moving but merging the two churches. "The level of unity and cooperation has been simply stunning," he reflects. "This clearly is something God had planned. We are all grateful that we allowed Him to lead us through the maze of personality, turf tendencies, and ownership issues."[1]

Moving into the First Building

Pastor Ned Barnes left an established, thriving congregation in Connecticut to start a new church in Jupiter, Florida, where he knew no one and where there was no United Church of Christ. Some of his friends thought he needed his head examined. He says that he wondered about it himself at times.

For the first two years, First United Church of Christ met on the top floor of the Jupiter Beach Hilton Hotel overlooking the ocean. After outgrowing the penthouse, the church met in the middle school, but members wanted a home of their own. A four-year search for just the right spot finally culminated in the purchase of an ideal five-acre parcel of land smack in the middle of a booming, high-density development with the option to buy an adjacent five acres. They had previously approached the developer, who wasn't interested in selling. This time, as a result of what Barnes describes as "the workings of the

Lord," the owner responded, "Yes, we might like to have a church at the entrance to our community. We'll rethink our plans and get back to you."

Recipients of invitations to the ground-breaking ceremony found a tiny, toy metal shovel tucked inside a small, one-fold, invitation-size mailer. Members and friends gathered for a ground-breaking ceremony on the church's fifth anniversary. Everyone wore a bright yellow construction worker's hard hat and was equipped with a shovel. They rented a large tent, hired a band, served lunch, and released five hundred helium balloons.

The church location on the property was outlined with ribbon, and signs marked the exact location of the sanctuary, choir loft, bell tower, kitchen, and offices. After the dedication ceremony, all the participants marched onto the site singing "The Church's One Foundation." The breaking of ground was accompanied by shouts of joy.

Once construction began, every Sunday the building committee took people on tours of the site and pointed out all that had been done the previous week. Barnes says that the building became a sanctuary long before it was even open. He recalls that one Sunday as he drove by, he noticed a car in the lot, so he stopped to see who was there. "Inside was a woman all alone leaning against the wall. She was in tears. I spoke to her and discovered she had been coming to church for two or three weeks and was in the midst of a difficult divorce. She said, 'I just needed to come here to be by myself.' There was a certain sense of God's presence in that place even before the roof went on."

After an annual leadership retreat, about fifteen of the participants went to the unfinished building and celebrated their first worship service in the new church. The first official service was held the Sunday before Christmas with all of the four hundred seats filled and people standing all around the walls.[2]

Moving Out from Town

Dr. Dennis Hochgraber, now pastor of Shiloh Terrace Baptist Church in Dallas, Texas, says that, realistically, a pastor pays a tough price both emotionally and physically in moving a congregation. Soon after he led Parkside Baptist Church in Denison, Texas, in successfully building and moving into their new facility, a New Mexico church invited him to come there and repeat the same scenario. His response? "God only asked Moses to lead the children of Israel out of Egypt one time. It was not really something I was ready to do again," he reflects.

When Hochgraber became pastor there in the early 1980s, Parkside was located in the middle of Denison, a town of about twenty-five thousand. It was landlocked with absolutely no room to grow and expand. The congregation had already voted to move and had purchased twenty-two acres of land outside of town in keeping with its vision to become a regional church. The original committee had knelt and prayed on the acreage and knew beyond any doubt that this was the place God wanted them. That day they made an "unbreakable vow" to build there.

"When I came, I had to buy into their vision. There was a learning curve in working together toward the same goals," Hochgraber recalls. He was there six years before the first phase of building was completed and they actually moved. He points out that it is easy to vote when it doesn't cost anything, but the picture sometimes looks different when reality sets in. For some, the obstacles began to seem insurmountable. For one thing, the population of Denison was shrinking. Members started asking, "Why should we build a larger church when there are fewer and fewer people around here? How will we pay for it?"

Hochgraber says that his role was "not so much a maker of decisions. That's the people's role. As their spiritual leader my job was to remind the people of God's faithfulness." He would tell them that "God is in the business of doing things bigger than we are. We can't totally explain how we can do it. Faith is a step of vision."

Hochgraber's sermons were filled with examples of God's faithfulness, especially in stories from the Old Testament, such as Moses leading the children of Israel out of Egypt and Joshua and Caleb returning from the Promised Land with their report. Hochgraber also reminded them of their vision as they considered their three options: to relocate, to split the church, or to start a mission and let another group fulfill their vision. As the church grew and changed, he had the congregation vote two more times on relocating just to make sure "everyone was on the same page." The results were positive with 88 to 94 percent voting to relocate each time.

During that period these are some approaches that helped in the transition.

- The church leaders held an annual picnic, usually on the Fourth of July, on the property to help keep up their enthusiasm. This included a worship service as well as ball games.
- As time went on, the church leaders held more and more events on the property.
- The church leaders conducted tours of the property.
- The vision was solidified by putting the plans down on paper.
- The church leaders kept the people totally informed through building-committee reports, bulletins, letters, committee meetings, and sermons.

- The church leaders bit off the project in bite sizes that were palatable.
- The church leaders kept the community well informed through the city council, the city planning commission, chambers of commerce, news releases, and full-page ads in the newspaper. They wrote a history of the church.
- From the time the church leaders broke ground, they involved as many people as possible to give them a feeling of ownership.
- Pains were taken to see that excitement and anticipation were built into the process.

It took three tries before the church leaders finally found the right architect, and it was costly paying for plans they didn't use. But the third architect really listened to the people. He created a master plan, which included four buildings and a picnic and park area, for the entire twenty-two acres. Roads were built, and the softball field was completed for church-league use before any of the buildings were finished.

The congregation was able to sell their building to another fellowship. When the first building, the sanctuary with carefully planned double-use space, was completed, the church moved. They lost fewer than 2 percent of their members in the process and immediately began a steady growth of 8 to 9 percent each year during the six years that Hochgraber remained there as pastor.

The church leaders invited the community to their opening "Week of Celebration," which included two evenings of musical concerts and two others with guest preachers. City officials and denominational leaders also participated in the festivities.

"This was one of the most exciting times in the life of the body, seeing God work in ways we never expected or anticipated," Hochgraber says. "Communications played a significant part in the entire process. Keeping the people consistently well informed is absolutely essential. "[3]

Communicating Effectively Through Publications, Advertising, and Computers

Declare among the nations,
Proclaim, and set up a standard;
Proclaim—do not conceal it.
              —Jeremiah 50:2 (NKJV)

12 Publishing a Dynamic Newsletter

A newsletter has the potential to be one of the most effective tools for a church or ministry. But it can also present a negative picture of your organization, depending on its quality. Two good questions to ask are:

1. Can my newsletter compete with the hundreds of other messages the average person receives each day?
2. Does the newsletter represent my ministry and what it stands for to those who receive it?

If you have a newsletter, you can use the following information to assist in evaluating and perhaps improving it. If you do not have a newsletter, this chapter should help you in setting up and producing a successful publication. In case terms such as *widow, bleed, bullet, gutter,* and *morgue* conjure up images for you that have little to do with a newsletter, a glossary of some publishing terms has been included in chapter 15.

Choosing an Editor

Ideally, the editor will have some background in journalism and experience with publications. At least it should be someone who can write concisely and clearly and is willing to invest considerable time in the project on a regular, continuing basis. A vision for what can be accomplished and enthusiasm for turning out a consistently excellent publication are also prime qualifications.

Considerations in Setting up a Newsletter

The decisions in this section should be made by the pastor, the communications director (if pertinent), the editor, and members of a communications committee (if available).

What Are Our Purposes in Publishing a Newsletter?

While you may have additional reasons, probably these purposes will be included on your list:
- to provide a record of the ministry
- to inform members and other interested people of what's happening in the church
- to create enthusiasm for programs
- to help in the recruitment of volunteers in various areas of ministry
- to engender financial support for various programs
- to give recognition for service
- to help create a caring community
- to help people keep track of upcoming important dates by providing a written calendar

Who Is Your Audience?

Usually this would include all members, visitors, news-media representatives, friends of the church or ministry who go elsewhere, members in the armed forces, missionaries associated with your ministry, former members who have moved away (if they desire to be kept on the list), people who have participated in church or ministry-sponsored activities, and contributors who are not members.

How Often Will You Publish the Newsletter?

Main factors to consider in making this decision are the resources that are needed in terms of time and money to produce a consistently effective publication. A weekly publication requires an enormous amount of time and can be quite expensive. Probably only rather large churches should consider publishing that frequently.

A decided advantage is the timeliness of the publication with the ability to keep members up-to-the-minute on what's happening. Those weekly deadlines, though, can become monotonous in a hurry, and it may be difficult to publish a top-quality newsletter that frequently.

A monthly newsletter can be effective for a small to medium-sized congregation, but, of course, it loses some of its timeliness. A compromise some churches find effective is publishing every two weeks or semi-monthly, which cuts down on some of the deadline pressures but provides more frequent and up-to-date communication.

What Will Be Its Name?
- The name should be short.
- The name should reflect the style and spirit of the organization.

- The name should be catchy and/or memorable.

If you're setting up a newsletter for the first time, you might try having a contest among members to come up with an appropriate name. This could create interest within the congregation for the debut of the publication.

What Size Will It Be?

If the newsletter will be published weekly, every two weeks, or even monthly, it probably is better to use either an 8½-by-11-inch page or an 8½-by-14-inch sheet. Going to a nonstandard size of paper will increase production costs. Usual sizes can be used in a variety of ways. The 8½-by-11-inch page can be printed flat front and back with copy broken up into columns or it can be folded in half, making four pages of 8½-by-5½ inches (see fig. 1).

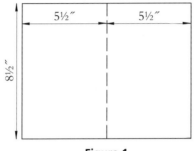

Figure 1

The 8½-by-14-inch page, of course, can also be used front and back. This size not only provides more space for stories, but it also can be nicely folded for mailing, with the bottom fourth of the page on the back side being reserved for the return address, mailing label, and, perhaps, an inspiring saying. This will save the cost of envelopes for mailing.

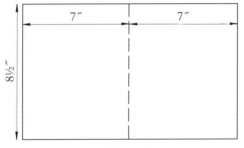

Figure 2

The larger size will also lend itself to more variety of format. You can fold the page in half, creating two 8½-by-7-inch sections on each side (see fig. 2); in thirds for three 4⅝-inch sections on each side (see fig. 3); or with two folds, making one panel smaller than the other two. This might break down on each side into two 8½-by-5½-inch and one 8½-by-3-inch section (see fig. 4). The smaller section could be used for the church calendar for the coming period and for other continuing information, such as the newsletter staff and the masthead (this contains information about the publication).

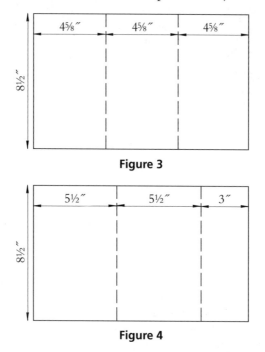

Figure 3

Figure 4

If the newsletter is to be published in a different time frame (for example, quarterly), you probably will want to consider going to multiple sheets in order to adequately cover the longer time span.

What Will Be the Cost?

Determine the approximate number of people on your list and add at least 10 to 15 percent for growth and for distribution to visitors who come to a service or activity. Since the price of paper varies, probably the best thing to do is get a quote on the type of paper you wish to use and add 10 percent for possible increases.

Church newsletters may be mailed at bulk rate with the purchase of a mailing permit that needs to be figured into the cost, unless it is already in place. Again, add 10 percent for possible postage increases. Also, preparing newsletters for mailing takes time. Usually they must be folded. Will you have that done by the printer or in-house? Address labels also must be attached. If they are to be mailed using a bulk-rate mail permit, they also must be sorted and bundled by zip code. Can this be handled by secretarial staff, volunteers, or will an extra hand need to be brought in at newsletter mailing time? Since postal regulations are subject to change, check with your local post office about current requirements. Most post offices are quite strict about only accepting mailings that are prepared according to their exact specifications. (See chapter 15 for additional information on mailing.)

Are you going to pay someone to edit the newsletter or will it be a part of a staff member's responsibilities or the work of a volunteer? If it is to be done by a staff member, then multiply the number of hours that it will probably require by the hourly rate of pay. Another cost will be film, processing, and picture screening for printing, if you plan to use photographs. Other expenses might include the purchase of clip art and cartoons.

Designing the Name Plate or Flag

The name plate of the newsletter containing its name (also called the flag, banner, or, sometimes, masthead) should be bold and eye catching. This section should include, in addition to the name of the newsletter, the name of your organization and its slogan. Too many ministry newsletters do not contain the name of the church or parachurch organization, and the person who receives it in the mail may not have even a clue as to where it came from. With the many tools made available by computer technology, a creative person can probably design a nice banner. But, even better, recruit an artist from your congregation as a volunteer or pay a commercial artist to come up with a professional-looking design.

Choosing the Paper

Some considerations in choosing the paper are:

1. The cost. Since this is an item that will not be saved for any length of time by the recipient, you probably will want to choose a relatively inexpensive quality of paper—but one that will look nice. However, be sure the weight of the paper is heavy enough so that the ink will not bleed through to the other side, especially if you are printing on both sides.
2. The finish. Slick papers look rather showy but are more difficult to read. A matte finish is probably better.

3. The color. The less the contrast between paper color and the type, the more difficult the newsletter will be to read. Black ink on white, off-white, or ecru is the best for legibility. Brown or blue ink with some black mixed in on buff or ivory is also easily read. Pastel papers are next in preferability, but, if you plan to use pictures, consider how people might look with blue or green faces.

While reverses (white letters on a black or dark background) decrease legibility significantly, if you want that effect, then it is better to use a sans serif typeface (without the narrow line endings at the bottom of letters such as l and r).

Once the paper is selected and the masthead designed, then it is time to have at least a year's quantity of the masthead printed. Using a different color of ink for the masthead than you plan to use for the body of the newsletter will give variety and a two-color effect.

Selecting the Type

The main consideration to keep in mind here is which typefaces and type sizes are most easily deciphered. The more legible, the better chance you'll have of getting the newsletter read all the way through.

Ten-point (the size of type in this text) is a good size for readability, yet is small enough to pack a lot of words into your limited space. You probably will want to use the next larger type size for the headline (for example, 12-point, if the body of the newsletter is done in 10-point). Also, the headline will stand out more effectively if it is done in boldface type.

There are many suitable typefaces to choose from. Among these are Courier, Palatino, Cheltenham, Fruit, Bookman, Geneva, and New York. Using a typeface, such as Old English or H P Techno, may look quaint or high tech and help create a mood, but will be much more difficult to read. This is also true of a long passage in italic print or script type. Sans serif typefaces are more legible for use in headlines, and the use of both upper- and lower-case letters in headlines helps readability. The same typeface should be used throughout a publication.

Getting the Necessities in Place

Certain items must be included in a newsletter for assistance to the reader and also to produce a publication that meets professional journalistic standards. Under the flag, each issue of the newsletter should have "Vol. 1, No. 1," if it is the first issue, or should be numbered accurately for whichever issue it is. The volume number would change to "2" the second year of the newsletter's publication and increase by one each year thereafter.

Also, each issue should contain a masthead (different from the flag), usually boxed or otherwise set apart in a consistent way. This should contain the name of the newsletter, the publisher, its audience, and the frequency of publication. For example: *"The Beacon* is published by Lighthouse Christian Center each month for its family and friends." The masthead should include the mailing address, telephone number, and fax number (including area codes), and e-mail and website addresses (if pertinent) of the ministry. It can also give the editor's name and the deadline for material to be submitted to the editor in order for it to be used. Another standby should be the usual schedule for services.

Deciding on Visual Material

Producing a newsletter that is appealing to the eye is critical to the success of the publication. If it looks too gray (type only with nonvisual material and little white space), most people will not go to the trouble to read it, even if the subjects are fascinating and the writing is terrific.

Excellent clip art is available at a relatively small price and, once purchased, may be used whenever desired. This can liven up a newsletter's appearance and underscore the subject of a particular item, if it is used tastefully and is not overdone. Original line drawings from a talented member of the staff or congregation can also be effective. Another possibility is to occasionally use a drawing done by a child in the congregation. This can be especially nice during the Christmas or Easter season.

Best of all are really good photographs that are appropriately cropped, identified with a well-written cut line, and artistically placed in the newsletter layout. If you are going to use photos, though, be sure to have them scanned for printing, which is a relatively inexpensive process, or purchase your own scanner. Relatively inexpensive scanners are available that would be adequate for many uses, such as a bulletin or flyer which might be produced in-house. However, for a piece such as a four-color brochure, it would be preferable to have pictures scanned by a professional printer as part of the job.

A picture that is simply photocopied results in a terrible reproduction and makes the whole newsletter look amateurish and second-rate. (See the section entitled "Helping Photographs Live Up to Their Potential" in this chapter.)

An occasional cartoon can be used to good effect, especially if it goes with a topic that is current to the life of the ministry. Several companies produce packs with multiple cartoons for a reasonable price.

Well-done charts and graphs, when appropriate, can add to the visual appeal of the newsletter as well as give emphasis and understanding for the reader. For example, a church that wishes to emphasize its involvement with foreign missions in an article can dramatize its efforts with a drawing of the globe and lines drawn to identify the ministries that are being supported in various countries.

Still another way to break up copy is to pull out a blurb, a quote or statement that captures the essence of the article, put it in boldface type, and either put lines above and below or box it.

Developing Regular Features

You will want to use some columns in every (or nearly every) edition. No doubt you will wish to include a calendar of events as a continuing feature in your newsletter. This can serve as a reminder for participants and potential participants of all the activities that will take place until the next newsletter is published. This is especially helpful for families with members of different ages who are involved in a variety of activities.

Another continuing feature will probably be a message from the pastor or ministry leader. This should be brief, to the point, and inspiring in nature. This can provide an opportunity to reinforce the vision of the ministry and to motivate readers to be involved in fulfilling it.

A welcome-new-members column can introduce newcomers to the body, especially if a couple of descriptive lines about each person or family are included. Using pictures of newcomers can go a long way toward helping them get acquainted with and assimilated into the congregation, if there is space to run them on a continuing basis. Another column, possibly titled "Pray and Praise," could detail prayer needs and reports of prayers answered. Deaths, births, and baptisms should also have a special spot in which to be reported.

Other occasional columns may be used, as space permits. For example, a kid's corner can give young children's answers to a question about God. One such column was titled "Out of the Mouths of Babes." Another occasional column might be a profile of a new staff member or a lay leader in the church.

Finding Material

Where can you find ideas for your newsletter? Everywhere is the answer. An editor who looks and listens with news antennae out will find too much material to cover, rather than having to dredge something up. Let readers know that you are always on the lookout for an interesting or inspiring story and encourage them to contact you with a lead.

Another approach is to ask each leader of a department or a major ministry to appoint a newsletter representative or reporter who will keep you informed about special programs and events coming up in his or her area of responsibility. The newsletter editor will probably want to meet with these representatives or at least send them a note to let them know the types of appropriate material, how to submit it in writing, and what the deadline is. You also may want to develop a "Newsletter Tip Sheet" (see page 172) to be made available to representatives as well as to members of the congregation.

Ask staff members and ministry heads to jot down questions they are asked or hear members discussing among themselves and pass them along to the newsletter editor. If the same question appears several times, it might indicate that an article on the subject in the newsletter would be worthwhile.

Here are some suggestions for types of stories you can include.

- If a major event is coming up, it should be given emphasis in the newsletter preceding the event. Several smaller articles probably will appear in earlier issues, but the issue just before the event will feature various aspects, preferably with an interesting picture to accompany the article.
- A guest speaker can be featured with biographical material about her or him along with some interesting highlights about the subject to be covered.
- The beginning of a new program with all the particulars, including how to become a part of the activity is a natural for a nice article. This should include the background, the need, the leader and his or her background or qualifications, time of meetings, and plans for the future.
- Highlights of a special sermon series or seminar can be presented. This would be especially valuable for those who were unable to attend or as a review for those who participated.
- A report on a missionary trip, complete with quotes from participants, could be detailed. An interesting action picture on the missionary field would greatly enhance the article.
- Financial support for a new ministry, such as a radio or television program, could be encouraged. This would also help members and other newsletter recipients become familiar with the program's time and station with a printed reference.
- An anniversary issue could give a brief history of the beginning of the church, those who have served in leadership, and significant events in the life of the church.
- Volunteer opportunities and needs can be listed with the appropriate person to contact.
- Honors received by members of the staff and congregation can be mentioned along with congratulations.
- Before major holidays, special observances being planned can be detailed. Also, an article giving the background for a certain

observance might be helpful to newcomers to the faith or to a certain denomination. For example, a liturgical church might detail a stations-of-the-cross service, so that those who had never participated in that particular type of service would understand its significance and have some idea of what to expect. And those who have attended year after year might learn something too.

- The first edition in January could give a recap of the previous year's activities and accomplishments, complete with quotes from representative members expressing what the church has meant to them during that year.
- Special features can be developed periodically. For example, a capsule profile of each person in the congregation who is an ordained or licensed minister might be given. Everyone may not know who they are.
- If rumors are floating around, a factual article on the subject can be used effectively to squelch untrue statements.
- A human-interest story or a humorous incident that occurred in the church can add warmth to the publication and provide pleasure for the reader.
- An article about pending changes can prepare members to accept and support future alterations in programs, responsibilities, and facilities.
- Giving reasons behind the decisions as well as the decisions made by the church board or leadership can provide information to promote understanding.
- Features about missionaries whom the church supports can help to interest and involve people in their work and engender enthusiasm and support for the church's involvement.

And the list could go on and on.

Writing a Newsletter That Will Be Read

Here are some suggestions for producing a newsletter that people will look forward to receiving and be eager to read.

- Use simple language. Most newspapers are written on an eighth-grade reading level on purpose—so they can be read by the average person. The ministry newsletter is not the place to showcase an outstanding vocabulary. The "Gunning Fog Index" is helpful to use as a periodic check of the reading level of any publication. In case the word processing software you use does not have this capability, you can do it like this by hand: (1) Count one hundred continuous words and divide by the number of sentences to get the average sentence length. (2) Count the number of three-syllable words within the one hundred words, omitting words that are capitalized, combinations of short, easy words such as *bookkeeper* or *butterfly,* and verb forms made by a suffix such as *-ed* or *-es*. (3) To get the Fog Index, add the average sentence length and number of long words and multiply by 0.4. The result will give you the approximate grade level you have written on. It is a good idea to count the Fog Index in two or three different parts of the newsletter for a reliable evaluation.

- Compose short, punchy headlines that nearly always contain an infinitive or a present-tense verb. If the headline doesn't grab the reader's attention, that article may well be skipped over. Besides attracting the reader's attention, the headline should present the gist of the story, sell the story to the reader so that it seems worth the investment of time and effort required to read it, and give the superficial reader a message that you want to leave with her or him. For an especially important story, you might also want to include a kicker, a short line in smaller or accent type above the main line of a head.
- Start the article with a colorful lead to get the reader into the story. Decide on the most important and most interesting aspect of this story that you can use to get the reader's attention.
- Keep articles brief and packed with action verbs. Talk about people as much as possible rather than about things. Even if the article must contain a lot of statistical information, try to translate at least some of the figures into the experience of, or impact on, people or a particular individual.
- Write in a positive, upbeat style—even if you're covering a problem area or a serious subject.
- Remember the five *w*s of journalistic writing: *who, what, when, where, why,* and also add *how* to make certain you've included all the pertinent information.
- Avoid "religionese" and terms that may not be understood by a person who is not in your church. Assume that the newsletter will be read by outsiders and that they will likely be turned off by a publication that they cannot understand.
- The first time acronyms are used within a particular article, be sure to write out the full name and place the initials in parentheses.
- Identify the person you are writing about or quoting, even if most people will know that person's position. For example, after the person's name, use the title, such as "minister of education" or "nursery director."
- Use interesting quotes liberally.

- Check the details carefully, so that your newsletter will be respected as a source of reliable information.
- With time-dated material, be sure that the newsletter will get to the reader before the event occurs. Remember: It's not news for your calendar if it's already happened.
- End a feature story with a bang. Some possibilities are a strong quote, a tieback to the lead, an anecdote, or a provocative question related to the article.
- Avoid editorial comments and subjective descriptions in stories. Relegate comments (such as "It was an inspiring evening") to quotes from someone who participated and said so.
- Edit what you've written. Write an article and then put it aside. Let it "cool off" while you work on something else. When you come back to it, you can read the material more objectively with fresh eyes. Is your meaning absolutely clear? Is it tightly and imaginatively written? An excellent way to ferret out awkward sentences and repetitive words and ideas is by reading your copy aloud.
- If possible, have someone else read the newsletter for clarity and interest.

Planning Your Newsletter

Taking the time to think through what you need to cover during the coming year will be invaluable as individual issue deadlines approach. Look at a calendar and note holidays that you may want to allude to. Also, it is important to determine the impact that they will have on your publication schedule. Then, take the ministry calendar and note the events that are already planned for the year. Probably you will be able to decide which ones will warrant a story and others that may just need to be listed on the newsletter calendar.

You will find it helpful to make a dated folder for each issue, along with the deadline date for material to be submitted and the date the camera-ready newsletter must be delivered to the printer (if an outside printer is to be used). Into each folder will go the materials for each edition that have been gleaned from the calendars. Then, as new information is received, it is an easy matter to place it in the appropriate folder.

When you get ready to plan the upcoming issue, take out the folder and see what information you already have. Then determine what is important to include in that issue. What is most important? That should become your lead story, preferably with a picture or other illustrative material. You may find that you have a lot of material to cover. That will cue you to make the stories extra tight when you write them, or if someone else has turned in a written article, plan to edit it drastically. Other things in your file, if they are not dated, may be postponed for a future edition. It also may be possible to combine some items. Brief stories, requiring only a line or two may be used together in one column under the heading of something like "Potpourri" or "To Speak of Many Things."

A good thing to do as time permits is to write several feature stories that might be used at any time. Then, when an issue is going to be lean because of little current news, just pull one story out and use it.

Giving Your Newsletter Visual Appeal

Eye appeal is one of the most critical factors in determining whether your newsletter will actually be read or be tossed aside, or even worse, be tossed into the circular file. A page crammed with tiny type that causes eye squint, and filled with narrow margins, long paragraphs, and little or no artwork presents a foreboding picture for even the person who would logically be interested in your ministry newsletter. So give your audience a break and make reading what you've spent so much time and money to produce a pleasant and easy endeavor.

Judges for a newsletter contest were asked to suggest ways in which editors could improve their publications. Here are some of their recommendations relating to design:

1. Limit your copy line to about three-to-four inches in width. Much longer slows down reading time, while much shorter has the same effect.
2. Do not print over illustrative material. While it may provide variety and look interesting, it will reduce legibility significantly.
3. Use copy-breaking devices when you have large blocks of text. Consider using the "dollar bill test." This entails taking a dollar bill and placing it on different parts of the page to see whether you have a copy-breaking device within the area of that bill. If not, put one in.
4. Avoid garish-colored stock for your publications.
5. Be creative, but don't let clever design overpower the content.
6. Do not use large blocks of reversed type. While reversed type can give an "arty" look, it can also decrease readability. One study concluded that reversed type cuts reading speed an average of 10.5 percent and results in a 30 percent drop in comprehension. This is particularly true when the reversal is done over a picture or where there is little contrast between the print and the background.
7. Use a few good-sized, action pictures rather than several small ones.
8. Avoid jumping stories or continuing the story on a different page. Every time you jump a story, you lose readers.[1]

Here are some additional angles to consider.

- Build white space into your layout for a readable, appealing, and modern look. Don't feel that every inch of space must be packed with print. White space, though, should not be "trapped" by other elements of the layout, but rather, these should be relegated to the outer parts of the page.
- Avoid being "cutesy" (for example, using a headline that runs down the page instead of across). It not only brands the publication as amateurish, but also makes it more difficult to decipher.
- If long lines of copy or a long article are necessary, an extra point of leading (space between lines) reduces the gray effect and makes the text more legible.
- Indenting the first line of each paragraph automatically provides some white space. It also increases legibility for the reader.
- Widows (a word or two left alone on a line at the end of a paragraph) also provide white space.
- Don't skimp on margins in order to squeeze in a few more letters. Also, space between columns can be used to good effect to create an airy look.
- Double space between the headline and the story and triple space or leave two-and-a-half spaces between news items.
- Underlining and boldface type, if used sparingly, can help break up copy and highlight important aspects of a story.
- Use bullets or heavy dots for emphasizing important points. These provide additional white space as well as call attention to a series of similar items or statements.
- Indented numbering of items can have the same effect.
- Use a box around an item for variety and to set it apart. A regular feature, such as a pastor's column, might have its own special identifiable border and contain a small bust shot of the pastor.
- Another way to provide variety is to use a light screen (pale gray when printing with black ink) behind a boxed item.
- Use a blurb within a relatively long article to break up the space and to highlight a quote or important statement.
- Another good device for providing white space in a long article and focus for the reader is to use a subhead in boldface type. These should be shorter than your regular headline, and probably only two or three words in length.
- A layout should have a single, dominant force. Too many little things to look at are distracting.
- The lead story or most important item should be the first item

in the newsletter and should be accompanied by compelling visual material, if at all possible.

• Remember, simplicity is the key to a contemporary-looking format.

• Using a justified right margin (with all lines on the right margin lined up as they are on the left margin—like in this book) or a ragged right margin (with lines of varying lengths depending on the number of character per line) is a matter of preference. Either is acceptable although ragged right is supposed to be somewhat easier to read.

Helping Photographs Live Up to Their Potential

Well-taken and effectively used photographs can add significantly to the eye appeal and interest of your newsletter. Pictures score higher in readership than any other part of the paper. And a person who will not take the time to read the entire newsletter will often look at the pictures and gain some information.

Here are some suggestions for getting good pictures:

1. For quality reproduction, use black-and-white photographs with a high-gloss finish (unless the pictures are to be run in color). Although sometimes color pictures will work, as a rule, they do not have the extreme contrasts necessary for quality reproduction.

2. Keep in mind the layout in which you will use a particular shot. Ending up with a horizontal picture when you need a vertical one for that particular spot can be a problem.

3. Have the subjects do something rather than just stare at the camera. Capture people in action so that you can give your reader a glimpse of what appears to be a real-life scenario. Of course, some stories lend themselves to this approach readily, while others require more imagination. For example, at the dedication of a new playground for preschool children, use a shot of a delighted child going down the slide rather than one of the pastor making a speech about it or a picture of the unoccupied playground.

4. Move your subjects closer together than they would normally stand or sit. Don't allow wasted space in the middle of the picture that is impossible to crop out.

5. Take close-ups of people, leaving out extraneous side details as much as possible.

6. Avoid cluttered, distracting elements in the background of the picture. A plain background is best, or next best is one that is uniquely appropriate to the message of the picture.

7. Make sure there are no shadows on the faces of the subject. Using a flash, even when adequate light is available, will eliminate this problem and also give a more vibrant look to the eyes.

8. Limit the number of people in the picture. One, two, or three are best. More than five gets cluttered.

9. If you absolutely must use a photograph of a large group, position the people on different height levels. The greater the width of the picture, the smaller the faces will be and the less effective the visual will become. Also, try to pose them in a more interesting configuration than in straight lines.

10. Plan to take several shots to get one really good picture. And if subjects seem tense with forced smiles, try talking to them during the shoot to get them to relax and loosen up.

11. Once you've selected the pictures for that issue, crop them to emphasize facial expressions and capture the essence of the moment. It's okay to remove outside shoulders and lower extremities that are not important to the picture's message. A cardboard picture mat cut into two pieces at two opposite corners can be helpful in deciding how to crop a picture. Just move the two pieces up and down, and in and out until you arrive at the most interesting image. Once you've decided, you can indicate crop marks in one of two ways. One way is to use a grease pencil to trace the opening made by the pieces of cardboard. You will probably have to move them back slightly to make the markings exact. The grease-pencil markings can later be rubbed off easily (never make crop markings with any kind of pen or pencil). Another way is to use a ruler, and make your markings at the tops, bottoms, and sides in the white margin of the picture (if there is one), rather than on the picture itself.

12. Usually you will have to reduce or enlarge the ratio of your picture for placement in your newsletter. Purchasing a photographic reduction wheel can simplify significantly the process of arriving at accurate figures.

13. Use rectangular pictures rather than odd shapes, such as a circle.

14. Pictures should sit squarely on the page, rather than be placed at an angle.

15. Research has shown that a picture placed immediately above the story it illustrates is more effective and that the article will more likely be read. Tests have shown that the eye has a tendency to move downward while viewing a photograph, so when the story is positioned below the photograph, you take advantage of this natural eye movement.

16. Adding a thumbnail photo to copy will increase the readership of a column. This, as a rule, should be limited to a bust shot.

17. Every picture should have a caption nearby, preferably below it. Placing captions for more than one photo together with a reference as to which ones they go with can be confusing and more time consuming for the reader.

18. If, because of the placement of a picture in the newsletter, the people are looking off the page, have the picture flopped or reversed. (If there is written material in the picture or other telltale signs, this would not work.)

19. When using two photos side by side, be sure that the sizes of the people in one picture are proportional to those in the other picture. Otherwise, it will appear that you have midgets alongside giants.

20. A dramatic effect can be achieved by using a portion of a picture, either a person or an inanimate object you wish to focus attention on, as a silhouette by removing the background. Do not try to actually cut the figure out of the photograph with scissors. Rather, indicate by drawing a keyline or outline on an overlay on tracing paper over the photo to indicate to the printer the portion you wish to use. Tape the overlay to the back of the picture so that it will fold over on top of the photo.

21. A partial silhouette can also be used for variety. The main portion of the photograph is used with the person or other element "poking out" of the picture in silhouette. Again, you would want to use an overlay over the photo to show the area you want deleted.

22. Develop a research file or morgue for used and unused photos and a method for filing them. You never know when you may need the same picture, perhaps cropped differently, or one you rejected for this issue, for a future publication, or perhaps for use in a display of some kind. Be sure to date the pictures and keep the negatives either with them or in a separate, labeled file.

Writing Cutlines for Pictures

Writing effective cutlines is a challenging assignment. Here are some guidelines:

1. The cutline should contain these elements: a description of the action that is taking place, identification of the persons or items in the photo, background information about the person, action, or occasion, and credit for the source of the picture (if credits are to be used).

2. Don't say what's obvious by just looking at the picture. For example, if all are smiling, you don't need to refer to their "smiling faces."

3. Identify the people who are pictured and tell where they are positioned. Usually this would be done from the left. In some pictures, though, it might be better to indicate the person at the far left and then point the others out in clockwise order. If the picture is of a large group, it's probably better to identify the group, such as the Children's Choir, rather than trying to list each person's name individually.

4. Try to summarize the story's idea in the cutline or, if that's not possible, at least give some of the article's flavor. This will give those who do not read the story some information and, along with the headline and subheads that stand out, they will have some idea of what the story is about.

5. The pictures of the people may be clear, but where they are and what they are doing may not be evident. The cutline should build on the picture, add the necessary information, and clear up any ambiguities in order to advance the idea contained in the photograph.

6. Don't lift a line from the story to use as the cutline. You may want to present the same information but say it in a different way. Add information by giving the cutline a slightly new angle, if possible.

7. Photographs used more as illustrations may not need a cutline; for example, the silhouette of a woman kneeling before a cross.

8. Treat each cutline as you would the beginning of a story. Begin with words that will attract the reader's attention.

9. Keep cutlines short, using only two or three sentences at the most. An exception would be in the case of the picture that is not accompanied by a separate article. In that instance, the cutline could be somewhat longer.

10. You may want to use boldfaced type for the first significant words of the cutline. This is called a legend.

Making Use of the Address Section

If you plan to fold your newsletter and use one section for the address, your return address, and postage, consider placing a short, bright saying to the left of the address and under the return address. These can be boxed with a variety of decorative borders or placed on different styles of clip art signs for variety. Besides the recipients of the newsletter, think about how many hands it will pass through from the time you mail it until it reaches the home mailbox. Who knows? The saying you select may be just the thing to inspire or give food for thought to several postal employees along the way.

Here are some sample sayings:

- Fishermen don't "influence" fish—they catch them.
- The best exercise for the heart is lifting someone up.
- Because of God's boundless love, He became what we are in order that He might make us what He is.
- I asked Jesus, "How much do You love me?" "This much," He said. And He stretched out His arms and died.
- Seven days without prayer make one weak.
- You can't expect to keep your lights on if you turn off your generator.
- If God sends you on a stony path, He will provide you with strong shoes.
- Wise men still seek Him today.
- Jesus is the reason for the season.
- God always gives you His best . . . if you let Him make the choice.
- Come as you are. God will have you no other way.
- Responsibility—Response to the ability God has given you.
- Never doubt in the darkness what God has shown you in the light.
- God's promises are never broken by standing on them.

Putting the Newsletter Together

Once you have the various elements of your newsletter—stories, columns, illustrative material—then comes the challenge of putting it all together and making it fit. Of course, the most important story will go at the top of the front page, or, if you use columns, in the top left-hand corner. After that, take an inventory of the remaining stories and visual material to see where you can use what for the most pleasing effect.

Of course, computers have made the work of the newsletter editor much easier. Being able to move articles around to see what looks best is a significant asset. And having the tools to scan in visual material saves messy paste-up jobs and will result in a more professional-looking end product.

After you have the pages the way you want them, print out copies, put them aside, and then pick them up later. Try to look at the newsletter as though you have never seen it before. Is the overall effect pleasing? Have you avoided a lopsided appearance caused by too much weight—in color, type, or illustrative material—at the top, bottom, or side of a page? Does the format have a consistent appearance in both layout and typography throughout the publication, or does it have a "split personality" due to multiple typefaces and styles of visual material? An interesting thing to do is prop the pages up in a standing position and step back several feet. Look at them with squinted eyes to determine where the focal points of interest are. Are they the same as the areas you wish to emphasize? Getting the opinions of others whose viewpoint you trust can also be helpful.

Proofing the Newsletter

One of the most challenging parts of publishing a newsletter is making sure everything's correct. For some reason, mistakes often seem to hide until they're in print. Then they leap off the page in flaming letters.

Since the newsletter represents the ministry, it is especially important to catch every error. Computer aids, such as spell and grammar checkers are wonderful tools, but they can't find everything. An editor who must write and type the newsletter can hardly be expected to see all the typos and other mistakes. He or she should do the preliminary proofing, taking special care to check for accuracy of dates and numbers. After that, call on the services of another knowledgeable person. If possible, get two others to proof as insurance. Otherwise, mistakes will be there for all to see and may prove to be embarrassing. For example, one church had an item inviting readers to attend its Harvest Craft & "Bizarre" Show. No doubt the intent was not to give the impression that something weird was going to happen there.

Evaluating the Newsletter

Informal evaluation of your efforts can be done on a continuing basis. Listen and ask staff members and lay leaders to listen for comments about the newsletter and report back to you. Keep track of responses to requests. For example, find out how many volunteers signed up in keeping with a plea for helping hands in an article about a new program.

Discussing the newsletter's effectiveness at a staff meeting can result in helpful feedback in planning future issues. Questions about its appearance, success in covering each staff member's area of responsibility, and suggestions for future issues can also be covered.

Another approach would be organizing and holding a focus group to discuss the newsletter (focus groups are discussed in chapter 10). In this case, you probably would want to have several categories designated to cover the following items: masthead design, overall graphic appearance, use of visual material, effectiveness of continuing columns, scope of coverage, and helpfulness of publication.

On an annual basis, preferably toward the end of the year (but not the last issue of the year), you will want to include an evaluation form to be completed by readers and returned. Limit it to one page, and make it easy to complete. If you want completely honest opinions, don't ask the respondents to sign their names. Also, be sure to facilitate the questionnaire's return. For example, it can be folded with the name and address of the ministry and postage already in place on one section of the backside of the questionnaire. Chances are, the easier you make it to complete and mail, the better the response will be.

The form itself can consist of a few open-ended questions. Here are some examples:

About how many issues of (name of publication)
    have you received? ____ _____
Do you think the newsletter helps to
    keep you well informed? _____
Do you usually take the time to read it? _____
Do you think this newsletter is worthwhile? _____
What would you like to see in the newsletter
    that is not covered? _____
What other suggestions do you
    have for improvement? _____

Or you may prefer to take a more formal approach with multiple-choice questions that can be easily tallied and analyzed. Included might be questions like the following.

How much of the newsletter do you read?
    all_____ most_____ some_____ none_____
Do you save it for future reference?
    always_____ sometimes_____ never_____
How would you describe the interest level?
    excellent_____ good_____ fair_____ poor_____
How informative do you think it is?
    very_____ somewhat_____ not very_____
How would you rate the visual material?
    excellent_____ good_____ fair_____ poor_____

Then you might want to add a line for suggestions. One question on both types of surveys should be whether the recipient wishes to keep receiving the newsletter. This will help in keeping a current mailing list of those who really are interested in reading the publication.

The results of the survey should be reported in a subsequent newsletter. Also, they should be used in planning future issues (more information on conducting a survey can be found in chapter 10).

Publishing an effective newsletter can be expensive, time-consuming, and, often, frustrating. Is it worth the effort? Definitely! It can be one of the most useful tools available for creating goodwill, promoting understanding, and keeping people informed about the work and the purpose of your ministry.

Newsletter Tip Sheet

Contact person_____

Phone_____ day_____ evening_____

Ministry area and head_____

What is the activity? _____

When will it happen?   Date _____Time _____

Where? _____

Who is involved? _____

_____

Why is it being done? _____

_____

How is it being done? _____

_____

Unusual features _____

_____

_____

_____

Date submitted _____

13 Developing Memorable Publication Pieces

E very printed piece carrying the name of your church or ministry makes a definite statement above and beyond the words it contains. It speaks loudly and clearly to the quality, attention to detail, and professionalism of your organization. Planning and producing excellent publication pieces takes time and talent and requires an investment of money. The positive impression that a memorable brochure or flyer makes, however, cannot be measured in dollars and cents. It's invaluable. (More information and suggestions relating to various publication aspects, such as photographs, typefaces and type-sizes, may be found in chapter 12, "Publishing a Dynamic Newsletter.")

Four principles should be considered in developing a kind of trademark look for your publication pieces. First, decide on an ink color and a background stock color for use in main pieces, such as stationery, business cards, and brochures. Be sure there is enough contrast between the ink and background for copy to be easily read. Some currently popular choices are burgundy on pale gray, turquoise on cream, and dark blue on light gray.

Second, choose a contemporary-looking typeface for the name of your church. A traditional style may give a subconscious "dated" reaction, while a modern typeface will give the impression of your being able to relate to today's challenges. Paying an artist (or enlisting the services of one in your church) to design the style and arrangement of the letters will be worth the investment.

Third, use a professionally designed logo that visually captures the main focus of your ministry to go with the church name on all pieces and even on your church sign. Fourth, if you decide to use a church or ministry motto, be sure that it succinctly sums up your mission in a few words, and place it on all important pieces.

Consistently making use of these four principles on most major publication efforts will result in a certain "look" that readily identifies your church at a glance.

Stationery

Think about the numerous places your stationery makes a one-on-one call. While you don't have to choose the most expensive stock available, paper of excellent quality is essential to making a good impression.

The usual placement of the letterhead is at the top of the page. This probably permits the greatest ease and versatility of use. Margins can be widened and extended toward the bottom of the page, especially if you need a little more space to get your message on one page. Another possibility is to use the name of the church with its logo in the upper right-hand corner of the page. The address, phone number, pastor's name, and so forth, may then be placed at the bottom of the page, perhaps with a heavy line above it.

Some groups prefer running the information down the left side of the page. Drawbacks are limiting the size of type that can be used for the organization's name and having to bring the left margin in. This arrangement also eats up some of the space that might be used for the letter.

Be sure to include the area code in the telephone number of your church or parachurch organization. Also, since so many people are now communicating by fax and e-mail, having your numbers printed on your stationery may prove convenient for the recipient and shows that you use contemporary approaches. Also, if you have a web site, include that address as well.

Business Cards

Using the same elements, colors, and typface that you use on your stationery gives a unified appearance and presents a visually identifiable cue on business cards. All staff members' business cards should be identical with the exception, of course, of the name and position.

Accomplishing Your Purpose with Printed Pieces

Whether you're producing a brochure, a flyer, a poster, or some other type of printed piece, here are some important questions to keep in mind:

What is my purpose? Ask yourself, "What exactly am I trying to accomplish with this piece?" Be able to answer the question succinctly. Then carefully select every element for that particular piece to meet your goal. The more elements that reinforce your intention—items such as type style, visual material, and colors—the closer you'll come to hitting your target, and the clearer and more powerful your message will be.

Who is my audience? Whom are you trying to reach? Describe the people you think would be interested in this particular program or activity. How old are they? What are their interests? How would this fit into their lifestyle? Then gear your material to that particular audience.

What's in it for the reader? Again, think about the type of people who will be reading your material. What are they looking for or needing in their life that your publication will fulfill? What are the benefits? Appeal to emotional needs and concerns.

How can I make this appear relevant to today and to current events? Perhaps a tie-in with an upcoming election or a controversial local issue can be made. Perhaps a testimonial from a well-known person might be possible for use.

What are the best methods for distribution? Are there places that this particular group gathers (such as a neighborhood recreation center for upper elementary students) where you might be able to place or have someone hand out information? Is the program general enough so that mailing to every household in one or more zip codes might be desirable?

How many do I need to have printed? Your answer to the previous question will help you estimate, but always plan to have extra copies run.

The Brochure

One of the most important printed pieces for your ministry is the brochure. This publication gives vital information about your church or ministry, its location, its programs, its outreaches, and, perhaps, its approach to worship.

Paper of good quality, excellent pictures, carefully worded copy, and an attractive layout are essential. Since the brochure may be used over a relatively long period of time, careful attention should be given to every detail. Photography, writing, and design should indicate professionalism.

A four-color brochure (allowing you to use full color pictures) is great but also expensive. Also to some, it may appear to have cost "too much" for a church or ministry. If four-color would be stretching the budget, consider using two colors of ink—black and another color. With two colors, you can use screens behind certain parts of copy or on photographs, producing different shades of gray and the other color. You thus can produce variety and the appearance of using more colors than you actually have.

Effective brochures can be produced in a variety of sizes. A commonly used approach is a 9-by-12-inch sheet, printed in three columns on each side of the page. The sheet is then folded twice, resulting in six panels in a 4-by-9-inch brochure that can be mailed in a regular business-size envelope.

Another popular size, which is less expensive to produce, is an 8½-by-11-inch page, also folded in thirds so that it fits into a business envelope. A variation that makes a sheet this size appear to be larger is to have the first and second panels 3¹³⁄₁₆-inches wide and the third one 3⅛-inches wide. On the inside of the brochure, print may run the width of the second and third panels. However, because of the smaller size of the third panel, approximately a ⅜-inch vertical strip will remain showing on the second panel. An effective possibility is to run a strip of color down the page in that space with type reversed out vertically with a heading such as "Programs Offered." While these configurations would usually be used vertically, they could also be used horizontally.

Suggestions for Effective Brochures

Here are several ideas you may want to consider in developing an attention-getting, appealing brochure:

1. Use the front section of the brochure as the title page. Use bold elements—large type for the church or ministry name, an enlarged logo, the pastor's or ministry head's name in type slightly smaller than the organization's name, along with the motto or mission statement. At the bottom of the brochure, give the address, phone number, including the area code, the fax number, and e-mail and website addresses. If the mailing address is different from the street address, include both. In case the church is located on a side street, a reference to a thoroughfare it abuts would be helpful.
2. Consider using an asymmetrical layout for the front panel for a contemporary look.
3. Don't pack every whit of space with type. Use white space effectively for a pleasing visual effect and so that the reader will not feel overwhelmed by a gray-looking page.
4. Use a current, smiling picture of the pastor or ministry head.
5. Feature close-up action pictures of people doing something interesting, and crop them to present the heart and message of the picture.
6. Gain variety by using boxes around a picture or a particular section of type. Other ways to prevent boredom are through the use of boldface type, screens, section titles in a different color of ink, and underlining.
7. Avoid using acronyms, unless the entire name has already been used in the brochure and the acronym given, such as: Women's Service League (WSL).
8. Ask several people, including some who know little or nothing about your ministry, to read the copy for clarity, correctness, and interest.

What to Include

Assume that the readers will know absolutely nothing about your program and that this is your opportunity to inform them in an interesting, exciting, and concise manner. These are some elements you may want to include, depending on your ministry:

- service times, and times and dates of other continuing programs
- education, experience, and awards of the pastor or ministry head
- the vision that you believe God has given for the church or ministry, along with a brief history of it
- denominational affiliation of the church, if any (if none, include a reference to the fact that it is nondenominational, independent, or interdenominational)
- a small map of the immediate area, if the location is difficult to find, complete with indication of the northerly direction
- a description of the main programs offered by the church
- information about special ministries and outreaches of the church
- missionaries and/or mission projects that the church supports
- an explanation of out-of-the-ordinary approaches to worship, such as raising hands, with scriptural bases for such practices

Uses for a Brochure

A brochure can play numerous roles in the life and work of your ministry. Here are some of them.

- Mail the brochure along with a letter of invitation to new people in the neighborhood.
- Include the brochure in a visitor's packet.
- Give copies of the brochure to members to use in inviting friends and family members.
- Provide copies of the brochure to the local chamber of commerce for distribution to interested citizens.
- Mail the brochure to those who inquire by phone about the church.
- Give the brochure to other ministers to inform them about your work.
- Try to get Welcome Wagon-type programs to hand the brochure out to newcomers.

The Visitor's Packet

The visitor's packet can take different forms—perhaps an envelope or a folder with pockets that can contain several items. Here's another good place to carry out the color theme, type style, and logo from your stationery and business cards. On the front you might want to have printed just the name of your church and "Visitor's Packet," or you might want to be less formal and use something like: "Welcome! We're glad you're here."

Inside you should place your beautiful brochure, the latest church newsletter, and flyers about upcoming events. As a small gift, you may want to include a pen with the name and address of the church on it. This is also convenient in case newcomers don't have a pen handy for completing the enclosed visitor's card.

The visitor's card should request vital information about the newcomer and her or his family. (For more information concerning this, see the form entitled "Visitor's Card," which you can find on page 181.) Be sure to ask visitors how they heard about your church. This information can help you to evaluate various communication approaches.

Flyers

Sophia Tarila, in her book entitled *Flyers That Work,* says that "you have approximately one to three seconds to make an impression and get the passerby's attention" with your flyer.[1] Her observation says volumes about the importance of the piece being eye-catching and interesting-looking. Elements must be bold, colorful, and intriguing or the flyer won't get a second chance to make a good impression.

The headline is probably the most important element of a flyer. Tarila says that 90 percent of response depends on the headline.[2] It must visually demand attention. This means it should be no smaller than thirty-six-points in size and be in boldface type. The message must also capture the reader's interest. Short and punchy is good. It should convey the idea, *Hey! This is for you!*

Being clever can be good—up to a point. Just don't be so cute that the message is obscured. Also, avoid negatives. Feature the benefit to the reader. All caps give a more formal look to a piece, while upper and lower case are more easily read. The name of the event, workshop, or whatever should be used either in the headline or in a subhead, and this should be the next size of type smaller than the headline.

Visual material is also important and should be large and attention getting. A compelling photograph that illustrates the activity is probably best, but creative artwork can also be effective.

Here are some other suggestions:

- What are the features of the event or program? You may want to use a bullet before each one and list them one under the other for aesthetic effect and to set them apart.
- Other variations to give relief to the eye include italics, boldface type,

underlining, and all caps for a word you especially want to emphasize.
- You do not always have to use complete sentences.
- In planning your layout, be aware that a vertical format connotes action, while the horizontal layout gives an impression of calmness and rest.
- A symmetrical layout is more formal and traditional than an asymmetrical one.
- Body text should be set in no smaller than 10-point type. If the audience is senior citizens, you might want to go to a larger type.
- You should use the same typeface throughout the flyer except, perhaps, for the headline and subhead. You might also want to use the larger typeface at the end for a message such as, *Enroll Now!*
- If appropriate, use a call for action. Some examples are: Space Is Limited. Make Reservations Today. Volunteer Today. Bring Your Rummage-Sale Items to the Church Saturday. Send Your Check to Help a Child Go to Summer Camp. Return This Coupon for a Free Tape.
- If you're asking for a reply by mail, make responding as easy as possible. Provide a stamped, self-addressed envelope or a card with a postage-paid stamp on it.
- Be sure that your phone number is prominently displayed in large type.
- Put A.M. or P.M. by a time, especially if there is a possibility that there could be confusion.
- Start in plenty of time, allowing for delays in photo processing (if a picture is to be used), printing, and mail delivery (especially if your event is near a national holiday).

Posters

Posters, which can be placed in a variety of places, can be effective in helping to promote a specific event. Here are some points to remember:

- Limit the copy to only a few lines set in large, bold type. Posters have to grab the attention of the passerby and convey a message in a matter of seconds.
- Ample use of white space helps the words to stand out.
- Use especially interesting visual material.
- Use bright, attention-getting colors.
- In deciding on the size, keep in mind that a small poster can be used in a greater number and a greater variety of spots. One that is large, say 16-by-20 inches, might take up too much space on the average-size bulletin board.

- Contact businesses, recreation centers, other churches (for instance, for a self-help program not offered there), laundromats, service groups, restaurants, waiting rooms, and libraries (if it's an educational program) about putting your poster in their facilities. If the poster is to be placed on a window, be sure to put two back-to-back so that they may be read from both sides.
- If you do place posters in public places, be sure to have someone go the rounds and remove them once the event is over.

Getting the Most for Your Money

If you're on a tight budget (as most nonprofit organizations are), you may want to consider these approaches to saving money on printed pieces.

- Black ink is cheaper to use than a color. On a flyer or a piece that you do not plan to use over a long period of time, try using a colorful stock of paper with black ink.
- The extra charge for using colored ink is due to the fact that the press must be cleaned when a different color is used. However, some printers have certain "color days" when no extra charge is made. For example, on Monday they may use brown ink, on Tuesday, blue ink, and so on. Check around, and have your piece printed on the day when there is no extra charge for the color you wish to use.
- Use a common size stock, such as 8½-by-11 inches or 8½-by-14 inches. Going to an unusual size will result in having to purchase larger, more expensive stock plus an extra charge for sizing the paper. Use your imagination to configure common sizes in interesting ways.
- Avoid cut-outs (where a building or person's head is partially cut out) and embossed pieces. While they may look interesting and produce a striking effect, they are also expensive to produce.
- Carefully select your paper for a quality look without picking the most expensive product. Costs can vary greatly. Some people think that a publication piece that looks too costly can be detrimental, for it may appear to be wasteful of precious funds that have been contributed to the ministry.
- If at all possible, have the piece "camera ready" before taking it to the printer. The less printer has to do before running it, the lower your cost.
- For best quality, submit your job for printing on a computer disk. A printer's high resolution image setter (film output unit) produces a quality four to five times higher than the laser printer used in a typical office. Along with the computer disk, include a hard copy (printed on paper by your laser printer) of the final

version of the file you are submitting on the disk. The hard copy serves as a reference for the printing company to ensure that the job will be printed exactly as you want it. Be sure to keep a copy of the computer disk and the hard copy.

- Have the printer run a "proof" of a major piece so that you can check for any errors.
- Make absolutely certain that the piece is exactly the way you want it before you have it printed. Once you have given your "okay," you will have to pay for the run even if you can't use it.
- Keep pictures that have been screened in a morgue file for possible use in the future to avoid another screening cost. This is especially true of bust shots of staff members, missionaries, and frequent speakers at the church, which you may have occasion to use periodically.
- Plan ahead so that a rush doesn't have to be placed on your printing job. Most companies charge extra for a quick turnaround.
- If the piece must be folded, have the printer deliver the job to you flat and have staff members or volunteers do the folding. Be sure, though, that they do it carefully and precisely. Otherwise, the total effect will be ruined.

An excellent approach to improving all your publications is to start a collection of outstanding and not-so-good newsletters, brochures, flyers, visitor's packets, stationery, calling cards, posters, and so on. Evaluating what is appealing and not so appealing about others' efforts will sharpen your eye and, perhaps, give you some ideas to use in polishing your own efforts.

Visitor's Card

Date _____

Name _____

Address _____

Phone number _____

Age range: Under 20_____ 21–30_____ 31–40_____

41–55_____ Over 55_____

Church affiliation or denominational preference _____

Names and ages of children _____

_____

How did you hear about our church? _____

Comments _____

_____

---

14 Communication with a Price Tag—Advertising

While publication pieces, such as newsletters and brochures definitely cost something in printing and people resources, other approaches—newspaper ads, billboards, and direct mail campaigns, for example—present an additional bill, unless, of course you can get space donated.

Advertising dollars can mount up rapidly. It's extremely important to define your audience precisely and to determine your specific message and which medium will most effectively deliver it to your audience. These are some of the questions to ask to enable your advertising bullet to be aimed precisely at your target, rather than just firing a shotgun blast in the dark and hoping it will hit your target:

- Whom am I trying to reach? The Christian who is a newcomer to the community and looking for a church home? The Christian who is unchurched? The unbeliever who has never heard the Good News but is searching for meaning in life? The skeptic who is convinced that religion is not for her or him? The hard-core, bitter antagonist who has an axe to grind?
- What age range am I looking at? Besides the faith status and outlook of the target audience, where are they located generationally?
- What is the marital status of the target audience? Married? Married with school-age children? Single? Single parent? Divorced? Widowed?
- What is the educational and career background of the target audience? Minimum wage? Blue collar? Human services? Professional? High tech?

Developing a profile of those with whom you want to communicate makes good sense, and it also saves time and money. Picture the target audience and what their life is like. What are their needs? What are their aspirations? If your picture is fuzzy, seek out some people who fit the profile and talk with them. Ask them what's important to them, what they like, and what turns them off. Also, much has been written about the lifestyles and mindsets of various generations, such as baby boomers and generation X. Do your homework before you reach for your wallet.

After you have your target audience clearly in mind, consider what kind of message will grab their attention. Using religious symbols in an ad aimed at the unsaved probably will not make a connection. Nor will copy that appeals to altruistic motives have much impact on a generation that is characterized by materialism. What words will catch their attention and interest? What kind of art will appeal to them?

Which Medium Will Be Most Effective for Your Message?

After delineating your audience and deciding how your message can be most effectively presented to that particular group, delivery systems should be given careful consideration.

A media mix of several approaches will probably produce the best result. In their article, "Spirit-filled Marketing," Kermit L. Netteburg and George Powell observe, "The mix of advertising through direct mail and through paid media adds credibility—and crowds." The late J. L. Shuler referred to various approaches as prongs in a rake—"the more you have, the more people you'll rake in." For example, handbills alone are not as effective as handbills reinforced with newspaper or radio advertising. People question whether the handbill can be real, for they haven't heard about it on radio or seen it in the newspaper.[1]

George Barna agrees with the approach of mixing media. He says, "Most communications experts will tell you that your best media strategy is one that relies upon a blend of several media to reach your desired audience. This multimedia strategy enables you to reach people in different contexts, with different messages geared to making the same impact and retards the potential for commercial wearout."[2]

Television reaches a wide audience, depending on the particular station and its viewership. However, it delivers more of a shotgun approach, unless a particular station specifically targets a segment of the population. For example, a station broadcasting in Spanish would definitely reach the Hispanic community in your area. Stations that feature religious programming probably would be a waste of money in trying to reach the unsaved and the unchurched. However, carefully placed television ads can be more specifically aimed at certain groups. An ad broadcast on a commercial station just after a particularly racy show might stand a good chance of being seen by the cynic. Advertising run immediately after a Billy Graham Crusade would in all probability be seen mostly by Christians.

Radio is much more specific in its programming. Stations are aiming to reach a certain segment of the population. They have the profile of their listeners carefully developed and their material and music tailored to their interests. Listen to various stations to determine whether their programming appeals to those you want to reach. Pay attention to their commercials. Call them if you're undecided. They'll be able to help you determine how effective your message will be on their station. Don't squander your resources by running ads on Christian radio stations if you're trying to reach the unsaved.

Newspapers also reach a wide audience. However, younger generations are not reading the daily newspaper as frequently as older people. Netteburg and Powell say, "Electronic media attract younger audiences; print media draw older audiences."[3] Weeklies featuring hometown or area news within a city, of course, have smaller readerships and are subscribed to more by settled adults. Then there are many newspapers that appeal to a segment of the population, such as business publications and occupational journals.

Placement, again, is critically important. Running your ad on the religion page will probably only reach Christians who attend a church or who are looking for a church home. If you specifically want to reach men, perhaps the sports section is your best choice. Try advertising a play or musical in the entertainment guide or section. But, if you want to reach the most readers of a daily as possible, Netteburg and Powell suggest that you opt for an upper right-hand spot in section A, and that, if you can only afford one ad, run it on Thursday. They also suggest that you provide camera-ready ads "to limit the potential for errors or 'sabotage.'"[4] Big-city dailies also have various editions. Running your ad in an edition that covers the area your church serves makes sense and saves money. Advertising in the state edition of a big city newspaper would be expensive and, for the most part, far less effective.

Shopper newspapers and others that are free and, perhaps, delivered to most residences in your area may provide good coverage. However, as a rule, they are not as seriously read as is a newspaper to which readers subscribe. Netteburg and Powell say, "Ads in paid newspapers draw better than those in freebies or shoppers. Paid newspapers have more credibility. Besides, your ad will get lost in the clutter of colorful inserts and commercial ads in a shopper."[5]

Christian newspapers usually fall into the freebie category as well. While distribution points may include grocery and drug stores and other locations in the community, there are probably more picked up at churches than anywhere else. Most Christian newspapers are monthly publications and so provide a long shelf life for your message to be read. You would want to limit advertising in this medium to events of interest to Christians, such as a seminar on marriage from a Christian perspective or a concert featuring a Christian music recording star.

Newspaper church directories are likely places to attract the attention of newcomers to the area and those looking for a church. Most ads in church directories have a sameness of appearance about them. What can you do to make yours stand out? Since ads are nearly always run vertically in one column, you might consider placing yours horizontally in two columns. You might experiment with screening the background for a different appearance. Of course, reversing out some of the type also results in an unusual look, but, due to the porous quality of newsprint and the small size of the letters, it may come out difficult or even impossible to read.

Billboards can prove effective, depending on their location. Of course, the more desirable the location and the greater the flow of traffic, the more expensive space will be. However, if a billboard has remained vacant for several weeks, there's a good possibility that a lower rate may be negotiated. And some companies give a price break to a nonprofit organization. Billboards-by-the-day are available for rental in most metropolitan areas. However, they are expensive and probably would not be cost-effective unless in advertising something like a huge, admission-paid concert of a major recording star.

Direct mail can be sent exactly where you want it to go. Corky Rogers, in his book entitled *Marketing Your Ministry,* cites these advantages of direct mail: pinpointing your specific market publics most likely to be interested in your ministry, capturing reader's attention with no conflicting media, and facilitating fast, simple response by the recipient via return of business-reply cards or envelopes.[6]

The secret here is developing a mailing list that will hit your target. No doubt your own membership and friends of the church mailing list will be used most frequently. Even that requires constant attention in order to keep it up to date. However, if you wish to reach out beyond those boundaries to the community or farther, you will probably need to work with a broker-mailing service to ensure that the selected subjects possess the greatest number of concrete characteristics directly related to your purpose. Lists may be purchased or rented depending on your future plans. Not surprisingly, mail addressed to a specific person by name rather than just "resident" receives more attention. Studies have shown that one of the tasks people look forward to the most each day is opening their mail.

Marriage mail or cooperative mail can be sent to every household with a mailbox in selected zip codes. Probably on a Tuesday or Wednesday you receive in your home mailbox a packet of mail in a folder containing grocery-store and other types of ads. While few churches use this approach, it is definitely the most cost-effective way to get your message delivered to each mail box in the area you wish to reach. Most companies that offer this service will help with the design of your piece, have it printed for you, and include it in their package for about one-fifth to one-sixth the cost of a first-class postage stamp. And, of course, you also save the expense of envelopes and having them addressed.

While marriage mail cannot be targeted to a special group, it can do a good job of blanketing your entire area at a bargain price. Consider one church that had recently moved into a new building several miles from its former location. The congregation created a cheery-looking flier that invited recipients to the new church. The flier was sent by marriage mail to two zip codes encompassing the new locale. Several people came to a service carrying the flyer and said something like, "I got this invitation in the mail." The consensus of opinion is that this was an effective means of reaching a wide audience at a relatively low cost and with minimum effort.

Handbills are another approach to blanket a specified area by placing them on house and apartment doors. This requires contracting for paid help to do the door-to-door legwork, or a team of committed volunteers. The cold call or pop-in visit from house to house that was popular in years past is used less frequently today. Perhaps one reason is the public's association of this type of approach with Jehovah's Witnesses and Mormons. Another consideration in some areas would be the safety of those calling on and going inside a stranger's house. Rogers says, "On the whole, it [home visitation without notice] is found to almost always be ineffective [less than 3 percent response] for the effort expended."[7]

Classified advertising in the Yellow Pages has a built-in audience of those who are looking for information about churches. Classified advertising, especially display ads giving more information than the name, address, and phone number, is not cheap and should be carefully planned, for it cannot be changed for a whole year. Visitors to the area and newcomers are trying to find basic facts, such as address, service times, and the name of the pastor.

In addition to the address, locating your church in relation to a major intersection will be well worth the extra words. In a metropolitan area, be sure to indicate the city. Any special services that your church offers, such as sign-language interpretation for the hearing impaired, should be included. Display advertising with some art will definitely draw the eye of the scanner, besides providing vital desired information. Using a different background color from the usual yellow and an additional color will guarantee that your ad will be noticed. Of course, it also costs more.

Moving advertising doesn't just refer to an emotional appeal but also describes what it actually does. Have you ever thought about having a billboard on the back or side of a bus on certain lines near your church? Another possibility is placard advertising inside the bus. Church ads can also be painted on benches at bus stops in prominent spots. A less expensive way to get your message moving is to have magnetic signs made that can be placed on the cars of staff members and church members who are open to the idea. (One congregation uses its church bus as a moving billboard with the legend on the back: "Follow me to _____ Church." They also periodically get permission to park the bus with large signs on the sides in various shopping centers.[8]) Also, bumper stickers can be effective in getting your church's name seen and recognized throughout the community. Another possibility for ads on wheels is the back of taxis.

Booths are suggested as one possible approach by Dan Danford. In his article, "Targeting Your Church Advertising," he tells of a church's renting a booth at a local baby fair to publicize a Parent's Day Out. It required having materials designed and printed and people to staff the booth throughout the fair. But a steady stream of interested parents— exactly the ones they were trying to reach—came by, talked, and picked up brochures and fliers. He says, "The baby fair was a real communication success."[9]

How Much Will It Cost?

The variables in advertising price tags are countless and ever changing. Here are some principles about costs of various media to keep in mind:

Broadcast media advertising costs are tied to the number of listeners for their particular station. The greater the number of people that they can demonstrate they reach through scientific ratings, the more they will charge to help you reach their listeners. Costs are usually also determined by placement. Radio charges more during drive time, while television ups the rates during prime-time viewing hours.

With its advantage of sight and sound, television certainly wins the award for the most sophisticated approach to advertising. Usually, though, for churches and other ministries, putting their message on a major television station is prohibitively expensive. With the advent of more and more channels, however, some stations offer less-prohibitive rates. Viewership will probably not be as great and will probably be quite difficult to predict, especially with many viewers opting to channel surf during advertisements. In addition to the air time, production costs for the commercial can also become quite expensive. This is particularly true if your spot requires an off-premises camera crew. Commercial production companies also charge high rates.

All-in-all, short of having an "angel" to pay the cost, television advertising is just too pricey for most churches. But it can be very effective. Donald M. Morgan, pastor of First Church of Christ in Wethersfield, Connecticut, recalls that one time more than half of a large class of new members first learned about his church through a TV ad following Schuller's "Hour of Power." As a result, he says that periodic television advertising is a regular part of their outreach effort.[10]

Unlike television, most radio stations include production costs for a commercial in the package you purchase. However, using a radio station personality in a large market may require a talent fee. Smaller stations usually make no charge. Besides time placement, your cost will be determined by the frequency of your spot, and the length, which may be ten, thirty, or sixty seconds. Frequency discounts are based on the number of programs or spot announcements, while dollar-volume discounts depend on total dollars spent. Corky Rogers warns, "Don't waste your money if you are not in radio to run a series of spots in various segments of time. . . . Unless you buy frequency, you are most likely to miss the majority of listeners."[11]

Newspaper advertising prices are also based, in large part, on readership. That's why different editions in a big city daily should be checked carefully. Your advertising can be maintained at a lower rate while you still reach your target audience. Frequency of publication and geographical considerations are also factored in. Cost is determined by agate lines. An agate line is 1¼ of a column inch that is 1-by-2 inches wide; in other words, there are fourteen agate lines in a one-inch, one-colum wide ad.

Some smaller newspapers sell space by column inches. Rates are referred to as open or flat. Flat rates are usually used for a one-time publication, while open rates provide discounts. Discounts are offered on the basis of agate lines purchased during a given time period. This is called a bulk contract rate and provides for discount scales, depending on the number of lines used. Earned rates involving no set contract can often be negotiated. After running so many inches for a length of time, you may be eligible for a discount. Some newspapers offer a so-called poverty rate for nonprofits, but probably fewer do so now than did in the past. Discounts may also be offered for cash payment. It can pay to simply ask what discounts are available.

Direct mail costs can be kept to a minimum in several ways. If your piece is just a letter or a brochure, consider making it a self-mailer by reserving one panel of the reverse side for your mailing label. You not only save the cost of the envelope but also time in stuffing the envelopes. James A. Vitti says, though, "Self-mailers usually don't generate as many responses as the 'classic' format for a variety of reasons. Primarily, it looks less personal and more like 'junk mail.'"[12] Another way to save labor is to use window envelopes and design and fold your piece so that the address shows through the window. Of course, if other pieces are to be included, such as a return coupon, an envelope will have to be used. Keep in mind the economic importance of limiting your mailing piece to a total weight of one ounce or less.

Billboard advertising prices are based on the size, location, and number purchased. Rates also will vary from place to place. A standard-sized billboard is about twenty feet long and nine feet high. This is called a "24-sheet" poster, a term that originated when lithograph presses were so small that twenty-four separate sheets had to be printed and then put together to cover the entire board. Today they are composed of about ten sheets pasted on the billboard to form the message. Some boards are somewhat larger and may be referred to as "30-sheet" billboards. Another alternative is the "junior panel" or mini-billboard. These are smaller and are usually posted at street level. The usual period of posting is one month, which gives an opportunity to try to evaluate outdoor advertising's effectiveness without signing a long-term contract. There is also the painted bulletin where the sign is painted directly on the board by an artist. The painted bulletin will last longer and is usually sold under a one-year contract.

How Can I Make My Message Stand Out?

Here are some possibilities for various approaches:

Bumper stickers should have the name of your church and, perhaps, its logo only. That's all the other drivers will be able to read. Adding any other information, such as the address, will decrease the effectiveness because of the smaller type.

Billboard, bus exterior messages can contain a few more words but not many. Try to limit your copy to no more than seven words with professionally done artwork and the name of your church. Ideally you will have one large illustration and one short copy block with vivid colors. Type must be plain and strong. Viewed from a distance of three hundred feet, your entire sign will be perceived as one inch high. And your audience is rolling along at high speed. Keep in mind that your board is going to be seen by many of the same people day after day. Will it wear well during rush hour if it's located on a freeway?

Handbills have to be interest-piquing or they'll be tossed aside. Here are some ideas using an 8½-by-11-inch piece of paper folded to make four 8½-by-5½ panels:

- On the front, scattered pieces of a jigsaw puzzle of the pastor's face with "Puzzled?" in large letters at the bottom. On the inside, the same picture of the pastor put back together with the words: "Put the pieces together at _____ [name of the church, address, phone number]."
- On the front, a picture of a woman looking in a shattered mirror with "Living in shattered dreams?" at the bottom. Inside, the same woman, smiling, looking in a regular mirror with the words: "Pick up the pieces at _____ [name of the church, address, phone number]."
- On the front, a picture of a man with a puzzled expression at a crossroads with several signs pointing in different directions with "Need direction?" at the bottom. Inside, the man starting to walk confidently with the words: "Get on the right path at _____ [name of the church, address, phone number]."
- On the front, a picture of a woman with a disgusted expression on her face looking under the hood of a car with "Can't seem to get started?" at the bottom. Inside, the same woman behind the wheel, smiling with the words: "Recharge your spiritual battery at _____ [name of the church, address, phone number]."
- On the front, a picture of a man's face out of focus in front of a city skyline that is in focus with "Life out of focus?" at the bottom. Inside, the same man's face in focus with skyline out of focus behind him with the words: "Remove the blur at _____ [name of church, address, phone number]."
- Picture of a disgusted-looking woman in baseball attire who has just struck at the ball with "Feel like you just struck out?" at the bottom. Inside, the same woman, smiling, with her foot on first base with the words "Get on base at _____ [name of church, address, phone number]."

Newspaper ads will be more attention-getting if you use some imagination to grab the reader's attention. Stereotypical symbols, such as a church steeple, will probably not attract the people you are trying to reach. Consider using an unusual border in all your ads, so that the reader will come to identify that border with your ministry as it becomes like a secondary logo.

Here are some ideas for ads with thought-provoking messages:

- Picture of a man playing a violin with broken strings with, "Has the music gone out of your life?" and the name, address, and phone number of the church.
- Picture of a woman's hand plugging an extension cord into a wall plug with "Make your spiritual connection at _____ [name of church, address, phone number]."
- Picture of a man's hand with finger on hold button on telephone with "Feel like your life's on hold?" and the name, address, and phone number of the church.
- Picture of a woman's hand unlocking a door with a key with "Find the key to abundant living at _____ [name of church, address, phone number]."
- Picture of a child with front teeth missing, looking in a mirror, with "Is something missing in your life? Fill the gap at _____ [name of church, address, phone number]."
- Picture of an archer aiming an arrow at the target with "Get your life on target at _____ [name of church, address, phone number]."
- Picture of a man inside an old car bogged down in ruts with "In a rut? Get out of it at _____ [name of church, address, phone number]."
- Picture of a child looking out through spread fingers with "Take a good look at what's really important," and the name of the church, address, and phone number.
- Picture of a hand flipping down light switch with "Turned off by religion? Get a new perspective at _____ [name of church, address, phone number]."

Try using an unusually shaped ad to gain attention. These are some possibilities for a one-column wide by 13½ inches ad designed to fill an entire column of a shopper newspaper:

- Picture of a ballet dancer stretching with, "Stretch your faith with us at _____ [name of church, address, phone number, service times]."
- Picture of a nurse measuring height of child with, "Come grow with us at _____ [name of church, address, phone number, service times]."
- Picture of a basketball player jumping and making a basket with, "Aim higher with us at _____ [name of church, address, phone number, service times]."

- Picture of a child walking on stilts with, "Walk taller with us at _____ [name of church, address, phone number, service times]."

Direct mail will usually get the receiver's attention, at least for the moment. The more personal your piece looks, the better your chances of having it read through. Generally, every touch of personalization you can use will add impact to your message. Addressing a letter by name to the recipient is ideal. Signing the letter in blue ink is good. If there are too many pieces to sign by hand, consider having the signature printed in blue ink for a more personalized touch.

Use simple words and short sentences. Write in a conversational manner as though you are just talking to the recipient. Use short paragraphs for easier readability. The first paragraph is critical to the success of the whole letter. Get to the point quickly, highlighting the benefits to the reader. Continue to weave in the benefits that the reader will receive from doing what you are suggesting. Tell the reader exactly what you want him to do and make it easy for him to do it by including a reply device, such as a postage-paid postcard or one with a stamp attached.

Vitti says, "People tend to scan letters, so we should put our main message in the letter three times: at the beginning, at the end, and in the postscript. Always use a P.S. It's the second-most-read part of the letter."[13]

Some Important Advertising Principles

Habakkuk 2:2 in *The Living Bible* reads, "Write my answer on a billboard, large and clear, so that anyone can read it at a glance and rush to tell the others." That's good advice, especially in today's society when everyone seems to be rushing around from place to place with their minds and emotions assaulted with dozens of messages from every side. How can you compete for their time and interest?

Principle # 1:

KISS. Keep it simple, saint. Limit your piece to a few bold elements that can be quickly seen and easily understood. Use familiar words that are easily grasped.

Principle #2:

Make it personal. Tell the receivers of your message what's in it for them as individuals. How are they going to benefit? Professional marketers know that people don't buy product features. They buy benefits. George Barna says, "The key to grabbing the readers' attention is to appeal to their self-interest."[14] Yale University researchers discovered that the twelve most persuasive words are: *you, love, discovery, proven, easy, guarantee, health, money, new, results, safety,* and *save.*[15]

Principle #3:

Avoid religious clichés both in language and art. Use symbols that have a contemporary look and that make a statement about your church's ability to relate to the challenges of day-to-day living in a complex society.

Principle #4:

Use imaginative ways to hook the reader's attention. However, don't be so clever that the message is not taken seriously, is obscured, or is ignored.

Principle #5:

Don't promise more than you can deliver. Barna comments, "Today's consumers have been burned often enough that they no longer take the claims of advertisers at face value. . . . Whatever claim your headline makes must seem reasonable and must have the facts to back it up."[16]

Also, don't use advertising that creates a false impression of any kind. One church aired radio spots that had a Woody the Woodpecker type character saying funny things that might have given the impression that going there was just one laugh after another with little serious purpose. Actually, the opposite was true.

Principle #6:

Be positive. Barna says that people do not like negative advertising. "Such approaches raise the prospect of conflict in the mind of the reader, causing the potential audience to steer clear of the situation. . . . The negative slant may position the sender of that negative message to gain an image as being one who is confrontational, defensive or aggressive."[17]

Principle #7:

Get to the point. People aren't going to take the time to figure out what you're trying to say, and they're unwilling to read a five-page letter that could have been said better in four paragraphs. Thus, edit mercilessly to get rid of extraneous words.

Principle #8:

Evaluate what you're doing. Effective evaluation is not easy. Part of the problem is the cumulative effect of advertising. Perhaps you drive by the same billboard every day for weeks without noticing it. One day, though, you read it and recognize its message. Perhaps you hear and see the same message from several different sources before you pay attention. If someone asked, you might not be able to tell them where you saw or heard it. You just know that you received the message somewhere along the way.

While evaluation of various advertising approaches is difficult, there are things that can be done. It takes the continuing involvement and reporting of several people. A key person is the one who answers the church phone. Any inquiries about the church's location, service times, or about an upcoming event should be responded to with the information, but then followed with something like, "May I ask how you found out about our church?" or, "How did you hear about the concert?" The answers should be duly recorded with the date and time of the call and the person's name, if known.

Other people in a prime position for collecting and reporting feedback are greeters and ushers. Train them to ask visitors casually how they learned about the church or particular program and then to write that information down and send it to the church office. Sunday school teachers and other small-group leaders can also be effective in getting feedback. Another approach is asking for a show of hands at an event to questions such as: "How many of you heard our radio spot? How many of you saw our ad in the newspaper? How many of you received an invitation in the mail?" And, of course, including the question on the visitor's card also results in valid feedback.

Designate one person to collect this information on a regular basis and see what kinds of patterns emerge. You may well find that one particular medium may be helping the most, while another is not worth the money being invested. This kind of information can be important in planning future advertising thrusts.

Communications Planning for a Particular Event

Getting the message out to those who would be interested in a particular seminar or concert is critical to its success. Effective planning takes time and effort. Since the lead time varies from one approach to another, it also requires starting in plenty of time and setting deadlines for the completion of various phases of the plan.

Planning an effective advertising program is complex and time consuming. The cost can be high. But a well-thought-out and well-executed program can also pay big dividends. Using an advertising project planning form (such as the one on the right) will prove helpful. Since several tasks probably will be ongoing at the same time, having a separate form for each communication project will assist in the juggling process.

Advertising Project Planning Form

Project _____

Date and time _____

Budget _____

Location _____

    reservations: make by_____ with _____

Special equipment needs _____

    to be purchased, rented, reserved by_____from _____

Seating configuration _____

Special guests to be invited _____

    Material to be printed: program_____flyer or brochure _____

                        handouts_____ agenda _____

    pictures needed _____

    deadline to photo lab_____cost _____

    printer_____ phone _____

    deadline to printer_____cost_____

Publicity: news release_____ deadline to mail _____

    Newspapers _____

    PSA_____ deadline to mail _____

    Radio stations _____

    Mail_____ deadline for printing _____

                 deadline to mail _____

    Other_____ deadline _____

Advertising: newspaper _____ deadline _____

    Radio spots _____ deadline _____

    Television _____ deadline _____

    Other _____ deadline _____

Follow up:

    equipment to be returned _____

    thank you notes to be written _____

    evaluation _____

15 Valuable Information You Should Know

Printing and mailing are major cost factors in preparing publications and getting them to their desired destination. Knowing and understanding regulations and requirements can save dollars as well as time and major headaches. The following information is invaluable. The final section of this chapter provides a glossary of some of the terms used in publication production. Since most of these words are not used outside of this field—at least not with these meanings—these definitions should be helpful.

From the Printer's Perspective

An interview with George E. Brian Jr., an electronic prepress manager, and Ron Regan, a prepress supervisor, at GAC South Press, Inc. in Garland, Texas, resulted in some valuable information for getting a quality printing job, avoiding common customer mistakes, and saving money.

The cornerstone of printing is that it is a customized manufacturing process, not something you can take off the shelf of a store. A good analogy is that the customer invents something and takes it to the printer to develop the first prototype. A part of its success will be determined by how well the customer understands the craft. Brian and Regan suggest that if you don't understand the process, ask to see what happens in the various production stages. Customers often make demands that are costly simply because they lack understanding.

Preplanning the job with the printer can save many headaches and much money. For instance, reducing the projected size to fit available paper size can reduce costs significantly. By way of illustration, consider shrinking a job from 8¾-by-11¾ inches to a standard paper size of 8½-by-11 inches. Also, for print jobs of less than one thousand, you can save a lot of money by using a smaller press that is geared for paper sizes of up to 11-by-17 inches. Using large presses where multiple images are printed on a sheet are much more costly to operate and also require cutting, which is another expense. Doing some reverse engineering on a project pays off.

These factors are also important in determining the final bill:

- Give adequate lead time. A realistic turnaround would be about seven to fourteen days. Putting a "rush" on a job costs extra.
- Getting a job to a printer far ahead of the time that it's needed—say, one to two months—may result in a price break, since the company can work it in between other jobs when it's convenient. Ask whether that's a possibility on something you can prepare in advance.
- Bringing a job in prematurely, before it's really ready, can cause major problems. Customers sometimes arrive with an incomplete project and say, "Get started on it" because of their deadlines. Brian says, "We usually make a lot of money on that." Regan adds, "Translate that into money that's thrown away—by the customer." Here's a saying in the printing industry: "They don't have time to do it right, but they have time to redo it."
- Another major problem is customers who okay the proof, but when they see the completed job, decide that's not the way they want it. Print shops have to pass the cost of redoing it along to the customer, who ends up paying twice.
- Since so much of the cost of a printing job is in the initial start-up, having a large quantity printed reduces the cost per copy.
- Printing shells in quantity of something you use on a continuing basis saves money. For example, you could have enough copies of the flag and return address for a newsletter and even the heading and border for a continuing column (if you're sure you want it in the same place in each issue) printed for a year or more. This could be in a color such as blue. Then when you have that particular issue printed in black on the preprinted shell, you pay at that time for only one color but have the second color you've already paid for at a reduced cost.
- The most reasonable approach is not to ask for anything unusual outside of standard printing procedures. Each of these things add to the expense: unusual size, additional ink color or colors (which require additional film, stripping, and plates), perforations, cutting, indices and mailing permits, unusual paper, die cutting, embossing, tab sealing, shrink wrapping, fulfillment kits containing various components in a package, binding, and unusual distribution.
- Another possible cost-cutter is asking whether a company will price all of the editions of your newsletter for a whole year as

one job. You might be able to get a break because of the higher volume.

- Submitting a job electronically done on professionally accepted software programs, such as QuarkXPress and PageMaker, results in major savings. The four major categories for software are: (l) page layout, (2) illustration, (3) photo editing and retouching, and (4) word processing. Many low-priced software packages say on the cover that you can do newsletters, layout, and so on. But what they don't say is that they're for home use and do not offer the necessary refinements for professional reproduction. Also, be sure that the fonts you use in your software are of high, professional quality. The old adage "You get what you pay for" is still true. Again, conferring with your printer in advance about compatibility can prevent costly and aggravating mistakes in your purchasing software.

And, as always, developing a good working relationship with the printer pays big dividends.[1]

Toward Swift, Accurate, and Frugal Mailing

United States postal business centers exist for one reason—to help nonprofit organizations and businesses do the most efficient and cost-effective job possible in regard to mailing. A call to your local post office station manager or postmaster will get you the phone number of the center that serves your area. Some of the services that they provide are:

- periodic seminars for representatives of nonprofit groups
- see-through templates that you can lay on a piece of mail to show where different elements on the package, such as address, return address, and bar code (if used), should be placed. Templates also contain information such as the maximum size that a piece may be without incurring an oversize surcharge.
- services of a design analyst who will look at a proposed major mailing piece and make suggestions for the most efficient design as it relates to mailing
- disks that contain information for every address in a designated zip code or certain area (available for a fee). Address-correction disks also may be purchased to update the information on the original disk that you purchase.
- information on how to take advantage of mailing discounts that are available to customers who provide greater levels of automation assistance. For example, the post office offers a lower

postage rate to an organization that is mailing in quantity with a bar code sprayed on the bottom of the envelope, for this helps significantly in using automated systems.

Here are some suggestions for getting your mail delivered safely and expediently.

- Use Zip-Plus-4 codes on material that you mail. The extra four digits enable sorting machines to separate mail to sector and segment or specific route and even the correct side of the street. This means your mail will arrive more swiftly and accurately than without the added four digits.
- Include your own Zip-Plus-4 in your return address and on your stationery.
- Have addresses computer printed or typed. Automated sorters can read addresses in type but not those written by hand. This means letters addressed by hand must be pulled off the conveyor belt and sorted by hand. This also applies to script fonts.
- Always put zip codes in the last line on the envelope, since electronic character readers in the post office scan the last printed line. If you write "Attention: Pastor Greenspan," underneath the address, the machine will reject the item, sending it to the human-sorting department. Place the "attention" information, instead, either on the first or second line of the address.
- Place apartment numbers on the same line as the street address.
- Drop Express mail off no later than 4:00 P.M. to guarantee next-day delivery.
- Place "Address Correction Requested" on your envelope to keep your mailing list up to date. You will receive a return card giving the new address. If you also place "Please forward" on the envelope, the mail will be forwarded to the addressee, and you will be sent the new address. In both cases, a fee per piece will be charged.

Of course, mailing regulations change along with postage costs. But working with your nearest postal business center can save you time, headaches, and money.[2]

Glossary of Some Publication Terms

Banner—The flag or masthead (the name of the newsletter, the organization, and the logo) placed at the top of the publication.

Bleed—To extend an illustration (usually a photograph) to the outside edges of the page without any margin.

Blind embossing—The impression of a design into the back of the paper so that it appears in bas-relief on the front side.

Blowup—An enlargement of a drawing or photo.

Blurb—A quote or statement pulled from the text of an article and set apart, usually in larger type.

Body type—Type used for the message, usually under 12-point in size. Also called text type. The opposite of display type.

Boldface—Thick, heavy type. Also, to mark copy for printing in this type, or to set or print in this type.

Bullet—A heavy dot used to highlight a particular item. Often used to set lists of similar items apart from the rest of the copy.

Camera ready—Description of a publication that is ready to be printed exactly as it is.

Caption—Descriptive lines of copy for an illustration or photo.

Collage—A placement of several pictures or drawings together to form one composition.

Color separation—Breaking down full-color copy into its component proportions of the primary colors in preparation for printing.

Copy—The text to be used for printing.

Crop—To trim a photograph to emphasize the main feature of the picture.

Cutline—The caption explaining the action and identifying the people in a picture.

Deckle edge—The irregular, ragged edge of a sheet of handmade paper, now produced mechanically.

Display type—Type larger than that used in the body of a publication. Used in headlines and blurbs.

Dummy—A mock-up of a printed piece in its sketched or pasted up form to indicate its desired appearance.

Flag—The banner or masthead, including the name of the newsletter, organization, and logo, at the top of a publication.

Flop—To reverse a photo or piece of artwork, making the old left-hand side the new right-hand side.

Font—All the letters and characters in one size and style of a typeface.

Gray—Overall appearance of a page that is nearly all type with little white space.

Gripper edge—Amount of paper left blank at the edge of a sheet to allow mechanical fingers to draw it into the printing press and hold it during impression.

Gutter—The inner margin of a printed page extending from the printed portion to the fold or binding.

Halftone—A process for reproducing tonal images by photographing a picture through a screen.

Head—The top of a book or a page. A headline or heading.

Italic—A style of printing type patterned on a Renaissance script with the letters slanting to the right.

Jump a story—To continue a story on another page.

Justify—To space a line of type to make it full to the right margin so that the copy will line up on the right as well as on the left margins.

Kicker—A short line in smaller or accent type above the main line of a head. Also called a teaser, eyebrow, or highline.

Lead—The introductory portion of a news story.

Leading—The spacing between lines, measured in points.

Lower case letter—A small letter in type, as distinguished from a capital letter.

Masthead—The listing in a periodical of information about the staff, operation, and circulation. Also, sometimes used to mean the banner or flag (name, publisher, logo) at the top of a newsletter.

Mechanical—A paste-up or working guide for the printer in which all the elements are pasted or indicated in their correct positions.

Measure—Width of a column or line of type.

Morgue—Also called research file, scrap file, swipe file, or clip file. A collection of pictures kept for reference and possible future use.

Overlay—A transparent sheet taped over the art to indicate the parts of the drawing to be printed in color or any other pertinent instructions.

Paste up—To put all the elements of a publication in place to present camera-ready copy for printing.

Pica—A unit of linear measurement. One pica is equal to twelve points, and six picas equal almost one inch. Picas are used to specify typographical dimensions such as line width, column depth, and column spacing.

Point—A unit of measure equivalent to about 1/72 of an inch, used to indicate type size and interlinear spacing.

Point size—The size of the type body on which the letters are cast. Point size can be estimated by measuring from the top of the highest letter (a capital or an ascender such as b or h) to the bottom of the lowest letter (a descender such as p or y).

Proof—Sample impression of the printing job that can be checked for errors before the full run is made.

Put to bed—Send the publication to the printer.

Ragged right—An unjustified right margin where the lines are of various lengths.

Register—To exactly fit together two or more elements to be printed together.

Reverse out—To print in white letters on a black or dark background.

Reverse type—White letters printed on a dark background.

Scan—To move a finely focused beam of light or electrons in a systematic pattern over visual material in order to reproduce it or sense and subsequently transmit an image.

Screen—A glass plate marked off with crossing lines, placed before the lens of a camera when photographing to produce dots of varying size for halftone reproduction.

Sans serif—Type having no serifs or finishing cross stroke at the end of a main stroke in a letter.

Serif—The finishing cross stroke at the end of a main stroke in a letter. Serifs resemble "feet" on the bottom of letters such as l and r.

Size a picture—To reduce or enlarge the size of a picture so that it will fit in a layout.

Stet—A proofreader's direction that means "let it stand" or ignore a change made inadvertently or incorrectly on the proof.

-30- (thirty)—The end. Used to indicate the final page in journalistic submissions, such as a news release. The symbol ### is also used.

Typeface—The size and/or style of the letter or character in a block of type.

Typography—The arrangement and appearance of printed material on a page.

Upper-case letter—A capital letter in print.

Widow—A single, usually short line of type (for example, one ending a paragraph) that is carried over to the top of the next page or column, or a short line at the bottom of a page, column, or paragraph.

16 Computers—An Effective Communication Tool in Ministry

The Internet has made an amazingly rapid impact on communication on a world-wide basis. "Awesome" is a good word to describe its potential for instant feedback, two-way communication, acquisition of information, opportunity for influence, and so on. Its popularity and fascination for people of all ages and backgrounds is undeniable. Certainly churches and ministries would do well to consider adding this potent tool to their repertoire of communication approaches.

Quentin J. Schultze, professor of communication at Calvin College (Grand Rapids, Michigan) and prolific author on the subject of communication via computers, says the following:

> There comes a time when the church of Jesus Christ has to be bold enough to lay claim to a new medium. As I like to put it, new technologies are part of the unfolding of God's Creation. We don't own these technologies; God does. We're stewards, caretakers and representatives on behalf of the King of kings. You and I have inherited God's command to Adam to take care of and develop the Creation.[1]

First Baptist Church of Richardson, Texas, has found the Internet and Web site to be effective and exciting additions to ministry. The church has a constituency with more than half its members on-line.

Ministries Assistant David Doom advises churches to take a good look at their congregations in assessing how effective the Internet would be for them. "Without member access, it won't do much good," he points out. "But e-mail is the fax machine of the 90s, the cutting edge. We want to be on that level. We don't want to get left behind. Our e-mail and Web-site addresses [which they include on business cards and in advertising] say 'We care about what's out there.' After all, you wouldn't *not* have a phone. You wouldn't *not* have an answering machine."

Here are some of the ways that First Baptist of Richardson has found the Internet useful.

- Members have immediate access to the office of Dr. Brian Harbour, the pastor. They can send him a message without an intermediary and without feeling they are intruding on his time. "He replies to the e-mail message during that same day," Doom says.
- Staff members use the Internet for research. For example, in a recent sermon, Harbour wanted to use television shows to illustrate the differences between today's culture and the past. He was able to find information about the Cleavers, the Bunkers, and the Simpsons quickly.
- Members can sign up for different events. About thirty participants registered for a recent basketball tourney through the Internet.
- Staff members remind participants in various ministries about upcoming events, such as a special choir rehearsal.

Staff members have been surprised at the amount of e-mail they receive. They feel that it saves them time. They can reply quicker, resulting in immediate feedback. It also saves money in mailing costs. One of the questions on their membership form now is "What is your e-mail address?"[2]

Schultze, in his book entitled *Internet for Christians,* suggests some other useful applications for pastors. He points out that they can commune on-line with other pastors, exchange ideas and concerns, discuss sermon topics, and follow current cultural trends. They can also participate in denominational discussion groups and avail themselves of on-line resources for Christian education.[3]

Schultze also gives these possible uses of e-mail for local churches:

- electronic prayer chains with requests sent to all in the chain
- church news for former members who are still interested in the congregation
- calendar lists that remind members of occasional responsibilities such as ushering
- sermon discussion questions
- congregational lists for weekly mailings about sermon topics, special services, committee meetings, and so on[4]

First Baptist of Richardson has had a Web site since the fall of 1996. These are some of the considerations Doom points out in designing a Web site.

1. Shop around for the best service provider. Get the best rate. Their cost averages about one hundred dollars to one hundred and fifty dollars per month.[5] Schultze suggests, "If you are a member of a denomination, check to see whether you can get access to the Net

through any denominational or cross-denominational networks. A growing number of churches are providing access to the Net as well as to denominational news and discussion services."[6]

2. Look at Web sites of other churches. Contact those whose Web sites you admire and get tips from them. *Christian Computing Magazine* (P.O. Box 198, Raymore, MO 64083) has a regular feature called "The Internet Page," which summarizes a variety of Web sites connected with ministries. It designates one of those covered as "Web site of the Month."

3. Appoint a planning committee composed of people with diverse backgrounds from high tech to no tech to provide balance. First Baptist's committee included a junior high student who is a computer whiz.

4. Purchase a Web site design software program that costs about one hundred dollars. Doom says that some of these can guide you step-by-step through the process of developing a professional-looking site without paying the hefty fee charged by a professional designer.

5. Decide on a general overall look for all the pages in your Web site. You want nice backgrounds that match in order to have a unified appearance.

6. Be aware that you will probably need more pages than you originally believe will be adequate. First Baptist now has grown to forty pages from the original thirty.

7. Establish policies about what will be permitted to be used. Doom gives a word of caution in this regard. "You don't want to let people link your pages to other pages on the Web that you have no control over."

8. Publicize your Web site. One approach First Baptist used was to project their entire Web site on a huge screen during a church service. They also list their address in their ad in the religion section of *The Dallas Morning News.* It's also noted in each Sunday's bulletin.

9. Have some watchdogs who will point out mistakes and make suggestions. "I have four—self-appointed. But they help me to do a better job," Doom laughs.

10. Last, but certainly not least, make sure that you have people who are committed to maintaining the Web site with current and pertinent information. About fifteen people at First Baptist of Richardson have the responsibility of updating their own pages, such as youth group and children's ministry. Sunday school classes have their own pages, which they use as newsletters. Doom usually spends about thirty minutes per day on this

responsibility. He says it's like landscaping a yard. "You just can't put it in. It requires upkeep and maintenance."

The Web is used for a variety of purposes. For example, children's Sunday school lessons are featured, giving parents an opportunity to know what their kids are going to be studying and to discuss the subject with them before or after their class. One page features the steps to becoming a Christian and asks users to let the church or another church know about their choice, if they have made that commitment.

A South Carolina family that was getting ready to move to Richardson discovered First Baptist of Richardson's web site. They liked what they saw. They started sending e-mail back and forth with staff members. By the time they arrived in Richardson, they had already established ties with the church through the Internet.

"We know that families are using the Internet for research when they're looking for a new church," Doom says. First Baptist of Richardson wants to have the opportunity to tell them about their ministry.[7]

Fellowship Bible Church North in Plano, Texas, takes a different approach to computer use with exciting results. It has had an on-line service of its own called FOL (Fellowship On-line) since November of 1996.

David Powers, Audio-Media Director for Fellowship Bible, also wears the hat of administrator of FOL. He says that a number of people have purchased computers and modems so that they can become a part of FOL. They now have between three hundred and four hundred people in the service out of a congregation of about fifteen hundred families. Several have dumped America On-line, preferring to participate in FOL.

Powers points out that an on-line service would be of little benefit for a small congregation or even for a larger one with a small number of computer users: "You have to have a user base." Fellowship Bible Church North does, and the response has been phenomenal.

Each ministry, such as men's and women's ministry, has its own area. An area just for staff members also enhances staff communication. The church has about sixty mini-church or home cell groups with several of them having their own area. Members can e-mail one another about a problem, a prayer need, or share a blessing with absolute confidentiality within that small group.

Subscribers are allotted one hour of time each day. They can chat with others who are logged in at that particular time. "We had to limit the time," Powers comments, "so that everyone could have access. Also, we didn't want members to neglect their families by spending too much time on FOL."

Moderators help "keep house" on the service. They keep conferences on topic. They also monitor incoming services such as Our Daily Bread,

Verse of the Day, and Christian news groups to which FOL subscribes. "They delete extraneous material and anything that might be in the least offensive. We want to keep this squeaky clean," Powers says. Moderators are given additional access time in exchange for their assistance.

One of the most dramatic results has been in the area of answered prayer. "We know prayer works," Power says. "Our prayer conference line lets people know immediately if there is a serious illness, injuries in an accident, a death, or another emergency so that they can start praying immediately. We can see the difference it's made."

The church, using a Macintosh server and First Class Software from Softarc, Inc., has eight modems to accommodate the service with the eight phone lines running about forty-five dollars each per month. Start up cost included about eight thousand dollars for software and hardware. In addition to staff time, costs also include about forty dollars per month for the ISP (Internet Service Provider), which handles the Internet e-mail. Churches cannot charge their members for access because of their non-profit status. However, one possible way to cut costs would be to have an on-line service located in a home since phone lines would be less expensive.

The service has recently linked with an Integrated Service Digital Network (ISDN). This enables Fellowship Bible Church North missionaries and other friends from all over the world to access the system via the Internet without paying long distance charges and without tying up the phone lines.

Powers gives the following tips for establishing your own on-line service:

- Make sure you have someone who is knowledgeable and is willing and able to spend a lot of time to administer the system.
- Investigate what software is available before you decide on the system you want to use.
- Dedicate ample funds.
- Ascertain that enough members are interested and would be able to access the system to justify the cost and effort.

Some of the advantages Powers points out are:

- It saves time. The same message can be sent to several people simultaneously.
- You have the ability to refer back to previous communications. "Messages on our system are kept for sixty days," Powers points out.
- The speed of communication is helpful.
- You can answer messages on your own time and terms without sudden interruptions.

"You hear people say that communication on-line is kind of cold," Powers reflects. "While there may be a little more sterility, you have to remember this is a whole different culture. We find that FOL is beneficial for us."[8]

Possibilities for parachurch groups are also varied and exciting. Schultze points out these opportunities:

- effective and inexpensive communication among staff at all geographic locations
- direct and immediate communication with supporters through e-mail and Web publication
- generation of more support through an on-line presence
- more effective communication with volunteers and part-time staff and as a means of locating new volunteers
- a much broader audience for the ministry's publications and other resources
- wider promotion of conferences and other meetings with registration being done on-line
- more effective post-convention follow-up through on-line interaction
- broader promotion of existing ministries
- reduced costs of sending out paper literature by referring inquiries to the Web or other on-line versions
- selling text-based materials on-line, with users downloading the material directly to their computers and printing the materials on their own home printers
- communication of supporters with ministry leaders
- product sampling, such as book excerpts, video and audio segments[9]

Schultze says the following:

> Our task as Christians, I believe, is to claim every new medium for Christ. If a new medium comes along, we should use it. Of course, all of the tough questions are in the decisions about how to use it. Our fundamental message, the Gospel of Jesus Christ, never changes. But the means of communication do change, just as they have since Christ walked the earth.[10]

Glossary of Some Terms Used on the Internet

Booleans—words or symbols used to connect numerous key search words in order to limit and refine the number of "hits" or positive responses. For example, you could combine the words "Christian" and "sportscasters" to ask for only pages that use both words.

Chat—talk using computerized keyboards to type messages over the Internet.

Computer server—a computer called a Net server because it serves or routes information to other computers. It stores common database files and gives access to the information to many users.

Computer-to-computer communication—communication transacted only through the use of computers without any voice or paper assistance. Also called "digital communication," it represents a worldwide web of computer networks.

Cybergap—the difference in cultures of those who are computer literate (are knowledgeable of computer usage and terminology) and those who are not.

Cyberspace—the collective computerized networks of telephone lines, coaxial cable (like cable-TV wire) satellites, and cellular phones.

Encryption—code to make private messages inaccessible to people who don't have the necessary passwords or encryption keys. It is available in software to prevent unauthorized access.

E-mail—an electronic message sent from computer to computer via the Internet.

E-zine—net lingo for on-line magazine.

Flamed—being bombarded by negative messages over the Internet.

Geek—A person whose whole life seems to revolve around the Internet and who constantly uses Internet jargon.

Home page—the first page on a Web site.

Hot spots—also called "bookmarks," these are favorite addresses of the places browsers visit regularly on the Web.

HTML—Hyper Text Markup Language—the kind of formatting (the way of creating the page) used on the Web.

Http:/www—hypertext transfer protocol, world wide web.

Hypermedia—words, icons, or graphics on which you can click the mouse to go to information about that subject.

Hypertext—specially marked words and phrases where you can click the mouse to automatically connect you to more information at other places.

Internet—also called "on-line," a digital, worldwide network that makes it possible for people to communicate from computer to computer using text, sound, still images, and moving images.

Internet access providers—also called Internet service provider (ISP), organizations that provide connections between computers with compatible modems and the Internet. They may be compared to long-distance phone companies that connect computers to other computers all over the world instead of telephones to other telephones.

Listservs—e-mail lists of addresses on the Internet.

Message pocket—call on the Internet.

Modem—a device that hooks between a computer and the telephone line, enabling the computer to exchange messages with other computers connected directly or indirectly to that phone line. Most new computers come with a built-in modem.

Mouse—a hand-held, button-activated input device that, when rolled on a flat surface (mouse pad), causes an arrow to move correspondingly around a computer screen. It enables the operator to select various computer operations and to manipulate text and graphics.

Netiquette—the established etiquette of Internet communication.

Page—place on the Web, even if it's more than one page long.

Snail mail—a physical message, such as a letter.

Search engines—computer programs that are used to search the Web for typed-in key words related to a specific topic. Among the most popular Web search engines and their Internet addresses are Alta Vista (http://www.altavista.digital.com), Excite (http://www.excite.com), Yahoo (http://www.yahoo.com), HotBot (http://www.hotbot.com), Lycos (http://www.lycos.com), and Webcrawler (http://webcrawler.com).

Software—the program that enables your computer to do what you'd like it to and gives the computer direction.

Surfing the net—searching the Internet for interesting or unusual information, similar to flipping through TV channels with a remote control.

Traffic—message flow on the Internet.

URL—uniform resource locator, address for a Web page that will begin with: http://www.

Vehicles—Internet lingo for specific software, databases, and directories.

Virtual—something created by a computer that replicates or imitates reality, thereby creating a new reality, such as a virtual office where a business person conducts business at home rather than in a real office in a business complex or corporate skyscraper.

Web site—a page on the Internet that tells about an organization, a person, or a product. Sound and motion may be included with visual material. A Web is a subset of the larger entity known as the Internet.

Webmaster—one who sets up and oversees a Web site.

Wired—the hooking up or connecting of a computer to the Internet.

World Wide Web—(www or the "Web") a visual, graphic means of showing where you can travel or surf on the Net, making it possible to communicate with people and organizations all over the world.

17 Respecting Copyrights—A Legal and Ethical Responsibility

Copyright provides protection to the authors of "original works of authorship" under the laws of the United States (title 17, U.S. Code). Included are literary, dramatic, musical, artistic, and certain other intellectual works.[1] A copyright clause (Article I, Section 8) was included in the United States Constitution when it was written in 1787.[2] Unfortunately many people and groups, including churches and parachurch ministries, either ignore copyright laws or do not understand their responsibility under the law. (See page 218, Copyright Checklist.)

The Bible speaks to a principle addressed by copyright law. First Timothy 5:18b (NIV) states: "The worker deserves his wages." Also, Jeremiah 22:13 (NIV) reads:

> Woe to him who builds his palace by unrighteousness,
> his upper rooms by injustice,
> making his countrymen work for nothing,
> not paying them for their labor.

Those who are not moved by scriptural injunctions should be aware that violating copyright laws is breaking federal law and is subject to penalties the same as any infraction of any law. Nonprofits are not exempt in any way.

Woody Young, in his book entitled *A Business Guide to Copyright Law—What You Don't Know Can Cost You,* says, "The misuse of copyrights of others can be very costly."[3] He goes on to say that violations of the copyright warnings are a serious offense and presume "an intent to violate the law. Jail may not be likely, but the fines can be very expensive." He points out that each unauthorized use of copyrighted material is an infringement and is considered a separate violation.[4]

Attorney Stephen Fishman says that "statutory damages are set by the copyright law and require no proof of how much the loss was in monetary terms." He says that statutory damages, when awarded, may

211

fall within the following range: between five hundred and twenty thousand dollars for all infringements by a single infringer of a single work, whether the infringement was done willfully or innocently. He states, however, that if the infringer took the material, knowing that he had no right to it, the court may increase the amount of statutory damages up to one hundred thousand dollars. If the infringer is determined to have acted innocently, the award might be reduced to as little as two hundred dollars. However, he also states, "if the work to which the infringer had access contained a valid copyright notice (©), the infringer may not claim to have acted innocently."[5]

Richard R. Hammar gives the following hypothetical example:

> The choir director assembles a compilation consisting of typed lyrics to fifty choruses (forty of which are copyrighted) commonly sung by the congregation, makes one hundred copies of the compilation, and inserts the copies in the hymnal racks in the sanctuary. This simple and seemingly innocent activity could result in minimum damages to the church of one million dollars under section 504 of the Copyright Act, and could be considerably higher.[6]

Hammar goes on to say: "Damages for copyright infringement can increase substantially in cases of willful violation. In the past, churches were treated with much greater deference. They were sued very seldom. Today, however, the reality is that churches are often the target of lawsuits."[7]

Obviously this complex subject with all its ramifications cannot be addressed within the limitations of one chapter in this book. A definitive work on the subject of copyright law, as it pertains to churches, is entitled *The Church Guide to Copyright Law,* by Richard R. Hammar (Christian Ministry Resources, publisher).

The following information should prove useful as a general guide for the use of copyrighted material.

What Does Copyright Provide?

"Copyright Basics," a publication of the Copyright Office of the Library of Congress, says the following:

Section 106 of the Copyright Act generally gives the owner of copyright the exclusive right to do and to authorize others to do the following:

- To reproduce the copyrighted work in copies or phono records;
- To prepare derivative works based upon the copyrighted work;
- To distribute copies or phono records of the copyrighted work

to the public by sale or other transfer of ownership, or by rental, lease, or lending;

- To perform the copyrighted work publicly, in the case of literary, musical, dramatic, and choreographic works, pantomimes, and motion pictures and other audiovisual works; and
- To display the copyrighted work publicly, in the case of literary, musical, dramatic, and choreographic works, pantomimes, and pictorial, graphic, or sculptural works, including the individual images of a motion picture or other audiovisual work.[8]

What Are the Limitations on Copyright Protection?

While it is illegal for anyone to violate the rights of the copyright owner in the areas mentioned, these rights are not unlimited in scope. A major limitation is the doctrine of "fair use," which is given a statutory basis in Section 107 of the Title 17, United States Code.[9] This is a reprint of Section 107.

107. Limitations on exclusive rights: Fair use

Notwithstanding the provisions of Section 106, the fair use of a copyrighted work, including such use by reproduction in copies or phono records or by any other means specified by that section, for purposes such as criticism, comment, news reporting, teaching (including multiple copies for classroom use), scholarship, or research, is not an infringement of copyright. In determining whether the use made of a work in any particular case is a fair use the factors to be considered shall include—

(1) the purpose and character of the use, including whether such use is of a commercial nature or is for nonprofit educational purposes;

(2) the nature of the copyrighted work;

(3) the amount and substantiality of the portion used in relation to the copyrighted work as a whole; and

(4) the effect of the use upon the potential market for or value of the copyrighted work.[10]

A frequently heard "myth" is that you may quote up to two hundred and fifty words of a copyrighted work as "fair use." This is not necessarily true, for two hundred and fifty words might be the entire length, or more, of a work, such as a poem. Section 107 does not specify a certain number of words. The best rule to follow is: if there is the slightest doubt in your mind, get permission from the copyright owner before using it.

Another limitation takes the form of a "compulsory license," under which certain limited uses of copyrighted works are permitted upon payment of specified royalties and compliance with statutory conditions. Compulsory license procedures are complex and are given in detail in pages 108–15 in Hammar's book.[11]

Ideas and facts are also not protected under copyright laws—only the way in which the writer uses particular words to express facts and ideas. Attorney Stephen Fishman says the following:

> To give an author a monopoly over the facts and ideas contained in his work would hinder intellectual and artistic progress, not encourage it. . . . Because copyright only extends its protection to words rather than the underlying facts and ideas, works in which the particular words used by the author are important and distinctive—such as poems, novels and plays—enjoy the most copyright protection.[12]

A work that is not protected by copyright is described as being "in the public domain," which means that it belongs to the public as a whole. Included are works for which the copyright was lost or has expired and those authored or owned by the federal government. Everyone can use such materials without asking anyone for permission. Anything published more than seventy-five years ago is now in the public domain.[13]

What Works Are Protected?

Original works of authorship, fixed in a tangible form of expression are protected by copyright and include the following categories:

- literary works
- musical works, including accompanying words
- dramatic works, including accompanying music
- pantomimes and choreographic works
- pictorial, graphic, and sculptural works
- motion pictures and other audiovisual works
- sound recordings
- architectural works

"Copyright Basics" points out that "These categories should be viewed quite broadly: for example, computer programs and most 'compilations' are registrable as 'literary works,' maps and architectural plans are registrable as 'pictorial, graphic, and sculptural works.'"[14]

What Is Not Protected by Copyright?

"Copyright Basics" lists several categories of material not eligible for statutory copyright protection. Included are:

- works that have not been fixed in a tangible form of expression, for example: choreographic works that have not been notated or recorded, or improvisational speeches or performances that have not been written or recorded.
- titles, names, short phrases, and slogans; familiar symbols or designs; mere variations of typographic ornamentation, lettering, or coloring; mere listings of ingredients or contents.
- ideas, procedures, methods, systems, processes, concepts, principles, discoveries, or devices, as distinguished from a description, explanation, or illustration.
- works consisting entirely of information that is common property and containing no original authorship, for example: standard calendars, height and weight charts, tape measures and rulers, and lists or tables taken from public documents or other common sources.[15]

What Is a "Work Made for Hire"?

A work made for hire is generally accepted to mean an original work that is done within the scope of a person's regular employment. Unless otherwise stipulated in a written and signed contract, the employer would become the holder of the copyright. Another instance would be when a free-lancer is paid to create a certain work. This kind of arrangement should be made in writing and signed by both parties, clearly stating to whom the copyright will belong.[16]

These relationships should be carefully delineated. For example, a church could logically claim ownership of all sermons preached by the pastor while he is an employee there. This issue should be addressed in contract form.

How and When Is a Work Copyrighted?

"Copyright Basics" says that a copyright is secured automatically when the work is created, "when it is fixed in a copy or phono record for the first time." The book gives these definitions:

Copies —material objects from which a work can be read or visually perceived either directly or with the aid of a machine or device, such as books, manuscripts, sheet music, film, videotape, or microfilm.

Phono records —material objects embodying fixations of sounds (excluding, by statutory definition, motion picture soundtracks), such as cassette tapes, CDs, or LPs.

No publication or registration or other action in the copyright office is now required to secure copyright.[17] The absence of the copyright notice—©—does not mean that the work is not copyrighted, even if it was completed on or after March 1, 1989. Most works will bear the copyright notice, which was required before that date.[18] Works created since 1978, when copyright laws were amended, usually remain in copyright during the life of the author plus an additional fifty years.[19]

What Are Frequent Areas of Noncompliance for Churches?

While the list could be extensive, these are some common mistakes churches make in failing to comply with copyright laws.

The Newsletter

Newsletters often contain an inspiring poem or a cartoon taken from another publication. Unless items such as this are in the public domain, using them without permission is a violation of law. However, if authorship cannot be determined after a reasonable effort has been made, "author unknown" should be placed on the item.

The Church Bulletin

Many churches today publish the lyrics to songs in their church bulletin or on an insert sheet. To do so without permission for a copyrighted lyric, again, is a breach of copyright laws. Copies of lyrics, printed with permission, as well as poems and cartoons should contain the notice of copyright symbol and the year and owner of the copyright.

Projection of Audiovisual Material

Projection of copyrighted song lyrics, prepared by a church without permission, is a violation of copyright law. Saying that only the words were projected, not the entire song, is no excuse. However, a purchased transparency or slide authorized by the copyright owner may be used legally.[20] Hammar says, "Many music publishers give churches the right to make a transparency for a nominal fee (e.g., ten dollars). Also, churches that obtain a blanket license from a publisher or an agent of one or more publishers often have the right to make transparencies of any song on a master list."[21]

Music

The Copyright Act exempts performances of copyrighted sacred music "in the course of services at a place of worship or other religious assembly." However, the exemption does not extend to secular operas, plays, or motion pictures, even though they might have an underlying religious theme and may be used in a religious service. This provision also excludes activities at a place of worship for social, educational, fund-raising, or entertainment purposes. Also, the provision does not extend to broadcasts of such works, even though they might be included in the broadcast of a regular church service. Churches should check with the radio or television station that is broadcasting their service about the station's authorization to air a copyrighted musical work.[22]

While limited copying of various copyrighted works may be made for educational purposes, the right does not extend to copying for the purpose of performance except in certain emergency situations.

In an emergency, the person responsible must contact the owner of the copyright for permission in order to legally make photocopies. Hammar says, "Some music publishers grant 'blanket licenses' to churches, authorizing them to make copies of any song in the publisher's repertory for an annual fee."[23]

A key point to remember is that no copying for the purpose of substituting for the purchase of music is allowed.[24] Also, no arrangement of a copyrighted work may be made without permission.[25]

Movies and Videos

Francis Anfuso, in his production manual entitled *Taking Your Church Off Pause*, reminds that the U.S. Copyright Act requires that you must have a public-performance license to show motion pictures released in home video format during youth-activities programs, adult-education sessions, or general church functions. He says, "This legal requirement applies equally to profit and nonprofit organizations, regardless of whether an admission or other fee is charged."[26]

The Motion Picture Licensing Corporation (MPLC, 13315 Washington Boulevard, Third Floor, Los Angeles, CA 90066) provides an MPLC Umbrella License that allows unrestricted use of several thousand authorized videos at church-sponsored functions for a one-year period. The annual fee is about one hundred dollars. Some of the types of titles that this license makes available are Walt Disney, Hanna-Barbera and its "Stories from the Bible" series, Best Film's "Great Bible Series," Inspirational Video's "The Living Christ Series," and American Portrait Films library.

Once licensed, a church may purchase videos, rent them from a video store, check them out at a public library, or use a church member's. However, it does not allow for usage of a videocassette taped from television. The Motion Picture Licensing Corporation's church-sponsored license does not represent all movie companies, which would have to be contacted individually in order to secure the right to show one of their titles. More information may be obtained by writing MPLC or calling 800-462-8855.[27]

Drama, Musicals, and Other Oral Works

Fishman says, "Be aware that performing a play, publishing an unauthorized copy, or reciting a written work in public also constitutes copyright infringement—unless the copyright owner's permission is obtained."[28]

Many published plays and musicals require that a royalty fee be paid for each performance, but there are many variations in arrangements. Some only require payment one time, while others will allow unlimited performances for the purchase of the required number of scripts. Few give permission to purchase only one copy of the script and make photocopies. A note must also be placed in the program stating that arrangements for production have been made with the play's or musical's publisher.

Another issue in regard to using drama is that of making changes in a script. This point relates to the right delineated in Section 106 of the Copyright Act, which gives the copyright owner exclusive right to prepare derivative works based upon the copyrighted work.

Paul M. Miller, editor of the Drama Division of Lillenas Publishing Co., was asked the following question: "How much can I change a script to make it fit our needs?" This was his reply, in part:

> Legally you can make no changes. Most publishers realize that many of us bend the law a bit, especially when dealing with secular scripts, by eliminating profanity and the like. In informal conversations with the large secular houses, that seems to be acceptable, even without written permission.

The following list represents some changes for which permission in writing must be secured:

- to eliminate a character, or combine him or her with another one
- to rewrite any scene to fit the purpose of your show or theology (frankly, you ought to look for a different script before undertaking such a task)
- to lift out a portion of one script to combine with some original or other script
- to edit to a shorter format in order to fit your time slot or format[29]

This would also apply to a copyrighted play or musical that has not been published.

Scripture

The King James Version of the Bible is in the public domain and may be quoted at will. More modern versions of the Bible, such as *The Living Bible* and *Holy Bible—New International Version,* are protected by copyright laws. Under the "fair use" provision, brief portions may be quoted in print, if credit is given.

Computer Programs

Section 117 of the Copyright Act allows the owner of a copy of a computer program to make another copy of that program in two instances: (1) when a piece of software is inputted into a computer as a part of its random access memory (RAM); (2) when a single backup copy is made for archival purposes. All other duplications constitute copyright infringement. However, some software makers will provide additional copies of particular programs at a reduced price and, in some cases, will not charge if duplicated copies are intended for nonprofit use.[30]

Moral rights is the doctrine "which purports to protect the personal rights of creators, as distinguished from their merely economic rights." This aspect has not been addressed in the United States to the extent that it has abroad.[31]

Article 6bis of the Berne Convention expresses the moral right this way:

> Independently of the author's economic rights, and even after the transfer of the said rights, the author shall have the right to claim authorship of the work and to object to any distortion, mutilation or other modification of, or other derogatory action in relation to, the said work, which would be prejudicial to his honor or reputation.[32]

While much more could be said on the subject of copyrights, hopefully, this information will help churches to comply with federal law and with professional and ethical practices.

Will your church end up having to pay a one hundred thousand dollar fine if you don't? Probably not. But it is a possibility. Hammar concluded from his survey of fifteen major publishers of religious music that, while many publishers are reluctant to take legal action against churches for copyright infringement, they would sue in extreme cases. A few of those contacted said they had already taken such action.[33]

In another and perhaps even more important sense than the legal implications, the church should be first in line to grant respect and sustenance to people who have labored diligently to contribute creative work worthy of its attention and use in enhancing worship services and programs.

Trademarks

A related issue is complying with correct trademark usage. The most usual misuse would be in a church publication or performance where a company's registered trademark is used instead of a generic term. Some examples are using kleenex instead of facial tissue or xerox copy rather than photo copy. If the registered trademark name is used, for example, in writing about the purchase of a Xerox® copy machine, then the trademark symbol should always be used. The trademark name should always be capitalized, followed by the trademark symbol (®) and a generic description; for example, Frigidaire® refrigerator. Companies are quite sensitive about this issue since they do not want to lose their trademarks as a result of the usage becoming so prevalent that their names are generally accepted as generic names.

Abiding by copyright law and correct trademark usage is the legal thing—and the right thing—to do.

Copyright Checklist*

_____ 1. Do I ever fail to get permission to use copyrighted poems, cartoons, and other material in publications?

_____ 2. Do I copy copyrighted materials, including music, scripts, and computer software, to keep from purchasing additional copies?

_____ 3. Do I print or project on a screen copyrighted lyrics without permission?

_____ 4. If permission has been granted, do I ever forget to include the copyright notice on printed and projected materials?

_____ 5. If an entire service is to be broadcast, do I just assume that copyrighted music used in the service is covered under the station's permission to broadcast without asking?

_____ 6. Do I permit films or videos to be shown in any services or meetings without permission?

_____ 7. If permission has been obtained, do I use a video tape that has been taped from television instead of purchasing one or checking it out from a library?

_____ 8. Do I ever neglect to see that all required royalties are paid for dramatic and musical productions?

_____ 9. Do I fail to ensure that notice is placed on the program that the work is being performed by arrangement with the publisher?

_____ 10. Do I allow dramatic and musical works to be altered without permission to fit the occasion or the desires of the director?

_____ 11. Do I allow arrangements to be made of copyrighted music without permission?

_____ 12. Do I let long passages of Scripture from modern, copyrighted translations of the Bible, such as *Holy Bible— New International Version* and *The Living Bible,* be reproduced for use in services without permission?

_____ 13. Do I use a trademark term when a generic reference is correct?

*"No" is the correct answer to all of the questions.

SECTION V

Communicating with and Through the News Media

Neither do people light a lamp and put it under a bowl. Instead they put it on its stand, and it gives light to everyone in the house.
                                                              —*Matthew 5:15 (NIV)*

18 Your Church Is Newsworthy

You have many good things going on in your church that your community should know about. Getting the good news out will be much easier and more successful if you learn to work effectively with the news media. That means getting to know their representatives, understanding their role and what constitutes news, and cooperating with them within the parameters of their operation.

While your angle is to get publicity for an upcoming musical program at your church, they are in the news-reporting business not a publicity-giving enterprise. But you may be able to present your story in such a way that both of you will meet your goals.

What Is Newsworthy?

First, what do the media consider newsworthy?

Timeliness. News is news when it is new. Fish and news both grow old and spoil in a hurry. An event may have been a terrific story two days ago. Today it is history.

Of consequence to the average person. A main criterion has to be: How many people want to know about this particular situation? Will this story appeal to a broad range of citizens?

From an important source. All of us are interested in knowing what the president of the United States has to say about a certain situation or challenge, especially in times of emergency and severe national problems. The higher the profile of the evangelist who is coming to hold a meeting in your church, the more likely it is that the media will be interested.

Of human interest. Stories of unusual courage, great sacrifice, outstanding service, and tremendous emotion pique the interest of the reader, listener, and viewer.

Suspenseful. Few people can resist being captivated by a story about real people in a dangerous or an unpredictable situation.

Some of the information in this chapter has previously been published in *How to Handle the News Media*, written by the author and Dean Angel (Betterway Publications, 1992) and is used with the permission of Dean Angel, joint owner of the copyright.

The unusual, the unique. The first time something happens, it's news. After that, it may be done bigger and better by someone else, but it probably will not receive that much attention.

Conflict or controversy. Get two major forces diametrically opposed to each other in action, and you will have instant news.

An explanation of progress. A developing story keeps everyone's interest.

Disaster or tragedy. Anything having an impact on the safety and lives of a number of people—or even a few, especially if they are well known— interests the majority of people.

Proximity to audience. A rule of thumb here is that the closer the action, the more people will be interested.

Famous people. People are interested in hearing about the rich, the powerful, and the famous.

Basically, those are the characteristics of news. The question is: How can you present your story to make it newsworthy?

Develop an Eye and Ear for News

Keep your antenna constantly tuned for the news angle in the activities, programs, and people associated with your church.

Many churches put on musical programs. What makes yours different? Perhaps the children used their creative ideas in designing and making their own costumes. You might include a picture of that cute little kid with the long, funny bunny ears and whiskers, standing in front of Noah's ark, and point out the angles that would make it an interesting feature story. Or perhaps the musical will be a premier performance, written by a member of your church, a well-known civic figure in your community.

Is your church going to sing at a shopping mall during the Christmas season? That would make a good television story at a time when there's usually not much "hard" news to cover. It would probably also increase your audience for the mall presentation.

Some of the possibilities for news coverage include:

Minister—call of a new minister, appointment, resignation, retirement, anniversary, special awards, publication of book or article, special speaking engagements, ecumenical involvement with other denominations or faiths

Organizations—staff changes, new programs, special training opportunities, courses, vacation Bible school, travel abroad with a religious emphasis by groups from the congregation, groups sponsored by the church such as scouts

Unusual services—outstanding guest speaker or artist; special choir and drama presentations; new approaches to worship; evangelistic meetings; seminars; and special services, for example, New Year's Day and Thanksgiving

Property—ground-breaking for a new facility, dedication of a new building or wing, new recreational facilities, new organ, significant contribution, memorial windows, historic room that could include requests for appropriate memorabilia

Service and involvement opportunities—recreational programs, get-acquainted and fellowship projects, study groups, performing groups, programs for special-needs groups, assistance programs, trips and field trips, volunteer opportunities such as staffing a food pantry

Also, be on the lookout for the human-interest angle for feature stories. These may be unexpected incidents, amusing happenings, strange coincidences or poignant little dramas. Mood and atmosphere may be created in these types of stories by the use of details that would be irrelevant in most stories. Use of an imaginative lead, suspense, humor, or a twist at the end often will spark interest with an editor.

A story about a young man with one leg who played baseball on a church's team, along with a picture of him hopping the bases made its way into five newspapers. His company also did an article, based on the newspaper stories, about him in their newsletter.

Role-play as the assignments editor who receives your information, and read it with his or her eyes to see whether it would make a good story from a news perspective.

Make News Happen

You can also make news happen. For example, plan an event to honor people outside your church who contribute significantly to your community, such as police officers or firefighters. Besides being a lovely thing to do and an excellent way to spark goodwill in your community, the occasion would also be an unusual, newsworthy event.

Be on the alert for opportunities to comment on a current issue. Many emerging stories in your local community relate to Christian ethics. As a Christian leader, you have a valuable perspective to offer. Call the reporter who is assigned to a particular story and state your viewpoint. Often reporters are searching for an intelligent, pertinent quote to add to their stories.

Don't overlook the letter to the editor to present your viewpoint on what's happening both locally and nationally. A well-written letter can sway public opinion, increase your personal credibility, and enhance the standing of your church in the community. Talk radio programs also present a forum for a Christian viewpoint as well as an opportunity to generate interest in your church.

Whatever you do, don't tell an editor that you want "some publicity." Using that terminology will be a real interest-killer, even if the story does have merit from a news angle.

Develop a Good Relationship

Developing a good working relationship with news-media representatives is the next step in getting your message out.

- Get to know the editor of your local weekly. Become acquainted with the religion writer of the big-city daily and his or her writing. Study the papers to see what kind of stories he or she likes to use.
- Find out the deadlines for each medium, and get your material to each one with plenty of lead time. Also, do not call in a story unless it is of high immediate news value and there is not time to write and get it in by the deadline. Especially, don't call with a story idea if it's the day the newspaper goes to press. Respect the pressures of news people, their job, and their deadlines.
- Make sure the names on your media contact list are up to date. Addressing a news release to a former editor gets you off on the wrong foot. Ascertain whether Kelly (or people with other unisex names) is a man or a woman. Also, don't risk spelling a name incorrectly. Keeping your news-media list in a loose-leaf notebook with a page devoted to each medium makes it easier and neater to keep your information up-to-date. (For more help on doing this, see the form entitled "News Medium Information," which you can find on page 236.)
- Return reporters' calls promptly. Help them get their story done as quickly and easily as possible.
- Be meticulous in the accuracy of the information you release. A few mistakes on your part will quickly earn you the reputation of being an unreliable source. Also, don't wear out your welcome by sending frequent news releases about trivial matters. Editors, deluged by inconsequential information from a group, have been known to toss its news releases in the round file automatically on sight of the return address, without even opening them.
- Point out how what you are doing can be tied in with something that is happening on a national level or can be a step toward solving a prevalent social or community problem. Share statistics and other pertinent material you have access to that may not be known by the reporter. This will help the reporter look good and may result in a favorable story for your church or ministry.
- Say "thanks" for a job well done. A phone call or, even better, a note to the reporter with a copy to the reporter's boss is a nice touch and may give you an opportunity to plant a seed for a future story.
- Be sure to let the news media know whether a scheduled event has been called off.

- Save complaints and criticisms for serious problems. Grievances to the editor should be made only if an issue is important and cannot be resolved with the reporter.
- Don't ask to see or hear a story before it is used.
- In addition to formal news releases, send the media copies of newsletters, notices of special events, annual reports, and information about meetings. It is amazing what a reporter sometimes will see, in what seems to be an unimportant item, to turn into a feature story.
- Offer to share your expertise for assistance with future stories. Reporters often need local sources to quote in connection with a national issue. For example, if you or a staff member is an authority or scholar on an issue, such as church and state or the situation in Israel, send the appropriate media editors your credentials and anything you may have authored on the subject. This should be accompanied by a letter stating your willingness to provide background information and be interviewed. Such references enhance your credibility in the community and give your ministry positive publicity.

Every radio and television station is required by the Federal Communications Commission (FCC) to complete an ascertainment list each quarter. This entails contacting community leaders each quarter for the issues and concerns that they feel are currently most important to their city and area. These may include categories such as crime, pollution, traffic, racism, education, and unemployment. The stations are then expected to develop public-affairs programming, including talk shows, to cover these main subjects.

Call and ask the public-affairs director for a copy of the current FCC ascertainment list. Then see how your expertise or church programs, which may relate to a concern area, might lend themselves for use in one of their future programs. Most public-affairs directors who are looking for a way to fulfill this obligation would welcome your input and your offer to appear on such a program.

A recent trend in the news media's approach to coverage, called public journalism or civic journalism, provides opportunities for community involvement in the news making process. Ministers and other citizens can play a role in determining issues that need to be covered. They can also voice their opinions to a greater degree and may be able to become recognized by the media as sources in certain fields of expertise. *U.S. News & World Report* commented as follows:

In theory, this means news organizations become involved in the process of finding solutions to community problems rather than only reporting them. In practice, news organizations become either moderators or advocates for change—often asking their readers what they want covered or bringing activists into gatherings where they hash out problems.[1]

Editors and reporters from the *Virginian-Pilot* in Norfolk, Virginia, summarize the changes they have made in order to become "public journalists":

> They look not just for sources at the opposite extremes of an issue, but for more moderate folks in the middle; they frame events in terms of people's daily experiences, instead of inserting them as incidental furniture in stories about official politics; they use people's emotions to show how they arrive at their decisions, instead of just as color to show how people feel about the issue; they describe the values people bring to an issue, including the gray areas and complexities, rather than simply describing the conflict; they value citizens' knowledge as well as the experts' knowledge; in writing about who, what, why, when, and where, they also try to explain to citizens why they should care; and they try to explore how people are resolving the issue, suggesting that solutions are possible and that the reader might play a role in them.[2]

Cheryl McCallister, producer of Family 1st for WFAA-TV, the ABC affiliate in Dallas, Texas, says that Channel 8 became involved in this approach in 1993, after several reporters returned from assignments talking about input they had received from police officers, teachers, and community leaders linking a dramatic increase in juvenile violence to the breakdown of the family. They started Family 1st public forums in which any citizen may participate.

A couple of years later, the station added News 8 Listens meetings, since all subjects did not relate to the family. In response to letters they receive from citizens and what's going on in churches and the community, the reporters select a topic to be discussed in the town meetings. They invite a panel of experts on the subject to participate. "We are the instrument to get the message out to the public," McCallister observes. Their approach is solution-oriented in focusing in on problems in the community. She says that their efforts have been well received by the public. Efforts such as those of Channel 8 provide an excellent opportunity for ministers and lay leaders to make their viewpoints known and to offer input on what is to be covered.[3]

Which Medium Should Get Which Message?

Which of the media would be interested in covering a particular story? Study the news media and notice the types of stories they use. What audience does a certain medium reach? What is its coverage area?

A big-city daily newspaper's goal is to reach the total population in that city and the surrounding smaller towns. It will also likely have a state edition, which appeals to an even wider readership. It thus is not likely to use a story about your promotion-Sunday activities.

However, a close perusal of the dailies reveals specialized interest columns and pages as well as various calendars, which may well give you a forum. Most dailies have columnists who write on pursuits and concerns of special ethnic, age, hobby, or community groups.

For example, your concert will not make the front page, but it probably would rate a small blurb in an activities column on the Saturday religion page. The same information might also be used in the arts section or an entertainment guide, especially if the group is well known. An item about a seminar on managing finances could find a home in the business section or on an events calendar, if the general public is invited. A youth group that adopts nursing-home residents as "grandparents" might make a feature story in a daily's living section around Grandparent's Day.

Find out the names of the editors or columnists who will likely be interested in the types of stories you want to see in print. Address your news release to those specific journalists by name. Do not assume that the right person will get the information if it's just sent to the newspaper.

The weekly newspaper in a city and the community newspaper that publishes once or twice a week in a smaller town have quite a different purpose than that of the metropolitan newspaper. They are interested in covering news about the people and events in their own communities. They welcome stories that the big-city press would turn up its nose at.

There is also the distinct possibility that your story will have a greater impact on those whom you want to reach, if it is in your community newspaper rather than if it is in the urban publication. It will almost certainly receive more space, which means that more details can be included.

Kathie Magers, editor of *The Oak Cliff Tribune,* a Dallas weekly, says, "Unlike the metro papers, we are not only willing, but enthusiastic about printing news of local events and local people . . . that means everything that happens in our circulation area."[4]

What About Pictures?

Sending an interesting, well-composed picture to a weekly will usually give your story a better chance of being used. Dailies, on the other hand, rarely use pictures that have not been taken by staff photographers, with the exception of a portrait-type picture.

Follow these guidelines in submitting pictures:

- Send a glossy black-and-white print, preferably five by seven in size or a good quality, black-and-white instamatic print with plenty of contrast. A sharp color print might be accepted, but the chances aren't as good.
- Be sure to identify the people as they appear in the photograph from left to right and tell what they are doing or what they did.
- Never write on the back of the picture or attach anything with a paper clip. Tape your caption to the back of the photo.
- Unless it is a portrait, have the subjects do something more attention-getting than staring at the camera. An informal group is more interesting than a lineup. Limit the subjects to not more than five or six.
- Close-ups of faces are more interesting and more attention-getting than full-length long shots.
- If pictures of objects must be shot, try to incorporate people with them in a logical way. For example, if the story is about a new, magnificent organ, take a picture of an organist playing the instrument.
- If you want a picture returned, write a note to that effect and enclose a self-addressed, stamped envelope. Usually you will get it back, but don't bank on it, especially if it is a one-of-a-kind, irreplaceable shot.

Know Different Needs of Radio and Television

It is important to keep in mind the unique qualities of radio and television. A story in which someone can be shown doing something unusual and interesting will be more appealing to television-assignment editors. Events that have strong auditory appeal and help a listener imagine a happening in his or her mind's eye are naturals for a brief spot on radio.

Also, while most television stations are trying to appeal to the masses with their news reports, radio stations usually have a more specialized audience. Many stations focus on a certain ethnic group, a particular age segment, or a specific socioeconomic cluster as their targeted listeners. Of course, Christian radio stations would be especially interested in your activities.

By putting a slightly different slant on the same story, you may well give it appeal for widely varying stations and newspapers. It is certainly worth the time and effort to individualize a story to meet the various media's needs and interests when the result is more coverage.

Check Out Community Bulletin Boards

Many radio stations, some television stations, and public-access cable-television channels have bulletin boards that you can use to help publicize a coming event of interest to the community. Such announcements should be typed and sent to the appropriate person at each station at least three weeks in advance. Be sure to include the name and phone number of the contact person in case more information is needed.

Try a Public Service Announcement

If you have a special event coming up that would be of interest to the general public, try the public service announcement (PSA). Radio and television stations are required by law to devote a certain amount of air time to public service. If your project is the most exciting or worthwhile event happening that week, you just might get some valuable free publicity.

These are general requirements for a PSA:

- noncontroversial (no topics like abortion)
- noncommercial (no reference to paid service)
- no lotteries (no events such as bingo or a raffle)
- no direct cash solicitation
- no other media promotional expenses

Announcements should be sent to a radio station to the attention of the public-service director at least three weeks prior to the date of the special event. Your public-service announcement should follow the following guidelines (for more information about this, see the form entitled "Sample Public Service Announcement," which you can find on page 238):

1. Put your return address in the top left-hand corner or use your printed stationery.
2. Center and type "Public Service Announcement" underlined or boldfaced.
3. Double space and type: "Contact:" followed by the person's name and phone number in case there are questions.
4. Announcements should be double-spaced.
5. Place "For use:" with beginning and ending dates that you want the announcement to run.
6. Include three lengths: a ten-second version, a fifteen-second version, and a thirty-second version.

The length that is used will depend on the time that is available.

January through April is a slower time for commercials, so your longer version has a better chance for use during those months.

Television stations also use public-service announcements, but it is usually harder to get them broadcast. Since requirements for visual material vary from station to station, contact the public-service director for information about his or her particular needs.

What About a News Conference?

News conferences should be used sparingly and be well done. Calling a news conference for a trivial reason will rapidly turn into a nonevent with little or no response. Trying to blow out of proportion the impact of information to be released in order to get reporters to attend will ruin your credibility with them and their editors. Make sure you have something to share that is important, timely, and of genuine worth.

When, Then, Should a News Conference Be Called?

- An event has happened that is of importance to thousands of people.
- A briefing to update developments in a continuing story is appropriate. An example is a natural disaster in which several people were severely injured.
- A nationally or internationally known expert or celebrity is going to speak at your church and is willing to appear before the news media. This person would need to be on the level of James Dobson, Billy Graham, or Chuck Swindoll.

Here are some guidelines to follow in setting up a news conference.

- Don't refer to the event as a "press conference." This term not only dates you, but it also irritates radio and television professionals who have nothing to do with presses. Use "news conference" or "media conference" instead.
- Carefully develop your list of journalists to invite. Make sure your announcement pertains to their areas of interest.
- If time permits, send a written invitation, even if it must be hand delivered. Follow up with a phone call to help determine an approximate number of attendees. In the case of a late-breaking news conference, invite reporters by telephone.
- Set the time for the reporters' convenience. Usually a midmorning conference is best, for it gives reporters time to file their stories by deadline.
- Notify United Press International (UPI) and Associated Press (AP) Day Book editors about the conference well in advance, if possible.
- Don't leak information. It is not only unfair to those attending,

but such a tactic will land you in their "bad books." Make information available to reporters who are unable to attend after the conference is over.

- Select a facility of appropriate size. One that is too large makes it seem as though few people were interested—even when there is a relatively good turnout. On the other hand, a crowded room is not only irritating to reporters and television crews but can hamper their getting the best possible story.
- Make sure that there are enough telephones available, and be certain you can accommodate television needs with heavy-duty extension cords and electrical outlets. Also provide a raised platform or sturdy tables at the back of the room for camera operators.
- If you have a logo for your ministry, display it in front of the lectern or behind the speaker.
- Anticipate all possible questions, and go over them with those who will be interviewed.
- Make certain that any audiovisual aids and equipment are in place, working properly, and that their use has been mastered by the person or persons making the presentation.
- Prepare a news kit to hand out to reporters that contains the following types of items: background information; appropriate pictures (for example, a name speaker or your new building designed by a nationally-known architect); any pertinent drawings or diagrams; a copy of the formal statement that will be given at the news conference; and a copy of any audio or video demonstration tape that will be used during the conference.

The Day of the Conference

Post someone at the door to greet reporters, pass out news kits, and assist them in any way possible. Provide refreshments, such as coffee, tea, soft drinks, mineral water, and pastries.

The news conference should begin with an introduction of the chief-executive officer, celebrity, or other key person. The formal statement would then be given, followed with an opportunity for reporters to ask questions of that person and perhaps a panel of experts, if appropriate.

If an important aspect of the program has not been covered, ask an appropriate question yourself. Or, if you are the person being questioned, say something like, "I am often asked . . ." Then proceed to answer the question you have raised.

Give the media adequate rein, but do not let the conference get off course. If the subject has been well explored and interest seems to be waning, state, "We have time for one or two more questions."

Thank the reporters for their time and attendance and end the conference.

Make What You Send Out Look Professional

Whether it's a PSA or a news release, make sure that your information is presented in an accepted, professional journalistic format, is easily read, and looks slick and appealing. Here are some general guidelines to assist you in preparing a professional-looking news release (for more help on doing this, see the form entitled "News Release Worksheet," which you can find on page 236).

1. Type it, double-spaced, one side only, on 8½-by-11-inch paper. Leave ample margins of about one and one-half inches. If you do not have special news-release stationery, use your ministry letterhead, or put your return address in the upper left-hand corner.
2. Space down three or four times and center the words *NEWS RELEASE* in caps or boldface type.
3. Skip a couple of spaces and put the word *Contact:* to the right with the name and phone number of the person whom the media should call for more information.
4. At the left, put the words *For release* with the date it may be used.
5. Skip a space and put a headline in caps, containing a subject and an infinitive or present-tense verb. Your headline probably will not be used, but it gives the editor an immediate grasp of what your story is about.
6. Double space and begin your story. If the release must run more than one page, center the word *More* at the bottom of the page. Then at the top of the next page, put *1st add xxxx,* followed by the headline in caps.
7. End each page with a complete paragraph.
8. Type "30" or "###" in the center of the page under the final paragraph. Be sure to keep a copy for your own files.

What Should You Include?

Try these suggestions for writing a news release that sounds smooth and professional.

- Include the five *w*'s—who, why, what, when, where—and also tell how. However, don't try to include all this information in the first sentence or even, necessarily, in the first paragraph. Pick out the most vital *w*'s and feature those first. You can include the others later as you expand on the story. Editors generally cut from the bottom, so you want to be sure to get the major facts into the first part of the story.
- Give your story a personal touch. For example, tell about one particular person who was helped by your outreach to the needy.

- Be accurate and objective. Avoid opinionated statements and adjectives. For example, if you want to say that a particular program made a difference in the lives of the participants, quote someone who actually said that. Keep opinions locked up in quotation marks.
- Use short sentences and words found in everyday conversation. Use strong, colorful verbs.
- Avoid religious terms that might not be understood by the person on the street (such as *prayer warrior*) and acronyms that are not spelled out.
- Include full names and identifying titles.
- Be as brief as possible, but be sure to cover the important facts about the event.
- List the date, along with the day of the week of an event. Abbreviate days of the week and months.
- Be aware that copy which requires little editing stands a better chance of being used.

Editors will either regard you as a dependable and discriminating news source (and thus use the material you prepare), or they will regard you as unreliable and indiscriminate (and thus toss your material in the wastebasket).

Keep Tabs on Your Coverage

Keep a notebook of the news releases and contacts that you make. Include clippings and records of such events as public service announcements and appearances on talk shows. Also, track the results of your efforts, such as attendance at meetings and comments you have heard about each story. This will help you determine the effectiveness of a particular approach and will serve as an impressive record of your communication efforts.

Becoming thoroughly familiar with the media in your area and developing an eye and ear for material that will appeal to them can result in many positive stories and good publicity for your ministry. Successfully getting your church's message out through the news media can be challenging, time consuming, and, at times, frustrating. But the results can be rewarding. And it's free!

News Release Worksheet

Subject_____

Who? _____

What? _____

Where? _____

When?_____

Why? _____

How?_____

Contact for further information _____

Publicity approaches. News release___Handbills___Posters _____

Bulletin_____ Pulpit announcements_____Newsletter _____

Public-service announcement____ Mailing____ Phone calls _____

Other_____

Pictures needed _____

Date for taking pictures _____

Date for mailing releases and PSAs _____

Notes_____

News Medium Information

News Medium _____

Mailing address _____

Phone number_____ FAX number _____

Owner or affiliate _____

Coverage area _____

Assignments editor _____

Reporter _____

Columnists and specialized reporters _____

_____

Special features (community bulletin board, events calendar, and so

forth) _____

_____

Publication day(s) _____

Deadline _____

Deadline for holiday material _____

Sample News Release

Joy in Life Church
4713 E. Main Street
Centerville, Colorado 73067

Contact: Heidi Windham
(717) 555-8176

FOR RELEASE: Dec. 7, 1999

JOY OF LIFE CHURCH
TO PRESENT CHRISTMAS PLAY

"Special Report: Bethlehem," a play based on the Christmas story but with a contemporary slant, will be presented at 6:30 p.m. Sun., Dec. 22, at Joy of Life Church. The church is located at 4713 E. Main St. in Centerville.

The 50-member cast includes participants from The King's Company Drama Ministry, tambourine teams and a sign-language choir. The play was written by and is directed by Judith Jernigan.

In the play, a television anchor in the newsroom and a reporter on location in Bethlehem are attempting to tell the story behind the brilliant star shining over a stable in Bethlehem. The reporter interviews the main characters in the Christmas story. Following each interview, a psychologist tries to explain away what each has said. For example, she says that Joseph is clearly in denial and refuses to face reality. The often humorous special report climaxes in a surprise ending.

The community is invited to attend the admission-free performance. For more information, call 555-8176.

###

Sample Public Service Announcement

Joy in Life Church
4713 E. Main Street
Centerville, Colorado 73067

Contact: Heidi Windham
(717) 555-8176

FOR USE: Dec. 15–22, 1999

ANNOUNCER: (10 seconds) Joy in Life Church invites you to see their Christmas production of "Special Report: Bethlehem" at 7 p.m., Sun., Dec. 23 at 4713 Main St. in Centerville.

ANNOUNCER: (15 seconds) Your whole family will enjoy seeing "Special Report: Bethlehem," a play with a fresh approach to the Christmas story. The production will be at 7 p.m., Sun., Dec. 23, at Joy in Life Church, 4713 E. Main St. in Centerville.

ANNOUNCER: (30 seconds) Your whole family will be inspired, entertained and surprised by seeing "Special Report: Bethlehem," a play with a fresh approach to the Christmas story. The 50-member cast production will be presented at 7 p.m., Sun., Dec. 23, at Joy in Life Church, 4713 E. Main St. in Centerville. There is no admission charge, and everyone is invited. It's rated "G" for great entertainment. Call 555-8176 for more information.

###

19 Communicating in a Crisis

A church bus carrying teenagers home from a summer church camp is swept away by flood waters. The fate of most of the occupants is unknown.

A church is heavily damaged by fire. Arson is suspected.

Parents bring charges against a youth minister for seducing their teenager.

The chairman of the church board is indicted for embezzling a large sum of money from his company.

How would you handle it if one of those situations happened in your church?

Most of us think, *That couldn't happen here, not in my congregation.* But situations like these do happen, and, with the news media's accelerated focus on what's wrong in religious circles, it certainly pays to be prepared.

Know What to Expect from the Media

Being prepared means knowing what to expect from the media and the way in which to respond that will be most advantageous to you and to your church in an emergency situation. Once a crisis occurs, the news media will be close on its heels. And they will not be put off. The reporters have been given an assignment. Their job depends on their getting in a story by deadline.

Saying, "No comment" or "I'll meet with you when I have more information" won't work. If you won't talk, they will get their information from someone who will—someone who may give opinion rather than fact or someone who has an axe to grind. If the media can't get something from the "horse's mouth," they will get something from somebody in time to meet their deadline. Here's the

---

Some of the information in this chapter has previously been published in *How to Handle the News Media*, written by the author and Dean Angel (Betterway Publications, 1992) and is used with the permission of Dean Angel, joint owner of the copyright.

point to remember: it is far better to have accurate information from a top official in tomorrow's newspaper than to have rumors quoted there from an outside source.

When the emergency situation occurs, it is a waste of time to quarrel with a reporter by saying something like, "I can't imagine why you're interested in this. After all, it's just a little matter between church members," or "Why don't you spend time explaining why millions of tax dollars are wasted by outlandish government spending, rather than worrying about one little church's finances?"

The reporter really doesn't care what you think of a story being done on your church's finances. His or her job is to get the assigned story, and the journalist is probably going to become very irritated at those kinds of comments.

Hassling the reporter, claiming no knowledge, or minimizing the situation will make the reporter suspect that you are hiding something. Refusing to return a reporter's calls will irritate him or her and usually result in a more damaging story.

As the official spokesperson, it is to your advantage to give the facts as you know them. Then state that you are looking into the situation and will hold a news conference at a certain time later that day. The reporter knows that an incident did occur, that the situation is under control, that you are not attempting to cover it up, that you know the importance of an immediate response, and that more information will be given at a specific time. This gives him or her something to report and you time to plan for the news conference.

News Conferences Provide Opportunities

At the news conference, give the information as you know it to be. Details that have not been completely verified should be prefaced with "as we have been able to ascertain so far" or "at this point, we believe . . ."

Give the steps that your church or ministry plans to take to rectify the problem or to keep the public apprised of the situation. For example, if the church has been destroyed by fire, try to give the location where Sunday services will be held. Make it a point to work in as many positive elements as possible—such as the quick-thinking and heroic efforts of workers in evacuating the young children from the building.

Donald W. Blohowiak, author of *No Comment! An Executive's Essential Guide to the News Media,* gives the following advice:

Reveal bad news in total. The slow drip, drip, drip of damaging facts piques public interest and surrounds the story in an air of a drama unfolding . . . revealing all there is to tell right off the bat allows the media to tell everything in one shot. The resulting bang may be deafening for a brief moment, but then it's in one ear, out the other, and quickly forgotten in the face of noise from other news events.[1]

In a controversial situation, avoid giving the reporters the opportunity to keep the story going over several days or even longer. You do not want them to keep coming back and prolonging and enlarging on the story. A one-time negative story is not nearly as damaging as one that is reported on at several points and by an increasing number of stations and newspapers. Telling about a plausible plan to rectify a problem may dim the reporters' interest in a return visit.

Respond in an Interview to Your Best Advantage

Becoming familiar with the news media in your area and how they operate before a crisis will give you a distinct advantage. What are the reputations and records of the stations and newspapers you might conceivably deal with? Who are their audiences? Who are the reporters who might logically be assigned to cover a story about your organization? Would they be familiar with your church or ministry?

If you've worked in advance to establish credible media relations on an ongoing basis, you have a distinct head start in dealing with the media in a crisis. Julia Duin, a writer for newspapers for more than a decade suggests, "Know whom you are dealing with." She points out that, according to the survey of media attitudes conducted by Lichter-Rothman, reporters are far more liberal than are the people they report on.[2] Don't expect most reporters to agree with your viewpoint. However, don't give them the impression that you think that the "heathen secular media . . . are controlled (with rare exceptions) by their father, the devil" as one televangelist wrote in his newsletter.[3]

Showing news people respect as professionals who are doing a difficult job will usually result in their showing respect for you as a professional who is doing a difficult job.

Decide What You Want to Say

First, pick the spot for the interview that will be most advantageous to you. Have in mind an alternative setting in case there is too much glare, noise, or other distractions in your first choice location.

Then decide what the overriding message is that you want to get across. Try to frame a statement in one sentence that will tell your story. You may even want to write it down and memorize it so you can speak smoothly and with confidence. Don't assume that the reporter will ask the right questions so that you can present the information you desire. Having a clear, concise statement already prepared will help you weave it into the interview.

Be aware that the anchor's introduction of the story and the reporter's comments probably will take up most of the time allowed for that particular report. There may be room for only one sentence from you as an interviewee. Be sure it says, in a nutshell, what you want to leave with the listener.

Anticipate Possible Questions

Cast yourself in the reporters' role and ask yourself what questions you would want answered about this particular story. Ask a colleague to help you brainstorm possibilities. Focus on the line of questioning that might come from a reporter who is not well informed or from an aggressive type who may ask abrasive and probing questions. Be prepared to field each question with a brief, well-thought-out reply.

Help the Reporter Understand the Situation

Remember, your best protection against an erroneous, slanted story is a reporter who fully understands the situation. He or she may be new to your city or may not know any of the background. Assume that the reporter is rather ignorant on the subject. It is better to be too basic than to assume knowledge that isn't there. Keep in mind that silence is not a good option, for it can appear that you have something to hide.

Use Set-up Time to Good Advantage

Even if the reporter and videographer appear rushed, they have to take time to get ready for the interview. As the person being interviewed, you can use that time to good advantage by talking in a friendly manner with the reporter. What you say during those few minutes can help plant ideas in her or his mind that will lead to questions that will allow you to say what you desire.

Also, be cordial to the videographer. Although the reporter is in charge, the videographer also can influence the outcome of the television interview. Too often the videographer is ignored by the interviewee as though he or she is only part of the equipment. But remember that the videographer determines the camera angle to shoot and whether to use an extreme close-up. Probably, too, the reporter will discuss the story on the ride back to the studio with the videographer. Sometimes, if the reporter has to go cover another story, it is the videographer who will decide how the story should be edited. Learn and use both their names.

Be Conversational in Tone and Use Simple Language

You do not want your replies to sound as though you are giving some kind of oration. Neither do you want your response to sound as though it is coming out of a textbook. Think of it as an opportunity to go into the citizen's living room and explain your point of view or situation.

Remember that a news interview is not the place to display your excellent vocabulary. Newspapers are written on an eighth grade reading level for a reason—so that everyone can understand them. A reporter will not use your reply if it is couched in language that is over the head of the average person. Rather, you will find your words rephrased in the final story in simpler terms by the reporter. It is especially important to avoid using theological terms and acronyms. Use words and terms that communicate your message precisely and concisely to the average person.

Be Enthusiastic and Spontaneous

People will be much more interested in what you have to say if your words and facial expressions are a matching pair. A deadpan expression is boring and turns viewers off. Also, be aware that a shot of you with the voice of the reporter over the picture may be used when you are not even speaking. Or you may be speaking, but your volume is lowered while the reporter tells the story.

Though your responses may be well prepared, they must appear to be spontaneous. The way you say what you want to share may be as important or more important than what you say.

Look at the Reporter; Leave the Microphone Alone

Never look directly into the camera in a news interview situation. It looks unnatural, awkward, and even shifty to the viewer, especially if the interviewee looks back and forth from the reporter to the camera lens.

The reporter will position the microphone in front of you for your reply. Resist any temptation to reach out and take it or even touch it. The reporter is not about to let you hold it. At worst, it may come off looking like you are in a physical struggle for possession of the microphone.

It is the reporter's responsibility to make certain that the audio is being recorded at the proper level. That, of course, involves knowing the type of microphone and the distance it should be from the interviewee's mouth.

Remember That Honesty Is the Best Policy

It is far better to admit to an error or mistake than to try to cover it up. Reporters seem to take great delight in exposing lies and misrepresentations. The next couple of examples back up the wisdom of going the honesty route. Not only reporters, but also the public seems to respect the integrity of someone who admits, "I was wrong."

When President John F. Kennedy acknowledged his responsibility for the Bay of Pigs fiasco, polls showed his popularity did not wane. In fact, it went up 10 percent.

Several years ago, Ford Motor Company recalled thousands of Montego automobiles because of faulty axles. They were not sure what the impact would be. Apparently, though, the buying public appreciated their diligence in not risking the safety of Ford automobile owners. After that, sales rose 77 percent.

If you made a mistake, present a plan for rectifying that error. Also, admitting a mistake removes the controversy, and the story may well die a natural death at that point. Not admitting to an error will usually result in deeper probing and more media attention. That tactic also can get you on a reporter's "hit list," which is not a good place to be.

Get to the Point Concisely

Chances are your interview for television news will last from three to five minutes. After the interview is edited, the story may last only about thirty seconds, and your statement will be even shorter. You may end up with only one or two sentences from the entire interview. The reporter may talk over a sentence in your interview, with only a part of the sentence of your actual words being used. Thus, you do not have the luxury of being expansive and elaborative on a statement. Make your point with the fewest words possible.

Interrupt Rather Than Submit to Unfair Questions

Don't be badgered into answering a question that you deem unfair, irrelevant, or inaccurate. Cut in with something like, "I would have to preface my answer with the real facts in this situation" and proceed to do so. If the question is a blatant trap, you might even say something like, "I'm sorry but I really can't answer a loaded question like that." Then you can add, "but I will say." Whatever your response is, be sure you say it in a pleasant way.

Bridge from the Question to What You Want to Say

Even though the reporter chooses and directs the questions, remember that you control the answers. You can briefly answer the question and, in the same sentence, expand the topic to include the message you want to put across. You can say something along the lines of:

"but it's also important to remember . . ."

"and that reminds me of . . ."

"while that is a problem, this is what we are doing to try to solve it . . ."

"Of course this is a challenge, but it's no greater than one we've successfully met in the past."

Turn the Question

If the question is one that you do not want to answer, don't answer it, but do so in a pleasant way that is not offensive. You can respond with something like:

"I don't really see that as the main issue here. The main issue is . . ."

"I would have thought your question would be . . ." Then proceed to answer it.

"I think most people are more interested in . . . and, of course, that's what we're concentrating on here."

Buy Time to Think of an Answer

If you are taken off guard by a question, stall for time in order to come up with a good answer. For example, ask the reporter to repeat the question. Or tell the reporter that you want to be sure that you understand the question. Rephrase it and ask him or her whether that is the correct interpretation. During this exchange you will have a good chance to order your thoughts.

Remember Who the Real Audience Is

While you are talking with a reporter, remember that your real audience is not the reporter. The listener or viewer is the person your message is directed toward. Don't think about that one individual with the microphone but rather about the public and what you want it to know. Your goal is to get beyond the "human filter" and reach the reporter's audience.

Avoid Answering Ranking Questions Too Specifically

If a reporter tries to pin you down to your number-one priority or major concern, you would do well to hedge the question by making it more inclusive. You might counter with, "Well, of course, we have several important priorities. Among these are . . ." Then discuss one or two.

Use the Reporter's Name in an Important Statement

Reporters are human, too. They like to have their name within the report as well as at the end. It makes them seem to be well known and respected in their field. Addressing the reporter by name gives you a better chance of getting your priority statement included in the story.

Realize That the Reporter May Know Something You Don't

If the reporter brings up something you are not aware of or an accusation someone has made, be careful in your response. Be prepared to say something like, "I am not aware of a problem in that area," or "I will be glad to look into that."

Sometimes a reporter may have a predetermined mindset about the situation. In the case of an obviously erroneous belief on the part of the reporter, the person being interviewed must be convincing to overcome the inability of the reporter to grasp the truth.

You might confront the reporter with an empathizing phrase, such as, "That's difficult to believe, isn't it?" or "That trend's been dead for several years." Or an even more forceful response, such as "Your story may already be written, but I don't believe it's complete" may help. Try to force a mental turnabout. Then back up your statement with solid facts, background, and reasons to drop the original hypothesis.

Do not allow a reporter to put you on the defensive. Be bold, ensuring that you present proactive elements of the story. If the reporter surprises you with rumors, say something like, "I don't know about the rumors, but I do know . . ."

Remember These Don'ts:

- Avoid responding with "no comment" or "talk to my lawyer," especially if the camera is already rolling. That will almost certainly be used on that night's news, particularly if you are scowling or shaking your fist at the reporter. Those types of replies put you in an adversarial role and make it appear that you have something to hide. It is better to be unavailable for comment, especially if you do not wish to be interviewed. If, in the case of a matter under litigation, your attorney has instructed you not to speak on the subject, make that explanation politely and with an apology as though you really wish you could oblige the reporter with an interview.

- Don't question the reporter's motive, for that only leads to the media's questioning your motives. Ken Muir, a school information director, has two questions he uses in deciding whether to release information. The first one is "Why should I not provide this information?" He says those who ask instead, "Why should I?" can always come up with a lot of lame excuses. The second question is: "If the questioner were to go to court to get this information, would he win?" If the answer is yes, he says you might as well give it gracefully and save yourself a lot of headaches.[4]
- Don't clam up. Remember that silence can be damning. A reporter will usually try to present both sides of the story. The Fairness Doctrine stated: "Broadcasters are charged by the Federal Communications Commission with the affirmative duty to seek out and broadcast contrasting viewpoints on controversial issues of public importance." While this is no longer in effect, many media outlets still abide by its principle. If only one side is available for comment, that, of course, is the only one the public will hear. It is almost always better to present your case.
- Don't ever become hostile. Unfortunately, there are television reporters who try to goad an interviewee into losing his or her temper, making an angry response, or becoming belligerent. Though that reaction might be justified in light of the provocation, the viewer, doubtless, will never know that. The questions, in all likelihood, will be cut, leaving the interviewee looking like some type of maniac. The interviewee has everything to gain and nothing to lose by responding consistently with politeness and restraint.
- Don't make any remarks off the record. Assume that any statement you might make will be used. There may be a misunderstanding about what you designate as off the record. Even if there is a firm off-the-record agreement, your remark may tip the reporter to an unknown bit of information. The reporter probably can then find someone else to interview and get the same facts. Play it safe and do not say anything that might come back to haunt you. Also, be aware that when a radio reporter calls for a telephone interview, the tape already may be rolling. Any flippant remark may end up on the air.
- Don't be evasive. The importance of at least appearing to be open and aboveboard cannot be overemphasized. An experienced reporter will home in quickly on an area that appears to be upsetting or sensitive to the interviewee.
- Don't give just a yes or no answer. Provide some additional information. Not only does this make for a more interesting

interview, it also gives you an opportunity to elaborate on a point. Sometimes a reporter will ask a loaded question and try to get only a yes or no response. Dr. Richard M. Adams, director of the School Health Services for the Dallas schools, shares his sure-fire method for guaranteeing that he has the opportunity to explain a one-word answer. "I always say, 'I would have to answer that with a qualified yes or a qualified no.' Invariably the reporter will ask, 'What do you mean by a qualified yes?' Then I get to tell more. It works every time."[5]

- Avoid saying "I don't know." Even if you don't know the answer, it is better to present some other response. For example, say something like this: "We're checking on that right now," or "I will have that information for you later today."
- Don't walk away. It is better to stay and face the reporter in a positive manner. You may be able to override the impact of the story with your response. The reporter who is counting on a negative reaction may decide that there really is not an interesting story there after all.

In brief, when a crisis does occur, remember the following:

- Respond quickly
- Don't deny what happened or be evasive.
- Have the highest official possible respond.
- Explain openly that information is being gathered and will be available at a specific time.
- Use media time to present your side of the story with positive facts that cast a more favorable light on your group.
- Prompt positive follow-up stories. If the emergency is a major incident for your town, the media will not let it be over in one day's news cycle. It will, in all likelihood, produce numerous features and side stories for readers, listeners, and viewers.
- Be sure you don't play favorites by giving information to one reporter and not to all of them.

Develop a Crisis-Communications Plan

Being prepared also means developing a crisis-communications plan before the dilemma occurs. The plan should be in writing and should be shared with all personnel. (For more help on doing this, see the form entitled "Emergency Communications Plan," which you can find on page 251.)

Points to be considered in drawing up a plan are:

- Select a spokesperson. Usually this should be the senior pastor or, in the case of a ministry, the group's president. Also, designate a second person in case the first choice is unavailable. Another possibility might be the director of communications. At any rate, that person should be capable of speaking with ease under the pressures of cameras, lights, heavy interrogation, and microphones. A single spokesperson insures that the message and stance of the church or ministry is consistent.
- Prepare and periodically update a fact sheet about your church or ministry. This will ensure that the media receive accurate and current information. This sheet should contain the official name and address of the church, office hours, a schedule of services and other major events, names and phone numbers of staff members, the number of members, major programs within the church, special ministries, the basic area it serves, and a brief history of the church.
- Agree on a location away from the church or crisis scene so that staff members can assess the situation and decide on a course of action.
- Assign specific duties to staff members. The plan should make it clear who is responsible for what. Alternative people should also be named in case someone is on vacation or out of town.
- Plan for an on-site newsroom for the media. In the event of a continuing emergency at a site, often the media become "based" at the location for updating or waiting on further developments. Such a situation means that telephones should be available for reporters. They may require a typewriter or computer, a facsimile machine, a copy machine, work tables or desks, and even an area for news conferences. Withholding assistance or making it difficult for the news people to work will be reflected in their reports. The more assistance the staff can give members of the media, the more understanding most will be about an organization's situation.
- Designate a staff member to keep detailed notes on the chain of events, recording the developments and announcements whenever possible. While this initially may seem trivial and a waste of needed manpower, you will find it to your advantage to document the happenings and related comments. This not only serves as a backup to the media itself, but it may also provide insight for responses and reactions to future emergencies.
- Appoint someone to track news media stories and public reaction to the event.
- Develop a plan for making key people available to reporters.

Although a single top-level spokesperson is essential, the media will want to talk to the individual who is closest to the action—the driver of a church bus involved in a serious accident, the sponsors of a singles' group whose member has disappeared and was last seen at a fellowship in the couple's home, a minister in charge of a youth camp where a child drowned. These key players should be briefed—before they face the media—about what to expect.

- Plan a strategy for keeping reporters informed on the progress of a developing story. For example, briefings could be scheduled at 10:00 A.M. and 4:00 P.M. with information promised immediately when something important happens. Such a schedule allows reporters to work on stories that they expect to file with their news outlets from interviews or photos that have been taken. They then can plan to be on hand for the briefings as scheduled.
- Identify all the critical groups with which you need to communicate. For instance, in the example of the church bus' being swept away by flood waters, there would be family members, church members, friends, and the immediate community to keep informed of the search, in addition to the news media and the general public.
- Decide who might be credible supporters and third-party sources for information and resources.
- Plan how to assume a leadership position in seeking to solve a crisis and ways to communicate from a position of strength.
- Keep media and contact lists up-to-date on a regular basis.
- Update the plan frequently. People and situations change. A communications plan will do you little good unless it meets your current needs.
- Periodically review your procedures and mode of operation to ferret out potential problems that could take on crisis proportions.
- Once the plan is developed, test it. Periodically try it out in a fictional crisis. Role-play with staff members by asking the kinds of questions a reporter might pose in that particular situation. This type of simulation may reveal weaknesses in the plan, which can then be improved.

Ken Fairchild, a Dallas-based media consultant specializing in crisis management, says about the need for an emergency plan, "It's only a crisis if you're unprepared. A good crisis plan won't tell you what to do. A good crisis plan tells how to decide what to do."[6]

There probably never will be a perfect emergency plan to take care of every possible situation. But without a plan, a crisis is sure to produce confusion and only make a bad scenario even worse. A well-thought-out and rehearsed plan can lessen the negative impact of a tragedy and help your church emerge with a more positive image and future.

Emergency Communications Plan

Official spokesperson _____

Alternate spokesperson _____

Current fact sheet _____

Person in charge of on-site newsroom _____

Location of area for reporters _____

Documenter of events _____

Groups to be kept informed _____

_____

_____

Plan for making key people available_____

_____

_____

Plan for keeping reporters informed on developing story _____

_____

_____

_____

Updated media and key contact lists _____

Monitor for media coverage and public reaction _____

Plan for assuming leadership position in solving problem and for communicating from position of strength _____

_____

_____

Dates of emergency communications drill _____

Communicating Beyond Your Congregation

What ye hear in the ear, that preach ye upon the housetops.
—*Matthew 10:27b (KJV)*

20 Reaching Outside the Four Walls

Norma stood far back in the shadows as she watched the laughing, well-groomed people enter the church. She often passed that way as she walked to work. She knew she needed help. She rarely slept, and when she did, often woke up shaken by horrible nightmares. She had finally gotten up the courage to leave her physically and emotionally abusive husband. Fearing for her unborn baby's life as well as her own, she had found a room in a boarding house and a job paying minimum wage. She lived in constant fear that her husband would find her.

Norma had gone to Sunday school as a child and wondered whether maybe someone inside that beautiful building would be able to help her get her life together. And so she had come, wearing the best she had. Now, however, she realized that she just wouldn't fit in with the well-dressed, beautiful people entering the building. Suddenly she felt more alone than ever. Fearing rejection, she looked longingly at the beautiful stained-glass windows and wearily made her way back to her dingy room.

No matter how many evangelical events you hold, regardless of how great your programs are, despite the intriguing appearance of your building, the fact is that many people who desperately need to be touched by the love of Christ will never darken your doors. Perhaps they have grown disillusioned with or perhaps been wounded by the organized church. Maybe, as with Norma, they don't feel that they would be accepted there. Or perhaps they have no hope. Whatever the case may be, there are many instances in which by expanding its concept of the church beyond its four walls, ministries can make a significant impact in the lives of those who need help the most.

This chapter describes dynamic outreaches into the community by several churches and parachurch ministries. Their stories are exciting and inspiring.

Ministering to Needs in a Changing Neighborhood

A decision had to be made. Should Calvary Baptist Church of Oak Cliff, located in one of the oldest parts of Dallas, follow the lead of several sister churches and move to the suburbs? Or should the church remain in its present location and develop new approaches to meeting the needs of the church's rapidly changing neighborhood?

Mostly middle-class Anglos had previously lived in the area in single unit homes. The population had shifted to about 60 percent Hispanic, 10 percent other minorities, and 30 percent lower income and older Anglos living in numerous multifamily dwellings, apartments, and boarding houses.

Pastor David Kuykendall knew that this important decision had to be made by the congregation. When members voted to stay, they ushered in an era of change, innovation, and exciting new challenges. A major change was a redefinition of *church*. Based on Matthew 18:20 (KJV): "For where two or three are gathered together in my name, there am I in the midst of them," Calvary's definition is anytime you meet, pray, study the Bible, and fellowship with other believers, you have church—regardless of the setting.

The settings have become some unlikely spots: halfway houses for former mental patients, alcoholics, and drug addicts; a vacant apartment that became a worship center for apartment dwellers; a cafeteria; nursing homes; and a high-rise apartment building. For the most part, lay leaders are the pastors of the home-type ministries. Qualifications for leaders include being able to walk by faith, knowing God's Word and being able to teach it, and being willing to get involved in the lives of their flock—just as a pastor does.

Kuykendall realizes that many of the people Calvary ministers to in the community and satellite programs probably never will come to the church, for they often don't feel comfortable in a traditional church setting. But members have found that when they are willing to meet them where they are, they are open to ministry. As a result of their involvement, the congregation's concept of missions has changed. They used to help with missions in other places. Now they have become missionaries themselves—right in their own back yards.[1]

Reaching the Inner City

Victory Ministries in Columbus, Ohio, has led thousands to Christ since its beginning in 1983. It has also distributed more than two million pounds of food and countless tons of clothing. Director Lloyd Craycroft points out that churches in the United States during the twentieth century, for the most part, abandoned the inner cities. He says, "When the cities began to be viewed as an undesirable place to live, families and businesses began an exodus to outlying areas. Eventually many of the spiritually alive churches left too. Having built our new sanctuaries as far away as possible from urban blight, we now wonder why the inner cities are filled with such crime and moral decay."

Craycroft believes that if we are to help the poor, we must go back to where they live and take the church with us.

> Problems like absentee fathers, crack cocaine, teenage mothers, third-generation welfare recipients, joblessness and the overall ethical breakdown will not cure themselves. These problems are great and may take a generation to overcome. Yet, with God and the gospel, we can reclaim our cities. . . . The present crisis in urban areas presents a tremendous opportunity for the gospel—if we are courageous enough to take action.[2]

Building Bridges Between the Inner City and Suburbs

Reaching and meeting the needs of people in the inner city is the ministry of Reconciliation Outreach, located just east of downtown Dallas. The Rev. Dorothy Moore, a former New York debutante, heads this dynamic ministry that is supported financially by about a dozen churches. Her own congregation, Hillcrest Church, located in far North Dallas, provides eighty-five volunteers. In the summer of 1996 more than one hundred teenagers from Cincinnati came to work in the ministry.

Reconciliation began about ten years ago when Moore started teaching a Bible study for women in the area and then added an after-school program for children. She says that she has watched many similar works die because the people tried to do it alone and lost their connection with the church. She believes that this relationship with those in the body of Christ is critical to the success of such an undertaking. "The church has to come together to fight against destruction," she says.

Ten years later the vision that God has given her has come to pass. Reconciliation Outreach now sponsors The Refuge, a shelter for women and children. The facility, an apartment building in dire need of repair, was acquired through a grant. Volunteers worked tirelessly to repair the apartments, each of which consists of a living and sleeping area, a small kitchenette, and a bathroom.

The Refuge currently has thirty-eight women and seventeen children as residents. They had all been abused or had lived in the streets and decided to try to turn their lives around. Applicants are screened to make sure they are really serious about wanting help. Adults must also agree to participate in a discipleship program. They work in a disciplined, structured program. There is no initial cost to the participants. Their shelter, food, and clothing are provided through grants and donations from individuals and churches. They receive training through a life-skills program that includes job training, preparation of a resume, and instruction on how to dress and answer the phone. Mothers are also required to attend parenting classes one day a week. As they become able to work, employment opportunities are provided through the ministry's employment agency, Samaritan Staffing.

Does it work? One of many success stories is Twanna, who was on drugs and living on the street when she came to Reconciliation. She had lost her children, was illiterate, and had no hope. She is now drug free, recently married, and will soon get her children back. She works in the ministry's thrift store and is learning to read.

There is also a shelter for men who, mostly, have been on drugs. The program began with seven men who are now as Moore says, "strong in the Lord and equipped to work." Each of the fourteen current residents is paired with another man as a mentor in a discipleship program. The leader of the shelter is the former drummer in a well-known heavy-metal rock band, who had been in prison on drug-related charges.

Another important aspect of the program is the East Dallas Crusaders and Junior Crusaders, a Thursday-night meeting that involves about one hundred teens and preteens who live in the area. Volunteers transport the children to and from the program each week. During the summer, they have programs for the eight- to twelve-year-olds from Monday through Thursday. All the Crusaders are invited to attend Kids Across America (a Kanakuk-Kanakomo Camp) in the summer. Expenses are paid through donations. After-school programs at various schools and at Reconciliation headquarters help the children with school work and relationships and provide recreation.

Sundays and Wednesdays find participants from Reconciliation worshiping and taking classes at Hillcrest Church. Part of Moore's original vision was to break down the walls between the inner city and the suburbs. Apparently that's happened to an amazing extent.[3]

Demonstrating Love by Being Servants

Steve Sjogren, pastor of Vineyard Community Church in Cincinnati, saw his congregation grow from thirty to three thousand in a matter of six years. About 50 percent of his membership comes from unchurched backgrounds.

Sjogren is convinced that demonstrating the love of Christ in simple, nonthreatening ways is the best approach to evangelization. Members put that precept into action in Vineyard's "servant evangelism" projects, which touch more than one hundred thousand people in the Cincinnati area in a year. Participants clean public restrooms for amazed restaurant managers, wash people's cars, offer cold drinks to joggers, and put quarters into expired parking meters—all free of charge. They find that they can build bridges to the unchurched by actions first and words later. "People don't necessarily remember what they are told about God's love," Sjogren comments, "but they never forget what they have experienced of God's love."[4]

Caring for the Homeless

"The Stewpot in Dallas is a free food center run by the First Presbyterian Church but looks more like a friendly restaurant. The dining room is spotless and decorated with plants. Incredibly, as if it was an elegant bistro, one of the diners played a piano to entertain the lunchtime crowd."[5]

This description of The Stewpot grew out of an article in the *National Enquirer* based on visits by reporters, posing as down-and-outers, to several free-feeding programs across the country.

"We have tried to create an environment as if Jesus were our guest," explains the Rev. Bruce Buchanan, associate pastor for community ministries at First Presbyterian Church in downtown Dallas since 1987. "We have to put our best foot forward if we expect people to change. When the door opens, it may be an opportunity for change. At the very least, it provides a safe oasis—a place where they can use the restroom and be treated fairly and with respect. And that's probably more important than the food."

Every weekday The Stewpot serves about 125 breakfasts, consisting of coffee, a sweet roll, and, sometimes, a sandwich. At noon an average of three hundred and fifty gather around the attractive, round tables for a "quality meal—but not four-star," Buchanan explains. He frowns as he notes, "That's an increase of about one hundred 'customers' over last year."

While the heart of the ministry is feeding those who are in need of a good meal, the scope goes far beyond providing food. Their purpose is to address the needs of the whole person: food, clothing, shelter, employment, and self-esteem. Since the program's inception in 1976, it has grown to include a dental clinic for free primary care and a dental-health program for secondary care, such as dentures. The two programs have served more than fifteen thousand.

Other services that are provided are assistance in obtaining documentation, like birth certificates and I.D. cards required for employment and other purposes; transportation for important matters, such as a job interview, a medical appointment, or for those who get stranded on their way to visit family in another city; counseling; clothing; basic computer training; and help in applying for appropriate entitlement programs, such as veterans' benefits and food stamps.

The Stewpot also allows those whose identity has been established through its I.D. identification program (with more than eight thousand registered names) to use its address to receive mail. Volunteers and caseworkers from other agencies provide medical and psychiatric care, veterans' counseling, haircuts, Alcoholics Anonymous and Narcotics Anonymous meetings, and General Equivalency Diploma courses. Too, the Stewpot serves as an independent advocate monitoring the public assistance of those who are eligible.

Buchanan describes all of the ministry's clients as being "at risk in one way or another." Most are homeless. Several work, but at minimum wage, and are unable to afford a permanent home. Some stay in shelters. Others are not allowed in shelters or simply won't go there. Some are mentally ill. Many have drug and alcohol problems, while others are domestically displaced. Most either grew up in Dallas or have been there more than five years.

Buchanan labels as a myth the idea that the homeless move from community to community. Their typical client is a young black man from Dallas in his twenties whom Buchanan describes as being a part of "the disposable generation." He points out that there are programs for veterans, women, and children, but the younger men are overlooked. The Stewpot serves some older men; some women, about 10 percent; and a few children. "We need to be where the pain is the greatest. That's where we can provide the most service."

One day several years ago, a situation gave rise to one unusual facet of the program. Lunch was not ready on time and people were hungry and were growing restless. As a diversionary tactic, Buchanan asked whether anyone could play the old piano that had been donated to The Stewpot. A man in his late sixties, who had once played in a piano bar, volunteered. His talent was obvious, and the late meal was no longer an issue. Buchanan was amazed, first of all, at the impact of the music, and, second, by the realization that there was probably much unrecognized talent in the people gathered there.

Out of that experience an annual contest developed with six categories: poetry, essay, art, music (original), music (performance), and stand-up comedy. The popular competition gives participants an opportunity for public recognition and a place to perform and showcase their work. Cash prizes are given to the winners. "People may be homeless, but they're not untalented," he observes. "They just had no opportunity to display their talents."

Buchanan also began paying one of the ministry's clients minimum wage to provide music for diners during the lunch hour. One of the pianists ended up playing the organ for a church, while another became a keyboardist in a piano bar.

A Bible study is also provided each weekday for those who wish to participate. First Presbyterian's tradition has always been: Don't force feed, so attendance is strictly voluntary. The group, led by volunteers, is not doctrinaire and is basic. They study the Bible, a chapter at a time. The format is joint reading, prayer, and discussion. Buchanan says that the study is affirming for those who participate. Some become quite involved. "Usually the homeless have a very deep faith," he observes. "It provides them with a way to survive."

First Presbyterian pays the salary of Buchanan, who has some other responsibilities, including some preaching, hospital visitation, and officiating at funerals, besides directing The Stewpot. The church also pays building costs, including utilities and phones. The remainder of the funding comes from donations from individuals, other churches and synagogues, foundations, and companies throughout the Metroplex. Ten full-time staff members, including a caseworker, and more than three hundred volunteers, keep the program going. Volunteers include members of various churches, synagogues, and mosques as well as those with no religious affiliation. Many say that their work there gives them a sense of "being the hands of Christ" and an opportunity for "practicing their faith."

Buchanan says that The Stewpot is "going full circle to prevent the cycle of poverty" with its programs for inner city youth and children. Programs include:

- Saturday School—an educational and recreational program offered on Saturdays and weekdays during the summer for more than one hundred children from a nearby elementary school.
- Summer Day Camp—a program for children that consists of small group games, gymnasium activities, computer lab, arts and crafts, and ceramics.
- Explorer Post—a coed scouting program involving forty junior and senior high school students.
- Youth Communication Project—a mentor project that produces ten thousand copies quarterly of the *Dallas Teen Age* newspaper.
- College Scholarship Fund—a program providing financial assistance for any former Saturday School or Explorer Post

student who wants to go to college or trade school. Currently seven students are enrolled in college in the program, and the first graduate recently received her degree.

"We see successes in small steps," Buchanan says. "Convincing an alcoholic to go to an AA [Alcoholics Anonymous] meeting, seeing someone trying to put a resume together, or deciding to go on a job interview—those are successes in our estimation. We try to affirm people, help elevate their self-esteem. By helping people feel positive about themselves, they can become willing to try to step out and help themselves."[6]

Helping Children in Traumatic Circumstances

Another parachurch ministry not associated with a particular church but supported by several is My Guardian Angel, a Dallas-based program that began in 1990 under the direction of Dr. Betty Spillman. Her vision is to create a safe place for children to heal from hurts that they experience as a result of losses in their lives.

The program recruits and trains volunteers to work with children who have been impacted by divorce and other significant losses, such as death, separation, and abandonment. Volunteers lead children ages four through seventeen, separated by age, in small peer-support, grief-recovery groups based on the Christian principles of love and forgiveness. Groups are also available for the step-families, blended families, grandparents, foster parents, and single parents of those children.

The program uses the Rainbows for All God's Children curriculum and is based on reflective listening skills undergirded with prayer. The culminating activity of the twelve-week semester is a forgiveness ceremony where, as Spillman says, "We as adults model for children and families by asking the children to forgive us for the painful things that we have done in their lives. We can't diagnose who's ready to forgive, but by modeling the divine pattern of forgiveness, we show how it can be experienced. Miracles happen every time. In fact," she muses, "miracles happen at every meeting."

Spillman lists the main items that are dealt with in the sessions:

- Helping children discover that what happened was not their fault. Either no one could help what happened or adults made choices, but the resulting consequences of those choices must be dealt with by all involved.
- Assisting the children in understanding that they can't "fix" everything and make things as they were. They learn that they can make decisions only for themselves.

- Giving the children language to empower them so that their pain can be dealt with instead of suppressing it, which often results in unwise actions, such as involvement in drugs, alcohol, or even suicide.

Children needing additional professional help are referred to appropriate youth serving agencies and services.

One family's story illustrates the power of the program. The week before school started the mother of three children—a boy, age six, and girls, ages ten and thirteen—suddenly left. The devastated father and children were distraught and didn't know where to turn. The grades of the girls, both honor students, nose-dived. The youngest child would ride the school bus, get off, and hide in the bushes until the principal came out, found him, and led him inside. The father searched for help and found several groups for support for himself, but nothing for the children. Finally, he heard about My Guardian Angel. He said that the program provided the only stable place in their world, gave them the time, the place, and the tools to heal. Two years later, the father has remarried, and the children are making excellent grades and winning awards.

The value of the program was nationally recognized in 1992 when President George Bush named My Guardian Angel as one of his "thousand points of light."

In its first seven years of operation, fifteen churches of various denominations helped support the program and provided sites for the weekly meetings. More than two thousand volunteers were trained, and about sixty-five hundred young people were helped. Referrals are made by about fifty area agencies, public and private counselors, pediatricians and other professionals, and families who have been helped themselves. A pilot project has served about three hundred children through a court-mandated program with Judge Frances Harris of Dallas County's 302d Family District Court.

The program is privately funded through donations from churches, civic groups, corporations, foundations, and caring individuals. Spillman said the following:

> The need is so great. Sometimes it seems like we're changing the tires on moving cars to keep things going, but God has always been faithful. God had to send His Son so that we could come into relationship with Him and understand His love. In the giving of our lives to children, they can experience and better understand God's love through relationships. We like to think that money and programs solve societal problems. But only relationships and the work of the Holy Spirit—the sustainer, comforter, and restorer—can truly provide lasting solutions.[7]

Steering Wayward Young People Back on Track

The goal of an impressive outreach sponsored by New Birth Baptist Church in suburban Atlanta, Georgia, is to rescue youth after they have had their first encounter with the legal system. Project Impact is a partnership program with the church and local government agencies. Nonviolent, first-time offenders are turned over by the court system to New Birth where they are enrolled in a Christian mentorship program.

Pastor Eddie L. Long comments: "Most hard criminals got started with misdemeanors. If someone could have turned them around at that time, they would not have gotten into bigger crimes. So we get the kids, provide counseling, get them through school and give them hope."

The program has an amazing success rate of 86 percent and is helping the judicial system seek an alternative to merely locking up wayward youth. A national outreach of Project Impact is planned with New Birth coordinating the ministry's efforts throughout the Southeast.

Another facet of New Birth's commitment to young people is local incentive programs. A scholarship program offers every high school graduate in the church at least $400 to help with tuition at any college. Also, the Joshua program offers funding for sports equipment, computers, and band uniforms to local schools whose students enroll in a Bible study class.[8]

Ministering to the Whole Person

The Parish Nurses Program at Episcopal Church of the Resurrection in Dallas was organized in 1993 by Lois Stanley, a registered nurse who is a member of the congregation. She heard about the national program from a friend who had attended a Christian Health Conference. Having just recently retired from the Veteran's Hospital, she could hardly wait to contact the International Parish Nurse Resource Center to learn more about the concept.

The program was started by Granger Westbrook, a former Lutheran pastor, hospital chaplain, and founder and director of Wholistic Health Centers, Inc. He believes that the church should be a place of healing and should minister to the whole person. The four areas that the program covers are: promoting wellness, assessing health problems, training volunteers, and organizing support groups. There are several different Parish Nurse models. More information may be obtained by writing International Nurse Resource Center, 205 W. Touhy Avenue, Park Ridge, Illinois 60068, or by calling (800) 556–5368.

This is the way the program works at Resurrection. On the first Sunday of each month, Stanley provides blood-pressure screenings between the two morning worship services. She also gives information about various health subjects around a theme for the month, such as poisons, eye care, and alcohol and drug abuse. She repeats the blood pressure-screenings each week at a morning service that is attended primarily by senior citizens. She also takes the time to talk with people about any health concerns they might have. A CPR course and a Healthy Living Seminar stressing Christian values have been presented on Saturday mornings. Blood screenings and flu immunizations have also been provided at the church.

Volunteers in the program provide services, such as driving people to the doctor, picking up a prescription for a mother with an ill baby, and providing relief for a caregiver for a few hours. Stanley goes to homes to make health-care assessments and see what kind of services are needed. She makes referrals to health-care agencies and programs, like Meals on Wheels, that the person or family may not know are available and suggests necessary services that may be less expensive than one that might be found just by looking in the Yellow Pages of the phone book.

Stanley is also available to interpret and explain medical terminology about an illness or condition in terms more understandable to a layperson. The program provides back-up for patients and families during immediate postsurgery or posthospitalization periods.

Stanley especially enjoys her weekly visits to Cathedral Gardens, a retirement center sponsored by the Episcopal church. She does blood-pressure screenings and talks with the residents about their health-care needs and whatever else they want to discuss. "I'm amazed at some of the things they want to tell me," she says with a laugh. She recalls one woman without any family in the area who became seriously ill while living there. "I visited her in the hospital and, later, in the nursing home. I became her family. As far as she was concerned, I was her daughter."

Another facet of the program is the loan of health-assistance equipment, such as shower stools and wheelchairs, to whomever needs it. The donated items are kept in a warehouse owned by one of the parishioners and are overseen by Stanley's husband, Stan. Her enthusiasm for the program and for the difference it is making in the lives of people is obvious. "It's one of the most rewarding things I've ever done," she says.[9]

Making Facilities Available to Secular Groups

Wooddale Church in Eden Prairie, Minnesota, reaches out to the community by bringing the community in. As part of its outreach strategy, the church gives priority for use of its facilities to secular groups rather than to other religious organizations. As a result, a wide variety of groups and people have become familiar with the church. Among the activities held there have been hospital-sponsored birthing classes, blood mobile visits, parties for local restaurant staffs, practice for NFL cheerleaders, city council and neighborhood meetings, out-processing of laid-off manufacturing employees, professional athlete's meetings, executive planning retreats for local businesses, secular music concerts, and Alcoholics Anonymous meetings. Pastor Leith Anderson says, "Between regular church activities and those outside secular events, there isn't much time or space left."[10]

Meeting Singles on Neutral Ground

The Single Adult Sunday School Class of Dallas has met in a meeting room at a major Dallas hotel every Sunday since 1971. The class grew out of two experiences. H. C. Noah, who was pastor of Oak Cliff Assembly of God in Dallas at that time, visited a church in California. He learned about a class in a hotel that the church sponsored and was fascinated by the idea.

About the same time Sam Monzingo, teacher of the college-career class at Oak Cliff Assembly, had a young woman come up to him after class and say, "Mr. Monzingo, I've visited your class three Sundays. I've really enjoyed your teaching, but I won't be coming back." When he asked why, she explained that she was in the right age bracket for the group, but, being divorced with three children, she just didn't fit in. "I don't fit into the class for couples . . . or this class . . . or the auditorium class (for older adults). I don't fit in anywhere. There's no place for me." She left Monzingo with her words ringing in his ears, and they continued to haunt him.

When Noah approached Monzingo about starting a class for singles in a nearby hotel, he was interested but somewhat apprehensive. "When you teach within the church, you have the protection and the comfort of the church," he explains. "I didn't know who would come or what to expect." The two men agreed that they wanted to make a place for the rapidly growing singles population, who felt that there was no place for them. The two men knew that there were many outside their denomination who needed ministry. They believed that meeting outside the walls of the church would overcome the prejudice that some might have about going to a church. "For some people, going to a hotel is less threatening. Many have been hurt in church but still have a need for ministry. Many people need to know that God loves them regardless of what they've done or what's happened in their lives. We actually targeted our audience," explains Monzingo, who was licensed as a minister by the Assemblies of God in 1994.

Letters were written, and announcements were made on the church's radio program about the new class. The first Sunday, twenty-four showed up. The unusual outreach quickly captured the attention of many singles across the Metroplex. Monzingo says that at first it was unique and provided a forum for singles to meet singles. Attendance grew rapidly, peaking one Sunday at about six hundred and fifty.

Over the years many have come who had never before been in a church. Others have showed up with what might be termed an "antagonistic attitude." For example, a doctor wearing a sports shirt unbuttoned nearly down to his waist and an expensive gold medallion on a chain, came up to Monzingo after a service. He said, "I enjoyed being here, but I want you to know I don't believe one bit in what you're doing. Knowing that, if you don't mind my coming, since it feels good here, I'd like to come." Monzingo assured him that everyone was welcome. A few Sundays later, the doctor approached him at the juice bar and said, "I've changed my mind. I believe in what you're doing here." He became a Christian, married a woman he met there, and later started teaching Sunday school in a church.

Another man was even more blunt. He said, "I'm a millionaire oilman. I came here looking for a wife. That's the only reason I'm here, and I'm a real hell-raiser." Monzingo told him that all were welcome as long as they behaved. When the teacher opened his eyes after the closing prayer, he was amazed to see the oilman standing in front of him with tears in his eyes. "If you don't quit that, you'll make a Christian out of me," the man blubbered. The same thing happened the next two Sundays, and then he trusted in Christ.

About two hundred consider the class their "church home" and come regularly. Others attend the class and then go to their own church for services. Many others come and go.

The class is still sponsored by Oak Cliff Assembly, but, after the first two years, the ministry became self-supporting financially. In fact, the class regularly gives gifts to the church.

Monzingo says that time after time class participants tell him and the other sixteen people, who have designated leadership roles for the group, statements like: "It feels good here. I like to come to this place." There is no doubt in Monzingo's mind that God made the place and that the Holy Spirit used the words of a lonely young woman years ago as an instrument in starting a work that has ministered to thousands of singles over the years. "You have to be a risk taker to move outside the four walls," Sam points out. "Taking that risk and seeing God move has been a very rewarding and faith-building experience for me."[11]

21 Special Evangelistic Events

M any churches have found that holding a special evangelistic event can be an excellent outreach. People who would never come to a traditional church service often will feel comfortable and enthusiastic about attending a sporting event, a cultural offering, or a neighborhood party. A church member may also find it easier to invite a friend or relative to this type of event.

The key word to the success of such an undertaking is *excellence*. Often that will mean spending much money to finance the program, but that is not always the case. Certainly every successful project of this nature will require a great deal of commitment and time on the part of many people. (For more information on this, see the form entitled "Evangelistic Event Planning Form," which you can find on page 277.)

Planning the Evangelistic Event

These are some helpful questions to ask before undertaking such a project.

Whom are you trying to reach? Children? Teenagers? A certain generation in the adult population? Singles? Families?

What are the interests of this targeted group in your particular community? If your area is business-oriented, perhaps a seminar on business ethics from a Christian perspective might prove to be popular. Perhaps you're located in a college town replete with avid sports followers. You might want to try a sporting event. If your community focuses on the arts, a drama production or excellent concert would probably spark a lot of interest.

What kind of event would be attention getting for your community to reach your chosen group? Has anything similar been done recently in your area? Has a church in another city sponsored a similar successful event from which you can learn?

How long will it take to plan and prepare for such a happening? What kind of timeline will be needed for each phase of the project?

Where will it be held? At your church or in another facility? If outside the church, how far in advance must you make reservations? How many can be accommodated? Is parking adequate? Is there a charge for using the facility?

What is the best time and date? Keep in mind what else is happening in your church at a certain time. Plan an event for a downtime when you will have more hands to help with the numerous details. Also, be aware of what's going on in the community. An event might be planned effectively in conjunction with a special community happening, such as a fair or a parade. Or it might be well attended if little else is going on at that particular time. Consulting the school calendar is also wise to do. Also, avoid dates too close to major holidays and sports highlights, such as the Super Bowl or World Series.

Who will be in charge of coordinating the event? Choosing someone with good leadership skills, enthusiasm, and a talent for detail will go a long way toward assuring the program's success. Who will the other key players be? What committees will be needed?

What people assets are available? What talents are needed for this particular event? Are they available within your church, or will some services need to be paid for? Are there enough enthusiastic, committed people in your congregation to take care of the numerous details?

How much will it cost? This might be figured two ways—top-flight approach and more conservatively speaking. Will you charge admission or will it be offered free to the public? If free, consider having tickets printed, even if you do not expect an overflow crowd. They contain all the pertinent information and make a convenient, easy way for members to invite friends and family members. Also, the experience of many groups has shown that this approach increases attendance.

Where will the money come from? Are there those with a vision for this type of outreach in your fellowship who might be willing to underwrite the event or make substantial contributions? Or are your people generous in responding to requests for funds for special projects?

How will you promote it? The key to the success of the event will be the development of an excellent communication plan that will target the segment of the population you wish to reach. How will you motivate members of your fellowship to invite their friends and family members?

If an altar call is to be given, how will you handle those who come forward? Will training be necessary in order to provide enough competent workers? Then, after the event, how will you follow up on them?

How will the event be evaluated? What criteria will you use? Determining approaches toward measuring its success in advance will assist in knowing what has been accomplished once it's over. Also, this step is important in planning future evangelistic events. A postevent meeting of those involved to discuss the successes and failures and to make suggestions for improving the process for future undertakings can be invaluable.

Events for Children

Ideas for events for children are limited only by the imagination. It usually takes little to excite children and get them to want to participate. However, children's events should be just as well done and, if anything, better organized than those for adults.

"The World's Largest Easter Egg Hunt" is the title given to Dallas' Pathway of Life Church's annual evangelistic outreach for children. Held the Sunday before Easter, the event attracted about two thousand children and parents the first year and approximately thirty-five hundred the second year. It is held in a nearby football stadium that is rented from the Dallas Public Schools.

Pastor Danny Wegman says that planning starts six months before the event. Forty to fifty letters are sent out in October asking businesses, such as fast-food places and toy stores, to donate gift certificates, coupons, and various items for prizes. He advises asking for donations in October in order to be a recipient for these kinds of freebies. The outreach costs the church about three thousand dollars. "I'm amazed at the way the extra money always comes in," he observes.

Besides the Easter eggs and the prizes, a boy's bicycle and a girl's bicycle are given away at the event in a special drawing. Two Saturdays before the egg hunt, parades are held in public housing neighborhoods and apartment complexes in the area. These consist of decorated vans, helium balloons, a boom box playing lively music, honking horns, and clowns giving away suckers. The Saturday before, flyers are left on apartment doors telling what time buses will come by on Sunday to pick the children up for the Easter egg hunt. Ten thousand flyers telling about the event and the special prizes are handed out to children as they leave school the Friday before it happens. Included are public schools as well as Christian schools. "You just have to be sure to stay on the sidewalk in front of the public schools," Wegman explains. "Then you're okay." The event is also plugged on the church's weekly television program and on radio.

Before the crowd arrives, seventy-five thousand individually wrapped candy eggs are scattered over the middle of the football field. Last year the first thousand who arrived received a free frisbee. An attempt is made to get parents and older students to fill out an information card when they are given tickets for the drawing and free coupons. Church members working security pick out children to play games on the football field, such as relay races and sweeping basketballs around a cone. This is followed by a dance routine on the field. A drama of the Crucifixion is the sermon and, afterward, an altar call is given. Last year about one thousand, mostly adults, responded. While some of those who come forward show up at the church later, even more from the community who heard about the program and admired the approach come as visitors.

The last part of the program is the drawing for the bikes and the egg hunt. Younger children are directed to one part of the field, while those in upper-elementary grades have their own area in which to hunt.

How does the congregation benefit? Wegman says that workers are "blown away by the sight of so many people's lives being changed. We have a lot of different departments and ages working together. Children witness to other children who have no concept of Christianity, so it helps them understand what ministry is all about. They realize that they need to be prayed up and ready to go. It's one of the most positive things we do and has a more lasting effect than any revival."[1]

A Baseball Clinic, sponsored by The Fellowship of Las Colinas in Irving, Texas, proved to be a highly successful event for children. Held in a local high school gym, the project capitalized on the high interest of boys and girls in the area in Little League Baseball. The church brought in four New York Yankees, who not only are top athletes but also outstanding Christians. Approximately six hundred and fifty girls and boys turned out for the popular program. The ball players gave baseball demonstrations on how to pitch, hit, and field. At the end of the demonstration, the Yankees shared their faith. As a result, a large number of children trusted in Christ.

The next Sunday, which was Father's Day, the boys and girls were invited to dress in their Little League uniforms and attend the church service. They flocked to the meeting, many with parents in tow, to see the Yankees once more—this time as speakers in the Sunday morning service. Pastor Ed Young, himself an athlete who attended Florida State University on a basketball scholarship, knows the fascination that young people have for outstanding sports figures. And he takes advantage of it for the kingdom of God.[2]

Kids Church is an outreach of Metro Church in Brooklyn, Ne" York. Many churches have a special service just for children while t¹ parents are attending "big" church. But Metro takes it a gian further. They take the church to the kids. A fleet of eigh Church" vehicles goes out every week to minister to more th thousand children right in their own neighborhoods.[3]

Events for Teens

Hell houses have been sponsored by churches throughout the nation during the last several years. The idea is to capitalize on the Halloween hype that takes over at that time of year and present a haunted house from a Christian perspective. Unwary customers usually think they're going to have a lot of fun in a scary atmosphere. Many of them, however, find themselves scared into confronting the question of where they will spend eternity.

Reconciliation Outreach, an inner-city ministry located near downtown Dallas, has sponsored several hell houses with positive results. The Rev. Dorothy Moore, who heads the ministry, recalls one of them in particular. "More than twelve hundred people stood outside in the frigid, pouring rain waiting to get in during the two nights." Of that number, there were more than four hundred salvations as a result of their visit to "hell." The event attracted teens by the busload from churches as well as drug addicts, swingers, and the curious. An unusual success story was the prostitute who propositioned a ministry volunteer who was helping to park cars. He said, "Hey, why don't you go with me?" and hauled her off to the hell house. She got saved and turned her life around.

While the ministry puts up a few posters in the neighborhood, they really don't have to worry about getting out the word. The secular media does it for them—at no cost—as they report on various Halloween-related activities in the area. No mention is made that it is a religious event.

The experience is divided into several scenes. Customers are guided through the house by a terrible looking man wearing a hideous mask. The first scene features an open casket with a "dead" young person. Family members are gathered around sobbing and moaning. Next is the party room where young people are drinking and doing drugs. Behind each of them is a demonic figure who has strands of florescent yarn tied to his victim's arms and is manipulating the revelers. A beautiful girl in a tight outfit is dancing. At first participants see only one side of her face, which is attractively made up, but then she turns and reveals the other side, which is made up to look depraved and demonic.

From there the guide takes them to a scene of domestic violence in which a drunken man takes a knife and tries to stab his wife in front of their son. The path then leads through a shower where a man has collapsed and "died" from an overdose of drugs. They emerge to a scene with a man lying on a dirty bed with a revolver. A recorded voice urging him amid evil laughs, "Go ahead and do it. Nobody cares." nally he "shoots" himself.

The next leg of the journey is through a casket that has been stood on end. As the customers enter, the door slams behind them and they find themselves in a scary representation of hell. After a few moments they emerge on the other side, this time with an angel guiding them to "heaven," replete with cherubic beings, clouds (generated by a smoke machine), and beautiful music. Jesus holds out His arms to them and explains how He died that they might have everlasting life. They then find themselves in the throne room, where a seated figure explains about the judgment seat of Christ. Those who wish may go to small rooms and talk with trained counselors about their experience.

More than fifty volunteers are involved in producing Reconciliation's Hell House over a period of two months. A large facility with at least four large rooms has to be secured. "It must be fire inspected and live up to the fire code," Moore cautions. Volunteers construct the sets, borrow and make props, plan and execute realistic sound and lighting effects, make costumes, design make up, and, of course, appear as actors in the production that requires extensive rehearsal to make every detail appear realistic. Counselors are also trained specifically to help customers afterward.

The reason for its success, Moore thinks, is that the experience focuses young people on the seriousness of drug involvement and wild, irresponsible lifestyles. "They face the realization that there is an evil force involved and that there is a day of reckoning."[4]

Events for Adults

The evangelistic outreach party has become one of the most effective tools in bringing new members into the fellowship of the Second Baptist Church in Houston, Texas. The parties are sponsored by the church, with some of them located in members' neighborhoods and others in a particular zip code. They are held throughout Houston, with some of them located as much as thirty miles from the church. Dr. H. Edwin Young, pastor of Second Baptist, has found that, while many people would not think of venturing inside the downtown church, they will come to a party in their neighborhood. The centerpiece of the gathering is fellowship, but a layperson will share a testimony of God's work in his or her life.

Once bonds of friendship have been established, participants are willing to come with their new found friends to the church. Th parties help break down the mental barriers that have been built u⁓ the thought of entering a large, unfamiliar downtown church.[5]

Large-scale musical dramatizations at Christmas and Easter have ⊦ community events in Jacksonville, Arkansas, a town of abou⁓ nine thousand in population. Presented by Second Bapt⁓

the productions are highlights of the year and are looked forward to by citizens. Pastor Ron Raines says, "We put a lot of effort and resources into making these outstanding productions. They are well attended." Members see the enormous investment of time and resources as a way to contribute to their community in a special way. "Presenting a top-quality musical makes a positive statement about our church, and it gets those who attend interested in what our church stands for," Raines points out.

Many people who, otherwise, would not darken a church door will come to see a friend or loved one act or sing in a production. And they will receive a message, albeit not in the form of a sermon.[6]

Hillcrest Highlights, a series of arts productions and exhibits, are presented periodically by Hillcrest Church in Dallas, Texas. The thrust is to return the arts to the church, where they originated. Artists, such as concert pianist Dino Karstonakis and Ballet Magnificat, have been presented through the series. Other attractions have included a folk music group from Russia; *Bamboo in Winter,* a film written and directed by Bill Myers about the underground church in China; and several Christian recording artists in concert. Art exhibits of professional area artists have also been featured around a theme, such as Easter. Admission is by ticket only. However, tickets are free and are distributed to church members, who are encouraged to bring their friends as guests. Donations are accepted, but they do not begin to pay for the considerable expenses involved.

Secular plays and musicals that are good family entertainment and are professionally done can also be an effective outreach. Once playgoers get to know some of the people and start feeling at home in their facilities, they are much more likely to come to a service.

First United Methodist Church in Dallas presents the Rotunda Theatre Series, which consists of six productions throughout the year, as a part of its Music and Arts Ministries. The choices are an interesting mix of drama, sacred drama, musicals, and sacred musicals. One was performed by children, another by youth, and others by adults and intergenerational casts. Two performances are free. The others require an admission charge that supplements the church's contribution for production costs.

The idea for the series originated when Dana Effler came to First United Methodist as Director of Music and Arts Ministries. The theater, which can be used for theater-in-the-round or proscenium productions, was there but had sat idle for years. A gift from a church member financed building dressing rooms and a new lighting system. Effler asked professional theatrical directors and actors in their congregation whether they would be willing to donate their gifts to the church. And so the series in honor of the sesquicentennial celebration of the large, downtown church was born.

In the brochure and the program for each production, it states: "As we strive to produce quality theatrical entertainment, we will also provide a Christian arena in which talented artists of all ages and races can exercise and share their art." People from the community can audition for parts and serve in technical production positions.

A Broadway musical has been staged each summer at First United Methodist for some forty years. "This is a big outreach tool," Effler points out. Many people from outside the church are involved. "They come to us because they want to be in a musical. They make friends. Often they return to become a part of the life of our church." One such person is now a director for the Rotunda Series and is involved in the church's AIDS Ministry. Another sings in the choir and runs lights for Rotunda. Their productions are a ministry to those who participate as well as to those who are part of the audience. "Many have been led into a relationship with Jesus Christ and with our church," she comments.

Mid-Day Music is another program of First United Methodist Church. The free nine-part series is held from noon to 1:00 P.M. the third Wednesday of each month from September through May. Those who come may either bring a brown-bag lunch or purchase a buffet lunch at the church for a nominal amount. Because of the church's downtown location, the program draws many people from the business community. "It's really catching on with people outside our church," Effler says. "It provides a vehicle to attract the unchurched and an easy opportunity for members to invite a friend. Once they've come, it becomes easier to invite them to a service. Relationships are growing as a result."

Emphasis is on entertainment and variety. The programs run the gamut both ethnically and in types of music—everything from jazz to classical and African drums to a Caribbean band. The idea is to give the audience a lift in the middle of the day. "It's our gift to the community," Effler comments.

The Music and Arts Ministries' mission statement is "Serving God and God's people with excellence in music and arts." "In everything we do, we believe in excellence," Effler remarks. "God deserves our very best not our leftovers." She also believes that "quality breeds quantity. A growing church can expand its number of ministries and still maintain the quality that helped it grow."[7]

A contemporary outreach show sponsored on a regular basis has proven to be a highly successful vehicle to reach the unchurched for Perimeter Church of Atlanta, Georgia. An example is a musical entitled "Back in Time," for which the church sold three thousand tickets. The program, which was designed to reach baby boomers, revolved around the music of the 1960s. The secular songs were accompanied by an explanation of the needs, hurts, and motivations revealed in the music. Afterward Pastor Randy Pope discussed what the people of that generation were searching for and how, then as now, Christ is the ultimate answer. No altar call was given, but the way Christ relates to their lives and needs was pointed out. After the show, members of Perimeter took their friends to a restaurant that had been reserved for dessert and conversation about what they had just experienced. This unusual approach to evangelism brought approximately two hundred new people into the church.[8]

Feeding the 5,000 is the name that Pathway of Life Church in Dallas calls its adult outreach program at Thanksgiving. A weekly area newspaper publicizes the program, and the court system helps in identifying families for the program. An application has to be completed, and a real need must be shown in order to participate. The entire family is required to attend one of two services the Wednesday before Thanksgiving in order to receive a complete traditional dinner that feeds fifteen people. The first service is in Spanish, for the church is located in a community with many Hispanics. The second service is in English. Tracts from the church are placed in the food baskets, and are followed up with a letter and phone call to each family. About one hundred and fifty families, who would otherwise have little for Thanksgiving, are treated to a traditional feast through this outreach.

Pathway's Pastor Danny Wegman believes that sponsoring large evangelistic outreach events can and should involve the whole congregation, and that they are of tremendous benefit to church members. "This type of outreach demonstrates to the congregation that we can break barriers," he points out. He believes that what happens in the lives of the members of the sponsoring church as a result of their participation in such programs is just as important as what happens in the lives of those whom they are trying to reach.[9]

Evangelistic Event-Planning Form

Type of event _____

Chairperson _____

Committee members and responsibilities_____

_____

Number of volunteers needed for various functions _____

_____

Date_____ On church calendar? _____

Projected number of participants _____

Location _____

Reservations made and confirmed for site _____

Projected cost _____

Funding sources _____

Admission charge _____

Talent _____

Contract signed (if applicable) _____

Promotion approaches and deadlines:

    Church publications _____

    News releases to newspapers and stations _____

    _____

    PSAs to radio and/or TV stations _____

    _____

    Handbills _____ Design _____ Printing_____

    Mailings _____ Design _____ Printing_____

    Advertising_____

    _____

    Posters _____ Design _____ Printing_____

    Placement of posters _____

Equipment needed _____

_____

Equipment rented (if not available at the church) _____

Decorations needed _____

Decorations rented or purchased _____

Program _____ Design _____ Printing_____

Follow-up:

    Return of equipment _____

    Return of decorations_____

    Thank-you notes to be written _____

    Evaluation of event _____

22 | Reaching the Unchurched

C hurch is boring! Those words rolled off the tongue of twenty-one-year-old David in his intriguing Australian accent. He had been brought up in church by his widowed mother, who saw that he was present at every service.

But now David was out on his own and was grazing far afield in strange spiritual pastures in his quest for the truth. He asked tough questions about the Christian faith. He appeared to be sincere, and seemed to innately know that God was more exciting than what he had experienced.

No doubt there are thousands of other "Davids" who still believe that there is a Creator but who have dropped out of the church program. And then, in increasing numbers, there are those who were brought up in a sterile faith atmosphere where they received their religious training in the form of TV commentators gleefully chronicling the fall of yet another minister.

George Barna concludes that most unchurched adults have made a conscious decision not to attend church. "It is the rare adult who avoids the local church out of lack of experience with such religious behavior."[1]

A 1992 *Newsweek* magazine article entitled "Talking to God," reported that 91 percent of American women and 85 percent of men say that they pray. And 52 percent of the unchurched claim that they have made a personal commitment to Jesus Christ. The article concludes that "in allegedly rootless, materialistic, self-centered America, there is also a hunger for a personal experience of God."[2]

George Gallup Jr. has said that "only four out of every 100 Americans are completely nonreligious—that is, have no religious preference, do not go to church, and say religion is not very important in their lives."[3]

Why, then, do so many opt out of church? The answers, of course, are many and varied. However, an impressive 91 percent of non-Christians believe that the church isn't sensitive to their needs.[4]

Christian communicator John Stott sums up their attitude with the phrase: "Hostile to the church, friendly to Jesus Christ."[5]

Bill Hybels, before starting Willow Creek Community Church in South Barrington, Illinois, enlisted the help of friends in conducting a survey of people in the area who did not attend church. They asked simply, "Why not?" Responses fell into four main categories.

1. The people felt churches were always asking for money.
2. The people said the sermons were boring and the services routine.
3. The people saw no relevancy between church and real life.
4. The people responded that pastors made them feel ignorant and guilty.

Hybels determined that Willow Creek, which has a weekly attendance of more than fourteen thousand, would not be guilty on any of those four counts.[6]

The question is: How do we reach the unchurched and convince them that the church is vital and necessary to their lives? While there are no simple answers, two basic elements emerge.

First, be willing to change—not the Gospel message, but the approaches used in presenting it. Because television plays such a major part in everyday life, our society has become visually oriented. Also, attention spans have shortened. Studies indicate that the average person's attention span is now seven minutes. What can be done to make a service more visually compelling and to give it more variety? How can it be related more clearly to real-life situations? Do the words of the hymns pertain to contemporary life, or are they even understandable to today's young person? Try looking at your service with fresh eyes as though this was the first time you had entered a church in ten years or, perhaps, in your entire life. Would what you experience there help you to cope with life, understand your problems, and make you feel that you are accepted and loved?

Second, decide on your target audience. While the term may have a less-than-spiritual ring to some ears, it is absolutely essential to know the kind of person you are trying to reach. That means becoming thoroughly familiar with your community. Elmer L. Towns speaks in his book, *An Inside Look at 10 of Today's Most Innovative Churches,* about the importance of a congregation finding its niche in the neighborhood and reaching the reachable. He says: "The local church of the future must know its neighborhood [do market research], its target person [develop a prospect profile], the method that will reach those who are responsive-receptive people [through media research] and it must then reach the reachable [advertise]."[7]

For example, Hybels decided on a target audience and developed a profile of the person whom Willow Creek is seeking primarily to reach. The target person is in the largest demographic group in the area. He is a 25- to 45-year-old professional male who is married, busy in the marketplace, and disenchanted with the traditional church. Hybels notes that, if you reach the men, you will in all likelihood reach their wives as well.[8]

Strobel says: "'Apologetics,' or using evidence and reasoning to defend the faith, is critically important in penetrating the skepticism of many secular people today. This is especially true for nonbelievers who are in professions that deal with facts and figures, such as engineering, science, journalism, medicine, and law."[9]

These are some approaches in reaching the unchurched that are working and are worth considering.

Develop a Special Seeker's Service

While the seeker-friendly service may vary in form, some aspects of it are fairly uniform.

- Religious terms or buzz words, that regular attenders are familiar with but that leave the unchurched scratching their heads, are eliminated.
- Music with a contemporary sound is used with words being projected on a screen or at least handed out. Assume that seekers have never heard the songs you're asking them to sing.
- A topic that relates to everyday living is chosen. The catchy title is publicized in advance.
- Drama and film clips are often used to set up the topic as a launching pad for the sermon.
- The sermon is informal and is delivered more in the style of a chat rather than as a fiery oration.
- Little is said about giving money. In fact, visitors are often told not to contribute to the offering.
- Visitors are given an opportunity to fill out a card (if they wish to) but are not put on the spot by being asked to wear a visitor's tag.
- Seekers are directed to an area afterward where they can meet with someone to ask questions and discuss the service.

Meadow Creek Community Church in Mesquite, Texas, basically follows this pattern. Pastor Russ Olmon explains how his congregation became a seeker's church primarily with every Sunday morning devoted to this type of service.

Olmon became pastor of what he describes as a typical Southern

Baptist church. It grew from sixty members to two hundred rapidly. "Oh, we had a net gain on the ground," he recalls, "but no net gain in heaven." He decided that Meadow Creek was going to reach the lost in the burgeoning Dallas suburb, or he was going to get out of the ministry. While the message didn't change, nearly everything else did. Bit by bit, he says, he dismantled the trappings. He substituted a Plexiglas lectern for the massive wooden pulpit. He scrapped the hymnals in favor of an overhead projector. He traded an organ for a keyboard and a choir for a singing ensemble. He removed "Baptist" from the name, even on the sign out front. He started using drama sketches to illustrate his messages and make them more understandable and relevant.

By June 1996, the church had grown to about three hundred and fifty in attendance on Sunday mornings, with nearly all the members having been saved at Meadow Creek. In August the congregation merged with Gross Road Baptist Church, and Olmon and Pastor Ronnie Yarber became copastors of the new congregation. The entire church's priority in the informal Sunday morning service, which averages about six hundred and fifty in attendance, is to reach the unchurched. The services deal with spiritual values with first-timers hearing something like, "What Would Jesus Say to Madonna?"

Members have their believers' service on Wednesday evenings, where they are constantly reminded that Jesus said to "go and tell." Training in relational evangelism is emphasized. This includes:

- Members building relationships with the unchurched
- Members giving their testimony
- Members inviting the unchurched to the Sunday seeker-sensitive service
- Members leading the unchurched to Christ

Olmon realized the possible impact of relational evangelism when he heard about the results of George Barna's survey of unchurched adults.[10] It indicated that one out of every four adults who do not currently attend church claim that they would go if someone whom they knew and respected would invite them.[11] Olmon says that Meadow Creek's motto could read something like this. "We love you enough to accept you where you are and too much to leave you there."[12]

Hold an Evangelistic Event

While an evangelistic event can take many forms, it is quite different from a revival. Instead it is a "happening" that, by its nature, will attract many people who do not usually attend the church that is sponsoring it (or for that matter any church). Often the event will be held at an off-campus location, such as a stadium, auditorium, or theater. The Fellowship of Las Colinas in Irving, Texas, has capitalized on the big-event venue to excellent advantage. About twenty-five thousand people turned out for a Celebrate Freedom! concert on the Sunday before the Fourth of July. The evening featured Phil Driscoll, and was sponsored by the church, Word Records, radio station KLTY, and the International Bible Society. A spectacular display of fireworks topped off the highly successful event held in Williams Square in Las Colinas.[13] Other events might include a dinner theater, a ballet performance, an art exhibit, or various types of concerts.

Organize Helpful Seminars and Support Groups

Take a cue from the advice of Dr. Robert Schuller: "Find a need and fill it. Find a hurt and heal it."[14] Seminar evangelism reaches people at their point of need through a nonthreatening approach. And the needs are rife and increasing daily. Single parenting, recovering from divorce, managing stress, getting through grief, offering help to blended families, and recovering from abortion are some of the areas where churches can offer programs based on Christian principles that will encourage and help the hurting. Other possibilities include helping people work through terminal illness, giving them advice on how to parent children with special-needs, and teaching them how to cope with unemployment. Churches can also organize support groups for victims of rape, abuse, and people with eating disorders as well as those trying to overcome a host of addictions.

Faith Presbyterian Church, located in a large retirement community in Sun City, Arizona, has a special program, Lifeline for the Grieving, for those who have experienced the loss of a loved one. Since Sunday is usually a family day which underscores the loneliness of suddenly finding oneself alone, several activities are planned for that day. After the Sunday morning services, small groups of Lifeliners have brunch together. An intensive grieving group for those with recent losses is held from two to three in the afternoon. Then, at 3:00, a larger group meets. At 4:00 the church's four pastors take turns leading a vesper service with communion. The Lifeliners then have supper together. One of the pastors always meets with the group.[15]

St. Mark's Evangelical Lutheran Church in University City, Missouri, offers a special ministry to "skip generation" parents—those who have the responsibility of rearing their usually single children's children. The church sponsors a monthly meeting called "Grandparents Raising Grandchildren." Participants share needs, ideas, and resources about this unexpected challenge.[16]

Offering various classes and services to the community is another way to find a need and fill it. Calvary Baptist is a Dallas church located in a neighborhood that has changed dramatically over the years. It has gone from being mostly middle-class Anglos in single unit homes to about 60 percent Hispanic, 10 percent other minorities, and 30 percent lower income and older Anglos with numerous multifamily dwellings, apartments, and boarding houses. The church decided to reach out to its "new" community in a variety of ways. Classes in adult literacy, English for the non-English speaking, and tutoring for school-aged children are offered. During the summer months, Backyard Bible Clubs spring up in city parks, at apartment houses, and in members' yards.

One of the latest projects is that of providing day care for babies born to teenage mothers. This service is offered at a nearby high school so that the moms can finish school. The congregation is providing support and encouragement to these young parents, who are little more than children themselves. Church facilities are used for baby aerobics, which is a parent-infant bonding program. Calvary has given each teenage mother a subscription to a parenting magazine. Social events for the parents are planned by members of the young-adult Sunday school department. Pastor David Kuykendall says, "We want to exhibit to the school and the students that Calvary is available for ministry whenever the need and opportunity arises."[17]

Church growth expert Dr. Win Arn notes that unchurched people are highly responsive to the Gospel during periods of transition. He points out that when normal behavior patterns are disrupted, an individual or family may be driven to their knees and to the church by their compelling needs.[18]

The Episcopal Church of the Resurrection in Dallas, Texas, has made an all-out commitment to meeting the needs of hurting people with its counseling center, which is staffed with eight professional psychotherapists, who are trained in a variety of specialities. Director Rosemary Johnson says that only about one-third of their clients are members of Resurrection, with the remainder coming from the community-at-large. She says that most have some kind of church background, and so they choose counseling with a Christian background. However, many are not involved in a local church. "We don't preach at them," she points out, "but, in the course of counseling, we do get into spiritual issues. Because of the influence and impact of our counselors, many decide, as they're getting their act together, that they need to become active in church."

Johnson points out that, while the counseling center is a ministry and outreach of the church, it is also a self-contained unit. There is a fixed-fee structure. Counseling ranges from play therapy with young children and assistance for a whole family to marriage counseling and working through geriatric problems. No one is turned away, though. If they simply can't afford the standard fee, a sliding scale is applied according to income. Appointments are offered during evening hours and on Saturdays for those who can't come during the day.

A variety of groups, such as Grief Resolution, Singles—Not by Choice, Addictive Disorders, and Incest/Sexual Abuse Recovery, are available. A new offering is group therapy for stressed and depressed women. The program's goals include improving self-esteem, increasing coping skills, developing satisfying relationships, and improving physical and emotional well-being. Workshops on various topics such as "Parenting Skills," "Aging," and "Caregiver Education and Support," are offered periodically.[19]

Central Community Church in Wichita, Kansas, uses what Pastor Ray Cotton terms "Seminar Evangelism" to reach the unchurched. The church's Family Life Counseling Center provides counseling and helpful resources plus creative seminars and family life activities based on biblical principles. Parenting, stress management, divorce recovery, and grief management are some of the subjects offered periodically. Also, instead of an adult Sunday school class, seminars on family life and other topics, such as self-image, are made available to members and the community. On one occasion a Family Life Seminar titled, "Your Family Can Be Fun," attracted more than 800 people with approximately half of the participants being first-time guests. A member said, "If we can get a new couple into a seminar for three or four weeks, we also get their kids in the Sunday School. Then the parents will return because their kids will like it, and it will make a difference in their home."[20]

Develop an Outstanding Program for Children and Youth

The Princeton Religion Research Center and the Gallup Organization, Inc., discovered in a poll that four out of five of unchurched Americans want their children to have some kind of religious education. Though they may have decided to shun church membership, 80 percent think that their children should be exposed to a good church program.[21]

Dr. Morris Sheats' experience in dedicating children at Hillcrest Church in Dallas, Texas, points to the same conclusion. He says that two out of every five families who have their children dedicated there have practically no connection with a church. But they want their children dedicated to the Lord.[22] And according to information in *The Unchurched American—Ten Years Later,* one of every four persons stated that they had returned to church because they wanted their children to receive religious training.[23]

In our consumer-oriented society, parents will shop for an interesting and exciting children's program. Sheats is aware of some of the "small" things that a parent considers in that shopping process. Though the Hillcrest facility is relatively new (built in the early 1990s), the interior in high-use areas has already been repainted many times. Repairs to scars and repainting soiled areas are done on a regular basis just as soon as they're noticed. Sheats points out that parents want their children in a spotless, well-maintained atmosphere at church just as they do at daycare.[24]

No parent could doubt the emphasis that's placed on children's ministry at Hillcrest Church. The recently completed children's wing features bold, colorful murals in the rooms for infants through sixth grade. Each classroom has a theme from a biblical story. Some rooms for the younger children even incorporate play areas into the theme or have cut-out figures that stand out from the walls. For example, the room with a Noah's ark theme has part of a wooden boat built so that children can go up on the decks and crawl into different parts of the boat. The Walls of Jericho room features a two-story wall with an inside ladder for climbing up to the second floor.

The area for children's church is equally inviting. The backdrop for the stage consists of a versatile street of permanent, beautifully constructed, painted houses, some with doors that open. Windows can be opened and closed for puppets and actors to pop out of. A regular puppet stage is another feature of the room. A screen rolls up or down at the push of a button for use of films and other audiovisuals. And the facility has its own sound system.

Offering infant care and programs for children while their parents are attending events, seminars, and support programs gives parents an opportunity to see the facilities and the priority that is placed by the church on nurturing their children. Children who feel at home and make friends will want to come back. Often they'll bring their parents with them.

Douglas Murren, senior pastor of Eastside Foursquare Church in Kirkland, Washington, says in an article entitled "Reaching Boomers," "If you show . . . Disney-quality concern for their kids, they will be there. If you are going to reach these parents, you had better put the bucks into a clean, easily found, efficient, and well-staffed nursery. They expect it." He points out that creativity is also a high priority. He advises the use of puppets, costumes, or anything that says, "We thought about your kids before you came."[25]

Church researcher George Barna concludes from a study of several successful, growing churches that ministering to kids is one way of attracting adults. He says that sometimes parents want to ingrain the values of the church in their kids, but they realize that they need help doing so. Others are moved by the genuine compassion a church shows their children.

Barna notes, "Regardless, many adults feel at home in a place that sincerely accepts their offspring." He also points out that "kids represent the highest potential for conversion." While the pastors he interviewed did not have actual statistics, they observed that a comparatively large proportion of the youngsters who came to their church accepted Christ as their Savior. Barna cites results of his nationwide research that suggests that two out of every three adults who are Christians made that decision before the age of eighteen.[26]

Create Side-Door Evangelism Opportunities

Side-door evangelism provides opportunities for the unchurched to have fellowship in perhaps what they might consider a less threatening atmosphere than the church building. Side-door evangelism has a three-step approach.

1. An attempt is made to win an unchurched person to a Christian as a friend.
2. Then the unchurched person is won to the church.
3. Finally the unchurched person is won to Jesus Christ.[27]

Organizing a church into small cell or home fellowship groups provides great opportunities for close relationships to be formed, both inside and outside the church membership. Many people will come to this type of informal meeting when they will not darken the doors of a church. However, most eventually find their way to a congregation as a result of their involvement with a group of Christians. These believers demonstrate the love of Christ and accept newcomers in an atmosphere that is warm and nonthreatening. (Chapter 6 covers home fellowships in greater depth.)

Win Arn says that 75 to 90 percent of the persons who are active in church today first came through a friend, relative, or associate already in the church. Small-group fellowships prove to be a natural, informal, nonthreatening atmosphere for members to invite friends and neighbors.[28]

A natural outgrowth of the small group is a potluck dinner or party where attenders feel free to invite nonchurched friends and relatives to a festive occasion. At Hillcrest Church, Growth Groups (as their home fellowships are called) plan such an occasion about once each quarter. Sheats believes that Christians should follow the example of the father in Jesus' parable of the prodigal son: "When the lost are found, throw a party."

Encouraging is the fact that nearly 25 percent of all church-going Americans were among the unchurched for a period of two years or more.[29] And George Gallup Jr. says that we don't have to convince most of the unchurched theologically. "Many already evidence high levels of belief in God, heaven and hell, the Second Coming, the divinity of Jesus Christ, and so on. The unchurched are overwhelmingly believers."[30]

Reaching the unchurched is a challenging assignment—but not impossible. It definitely requires concerted time and effort, flexibility in trying new approaches, and creativity. But then God is a creative God. He is not boring!

Endnotes

Chapter 1

1. George Barna, *User Friendly Churches* (Ventura, Calif.: Regal Books, 1991), 88.
2. Dorothy Moore, interview by the author, Dallas, Tex. (11 October 1996).
3. Terry Kendrick, interview by the author, telephone (21 October 1996).
4. Russ Olmon, interview by the author, Mesquite, Tex. (22 October 1996).
5. George Barna, *The Power of Vision* (Ventura, Calif.: Regal Books, 1992), 115.
6. Ibid., 134.
7. Ibid., 144–45.
8. Ibid., 135.

Chapter 2

1. George Barna, *Step-by-Step Guide to Church Marketing* (Ventura, Calif.: Regal Books, 1992), 46.
2. Ibid.
3. Ibid., 47.
4. Marriage mail "weds" several pieces of advertising that are sent out together as a weekly packet in the U.S. mail. Cost is only a few pennies per piece—a major savings over mailings done through a postal permit. You can select just the zip code or zip codes you want covered, and every resident with a mail box will receive your informational piece. More information about marriage mail is included in chapter 14.

Chapter 3

1. Ginny Thornburgh, ed., *That All May Worship* (Washington, D.C.: National Organization on Disability, 1992), 20.
2. Russ Olmon, interview by the author, Mesquite, Tex. (22 October 1996).

Chapter 4

1. George Barna, *User Friendly Churches* (Ventura, Calif.: Regal Books, 1991), 100.
2. Ibid.
3. Robert L. Burt, ed., *Good News in Growing Churches* (New York: Pilgrim Press, 1990), 166.
4. Francis Anfuso, "Strategies to Reach the Unchurched," *Ministries Today* (July/August 1995), 33.
5. John W. Bullock, "Evaluating Your Church's Friendliness," *Growing Churches* (Nashville: Sunday School Board of the Southern Baptist Convention, 1994), 43.
6. Barna, *User Friendly Churches,* 177.
7. Win Arn, *The Pastor's Manual for Effective Ministry* (Monrovia, Calif.: Church Growth, 1988), 8.
8. David Goldstein, "How to Use Video for Ministry," *Ministries Today* (March/April 1991), 57–58.
9. Danny Wegman, interview by the author, Dallas, Tex. (17 September 1996).
10. Arn, *Pastor's Manual,* 14.
11. Ibid., 74.
12. Ken Houts, *You Are a Miracle Waiting to Happen* (Shippensburg, Pa.: Treasure House, 1996), 50–51.
13. Trinity Church, Bulletin (DeSoto, Tex., Trinity Church, n.d.).
14. Houts, *You Are a Miracle,* 5.

Chapter 5

1. Win Arn, *The Pastor's Manual for Effective Ministry* (Monrovia, Calif.: Church Growth, 1988), 72.
2. Ibid.
3. Elmer L. Towns, *An Inside Look at 10 of Today's Most Innovative Churches* (Ventura, Calif.: Regal Books, 1990), 231.
4. Charles E. Fuller, Institute of Evangelism and Church Growth Seminar, Dallas, Tex. (1993).
5. William D. Hendricks, *Exit Interviews: Revealing Stories of Why People Are Leaving the Church* (Chicago: Moody Press, 1993), 278–79.
6. George Wade, interview by the author, Dallas, Tex. (12 October 1996).
7. Robert L. Burt, ed., *Good News in Growing Churches* (New York: Pilgrim Press, 1990), 173–74.
8. Donald P. Smith, *How to Attract and Keep Active Church Members* (Louisville: Westminster/John Knox, 1992), 76.
9. Lyle Schaller, *Assimilating New Members* (Nashville: Abingdon, 1978), 76–77.
10. Ibid., 81.

11. Towns, 85.
12. Smith, 81.
13. "California Approaches to Reaching Unchurched 'Baby Boomers'" (San Juan Capistrano, Calif.: Church Growth Division, California Southern Baptist Convention, 1989), 17.
14. Elmer L. Towns, *The Complete Book of Church Growth* (Wheaton, Ill.: Tyndale House Publishers, 1982), 292.
15. Lyle Schaller, *Looking in the Mirror* (Nashville: Abingdon, 1984), 107.
16. Schaller, *Assimilating New Members,* 96.
17. Arn, *Pastor's Manual,* 80.
18. Ibid.
19. Towns, *The Complete Book of Church Growth,* 85.
20. Burt, 238.
21. Smith, *How to Attract and Keep Active Church Members,* 87–88.
22. Ibid., 88.
23. Burt, 177.
24. Hendricks, 282.
25. Ibid., 20.
26. Ibid., 281.
27. Smith, 16.

Chapter 6

1. Win Arn, *The Pastor's Manual for Effective Ministry* (Monrovia, Calif.: Church Growth, 1988), 67.
2. Ibid., 68.
3. Charles E. Fuller, Institute of Evangelism and Church Growth Seminar, Dallas, Tex. (1993).
4. Elmer L. Towns, *An Inside Look at 10 of Today's Most Innovative Churches* (Ventura, Calif.: Regal Books, 1990), 77–84.
5. Ibid.
6. Larry Stockstill, "'Celling Out' to Win the Lost—An Interview with Larry Stockstill," *Ministries Today* (July/August 1996), 37–41.
7. Bill Atwood, Seminar, Dallas, Tex. (1993).
8. George Barna, "Stop Playing Church," *Ministries Today* (January/February 1989), 55.
9. Stockstill, 41.

Chapter 7

1. Tony Crawford, interview by the author, Dallas, Tex. (1992).
2. Donald P. Smith, *How to Attract and Keep Active Church Members* (Louisville: Westminster/John Knox, 1992), 157.
3. Larry Pitcher, "Ministering to and through Blind and Deaf

Individuals," *Ministry* (Silver Springs, Md.: Ministerial Association General Conference of Seventh Day Adventist, 1996), 29.

4. Laurie Vassallo, interview by the author, telephone (5 December 1996).
5. Barbara A. Buttweiler, "Helping the Hearing Impaired," *Ministries Today* (July/August 1988), 86–89.
6. Vassallo, telephone interview.
7. Ginny Thornburgh, ed., *That All May Worship* (Washington D.C.: National Organization on Disability, 1992), 28.
8. Ron Raines, interview by the author, Fort Worth, Tex. (1993).
9. Jean Warner, interview by the author, Dallas, Tex. (1992).
10. Smith, 158.
11. Gordon Moore, interview by the author, Dallas, Tex. (1990).
12. Thornburgh, 35.
13. Leith Anderson, *A Church for the 21st Century* (Minneapolis: Bethany House Publishers, 1992), 168.
14. Robert L. Burt, ed., *Good News in Growing Churches* (New York: Pilgrim Press, 1990), 232.
15. Smith, 157.
16. Thornburgh, 8.

Chapter 8

1. Robert W. Jeambey, "Helping Communication within Church Groups," *The Clergy Journal* (April 1996), 18.
2. Ibid.
3. Ibid., 19.
4. Ibid.
5. Ibid.

Chapter 9

1. Bell and Howell Corporation (publication unknown).
2. "3M Guide," n.d.
3. Jeff Burger, *Multimedia for Decision Makers—A Business Primer* (New York: Addison-Wesley, 1995), 115.
4. Ibid., 115–16.
5. Ibid., 116.
6. Ibid., 117.
7. Ibid., 117–18.
8. Ibid., 126.

Chapter 10

1. George Barna, *User Friendly Churches* (Ventura, Calif.: Regal Books, 1991), 65–66.

2. Leith Anderson, *A Church for the 21st Century* (Minneapolis: Bethany House Publishers, 1992), 108-10.

Chapter 11

1. Russ Olmon, interview by the author, Mesquite, Tex. (22 October 1996).
2. Robert L. Burt, ed., *Good News in Growing Churches* (New York: Pilgrim Press, 1990), 14–23.
3. Dennis Hochgraber, interview by the author, Dallas, Tex. (18 November 1996).

Chapter 12

1. From materials collected during the 1970s, source unknown.

Chapter 13

1. Sophia Tarila, *Flyers That Work* (Sedona, Ariz.: First Editions, 1994), 4.
2. Ibid., 27.

Chapter 14

1. Kermit L. Netteburg and George A. Powell, "Spirit-filled Marketing," *Ministry* (Silver Springs, Md.: Ministerial Association General Conference of Seventh Day Adventists, February, 1993), 11.
2. George Barna, *Step-by-Step Guide to Church Marketing* (Ventura, Calif.: Regal Books, 1992), 208–9.
3. Netteburg and Powell, 12.
4. Ibid.
5. Ibid.
6. Corky Rogers, *Marketing Your Ministry in the Nineties* (Arvada, Colo.: Directory Services, 1992), 61–62.
7. Ibid., 145.
8. Ibid., 137.
9. Dan Danford, "Targeting Your Church Advertising," Ministries Today (Palm Beach, Florida: Strang Communications, May/June, 1988), 52.
10. Robert L. Burt, ed., *Good News in Growing Churches* (New York: Pilgrim Press, 1990), 143.
11. Rogers, 59.
12. James A. Vitti, *Publicity Handbook for Churches and Christian Organizations* (Grand Rapids: Zondervan, 1987), 76.
13. Ibid., 80.
14. Barna, 203.
15. From material collected during the 1970s by the author, source unknown.
16. Barna, 202.
17. Ibid., 203.

Chapter 15

1. George E. Brian, Jr., and Ron Regan, interview by the author, Garland, Tex. (15 November 1996).
2. U.S. Post Office official, interview by the author, Dallas, Tex. (30 December 1996).

Chapter 16

1. Quentin J. Schultze, *Internet for Christians—Everything You Need to Start Cruising the Net Today!* (Muskegon, Mich.: Gospel Films, Inc., 1995), 11–12.
2. David Doom, interview by the author, Richardson, Tex. (23 April 1997).
3. Schultze, 26.
4. Ibid, 77–78.
5. Doom, interview.
6. Schultze, 44.
7. Doom, interview.
8. David Powers, interview with the author, Plano, Tex. (30 April 1997).
9. Schultze, 83–84.
10. Ibid., 27.

Chapter 17

1. Copyright Office, "Copyright Basics" (Washington, D.C.: Library of Congress, 1994), 2.
2. Stephen Fishman, *Copyright Handbook—How to Protect and Use Written Works* (Berkeley, Calif.: Nolo Press, 1992), 2:2.
3. Woody Young, *A Business Guide to Copyright Law—What You Don't Know Can Cost You* (San Juan Capistrano, Calif.: Joy Publishing, 1986), 30.
4. Ibid., 26.
5. Fishman, 12:20.
6. Richard R. Hammar, *The Church Guide to Copyright Law* (Matthews, N.C.: Christian Ministry Resources, 1990), ix.
7. Ibid., x.
8. Copyright Office, 2.
9. Ibid.
10. Section 107 of Title 17, United States Code, vol. 8 (Washington, D.C.: U.S. Government Printing Office, 1995), 912–13.
11. Hammar, 108–15.
12. Fishman, 2:4.
13. Ibid.
14. Copyright Office, 3.
15. Ibid.

16. Fishman, 8:11.
17. Copyright Office, 3.
18. Ibid., 4.
19. Fishman, 2:5.
20. Hammar, 146–7.
21. Ibid., 155.
22. Ibid., 101–2.
23. Ibid., 116–17.
24. Ibid., 91.
25. Ibid., 10.
26. Francis Anfuso, *Taking Your Church Off Pause* (Yuba City, Calif.: Twenty-first Century Ministries, 1993), 146.
27. Ibid., 146–47, 149.
28. Fishman, 12:2.
29. Paul M. Miller, *Lillenas Drama Newsletter* (Kansas City, Mo.: Lillenas Publishing, 1994), 2.
30. Hammar, 115.
31. Sheldon W. Halpern, David E. Shipley, and Howard B. Abrams, *Copyright Cases and Materials* (St. Paul, Minn.: West Publishing, 1992), 274.
32. Ibid., 273.
33. Hammar, 157.

Chapter 18

1. Mike Tharp, "The media's new fix," *U.S. News & World Report* (18 March 1996), 74.
2. Ellen Hume, "The New Paradigm for News," *The Annals of the American Academy of Political and Social Science* (July 1996), 150.
3. Cheryl McCallister, interview by the author, telephone (10 September 1997).
4. Kathie Magers, "Attracting Your Community Newspaper," Positive Parents of Dallas Seminar, Dallas, Tex. (26 October 1991).

Chapter 19

1. Donald W. Blohowiak, *No Comment! An Executive's Essential Guide to the News Media* (New York: Praeger, 1987), 147.
2. Julia Duin, "How To Beat Media Phobia," *Ministries Today* (March/April 1992), 55.
3. Ibid., 59.
4. "Why Would You Want to Know That?" *Trends for the Secondary School,* 1974.
5. Richard M. Adams, interview by the author, Dallas, Tex. (1985).
6. Steven H. Lee, "Crisis and Conscience," *The Dallas Morning News* (5

January 1992), sec. H, 1–2.

Chapter 20

1. David Kuykendall, interview by the author, Dallas, Tex. (1990).
2. Lloyd Craycroft, "Ministering to the Poor," *Ministries Today* (July/August 1995), 32.
3. Dorothy Moore, interview by the author, Dallas, Tex. (11 October 1996).
4. Francis Anfuso, "Strategies To Reach the Unchurched," *Ministries Today* (July/August 1995), 34.
5. John Blosser, "You Can Always Get a Wholesome Meal in America— Even If You Don't Have a Dime," *National Enquirer* (8 September 1992), 40.
6. Bruce Buchanan, interview by the author, Dallas, Tex. (26 November 1996).
7. Betty Spillman, interview by the author, Dallas, Tex. (23 November 1996).
8. Valerie G. Lowe, "The Long Way To Build a Church," *Ministries Today* (September/October 1997): 38, 40.
9. Lois Stanley, interview by the author, Dallas, Tex. (13 December 1996).
10. Leith Anderson, *A Church for the 21st Century* (Minneapolis: Bethany House Publishers, 1992), 133.
11. Sam Monzingo, interview by the author, Dallas, Tex. (5 December 1996).

Chapter 21

1. Danny Wegman, interview by the author, Dallas, Tex. (17 September 1996).
2. Ed Young, interview by the author, Irving, Tex. (1992).
3. Francis Anfuso, "Strategies to Reach the Unchurched," *Ministries Today* (July/August, 1995), 34.
4. Dorothy Moore, interview by the author, Dallas, Tex. (11 October 1996).
5. Elmer L. Towns, *An Inside Look at 10 of Today's Most Innovative Churches* (Ventura, Calif.: Regal Books, 1990), 143.
6. Ron Raines, interview by the author, telephone (1993).
7. Dana Effler, interview by the author, Dallas, Tex. (15 October 1996).
8. Towns, 102–3.
9. Wegman, interview.

Chapter 22

1. Lee Strobel, *Inside the Mind of Unchurched Harry and Mary* (Grand Rapids: Zondervan, 1993), 47.

2. Ibid., 46–47.
3. Delos Miles, "Can We Reach the Hard-Core Unreached?" *Growing Churches* (January/February/March 1991), 48.
4. Strobel, 47.
5. Ibid.
6. Ibid., 45–46.
7. Ibid., 17.
8. Ibid., 46–47.
9. Ibid., 43.
10. Russ Olmon, interview by the author, Mesquite, Tex. (22 October 1996).
11. George Barna, "Stop Playing Church," *Ministries Today* (January/February 1989), 55.
12. Russ Olmon, interview.
13. Ed Young, interview by the author, Irving, Tex. (1992).
14. Elmer L. Towns, *An Inside Look at 10 of Today's Most Innovative Churches* (Ventura, Calif.: Regal Books, 1990), 77.
15. Donald P. Smith, *How To Attract and Keep Active Church Members* (Louisville: Westminster/John Knox Press, 1992), 157.
16. Leith Anderson, *A Church for the 21st Century* (Minneapolis: Bethany House Publishers, 1992), 167-68.
17. David Kuykendall, interview by the author, Dallas, Tex. (1990).
18. Win Arn, *The Pastor's Manual for Effective Ministry* (Monrovia, Calif.: Church Growth, 1988), 23.
19. Rosemary Johnson, interview by the author, Dallas, Tex. (1994).
20. Elmer L. Towns, *An Inside Look at 10 of Today's Most Innovative Churches* (Ventura, California: Regal Books, 1990), 131-32.
21. Princeton Religion Research Center and the Gallup Organization, Inc., *The Unchurched American—Ten Years Later* (Princeton, N.J.: Princeton Religion Research Center, 1990), 35.
22. Morris Sheats, Seminar, Dallas, Tex. (1993).
23. Princeton Religion Research Center, *Unchurched American,* 16.
24. Morris Sheats, interview by the author, Dallas, Tex. (1994).
25. Douglas Murren, "Reaching Boomers," *Ministries Today* (January/February, 1989), 32.
26. George Barna, *User Friendly Churches* (Ventura, Calif.: Regal Books, 1991), 123.
27. Towns, 77.
28. Arn, 20.
29. The Princeton Religion Research Center, *Unchurched American,* 18–19.
30. Miles, 49.

Index